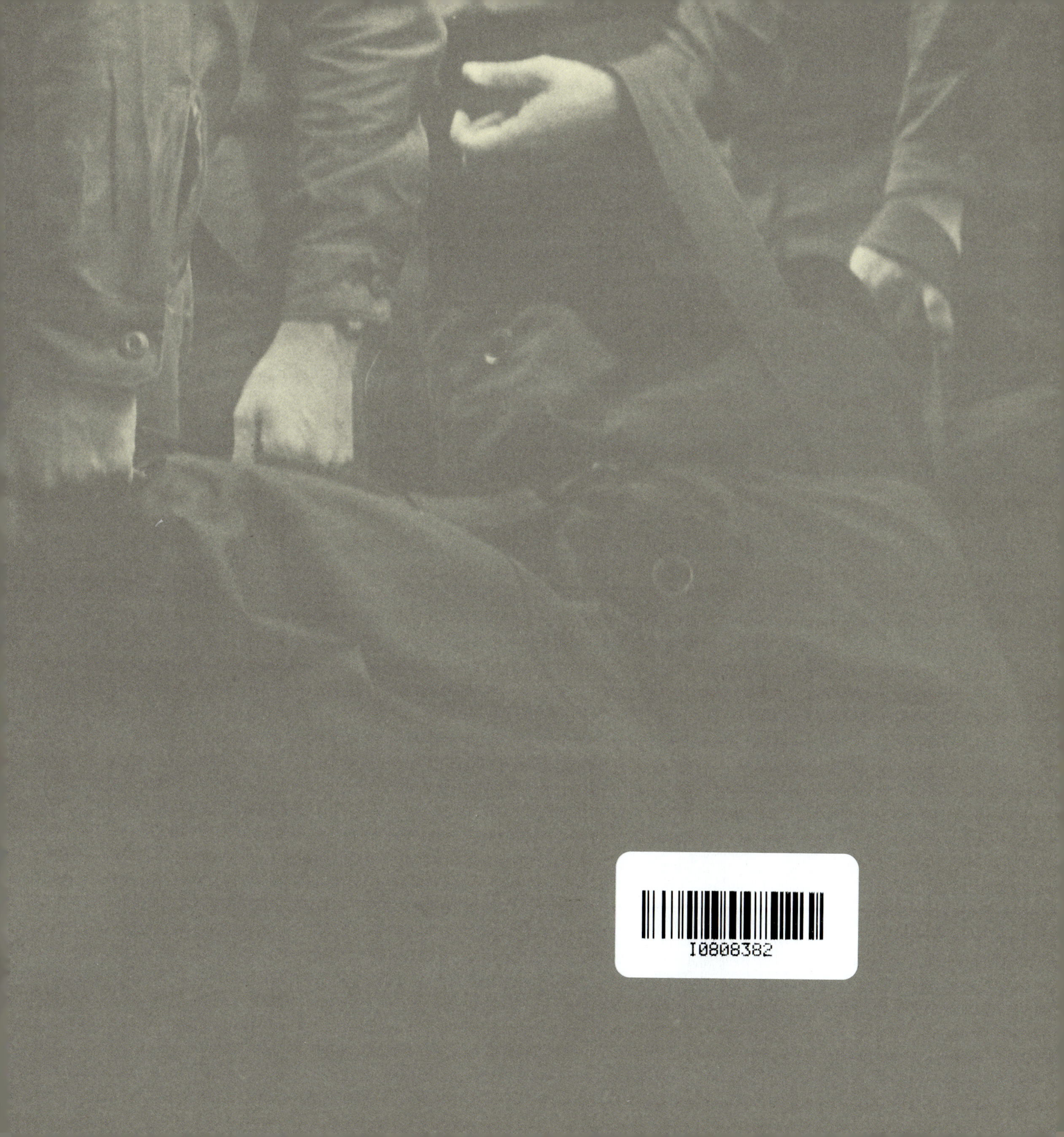

GRUNTS

THE LAST US DRAFT, 1972

ED ECKSTEIN

Schiffer Publishing Ltd
4880 Lower Valley Road • Atglen, PA 19310

Library of Congress Control Number: 2017930635

Designed by Justin Watkinson
Cover design by John Cheek
Type set in Compacta Bd BT/ITC Officina Sans

ISBN: 978-0-7643-5302-4
Printed in China

Published by Schiffer Publishing, Ltd.
4880 Lower Valley Road
Atglen, PA 19310
Phone: (610) 593-1777; Fax: (610) 593-2002
E-mail: Info@schifferbooks.com
Web: www.schifferbooks.com

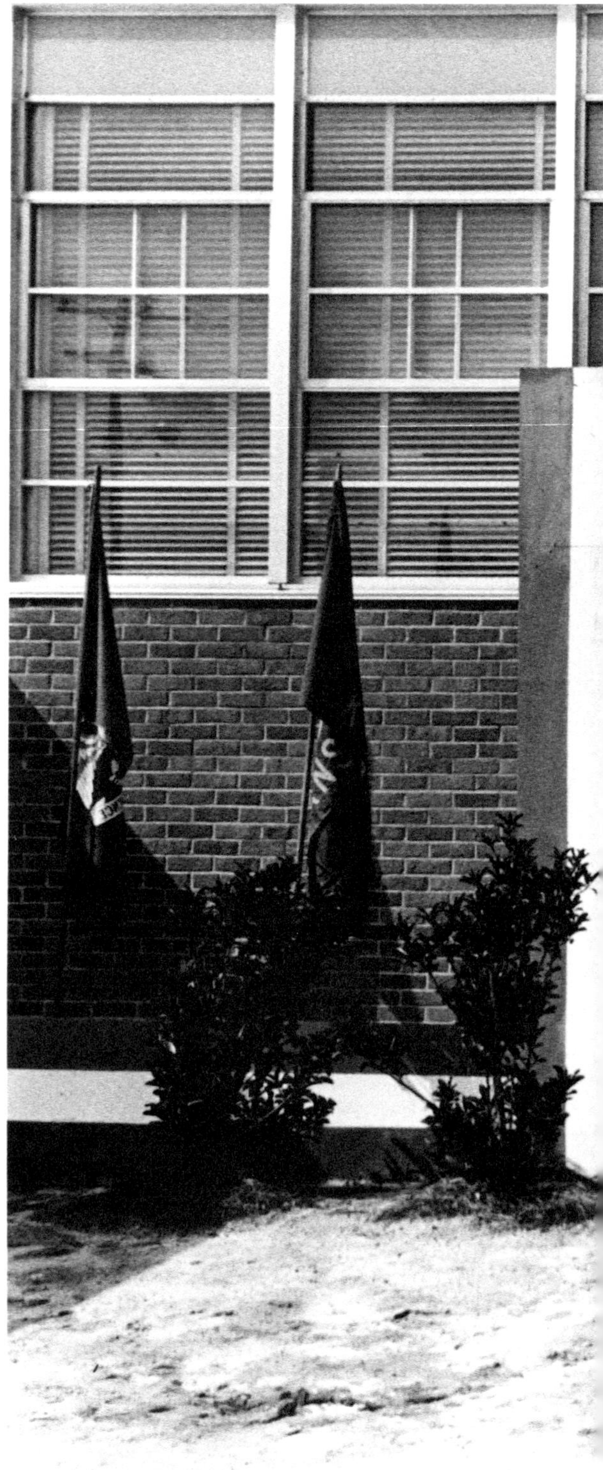

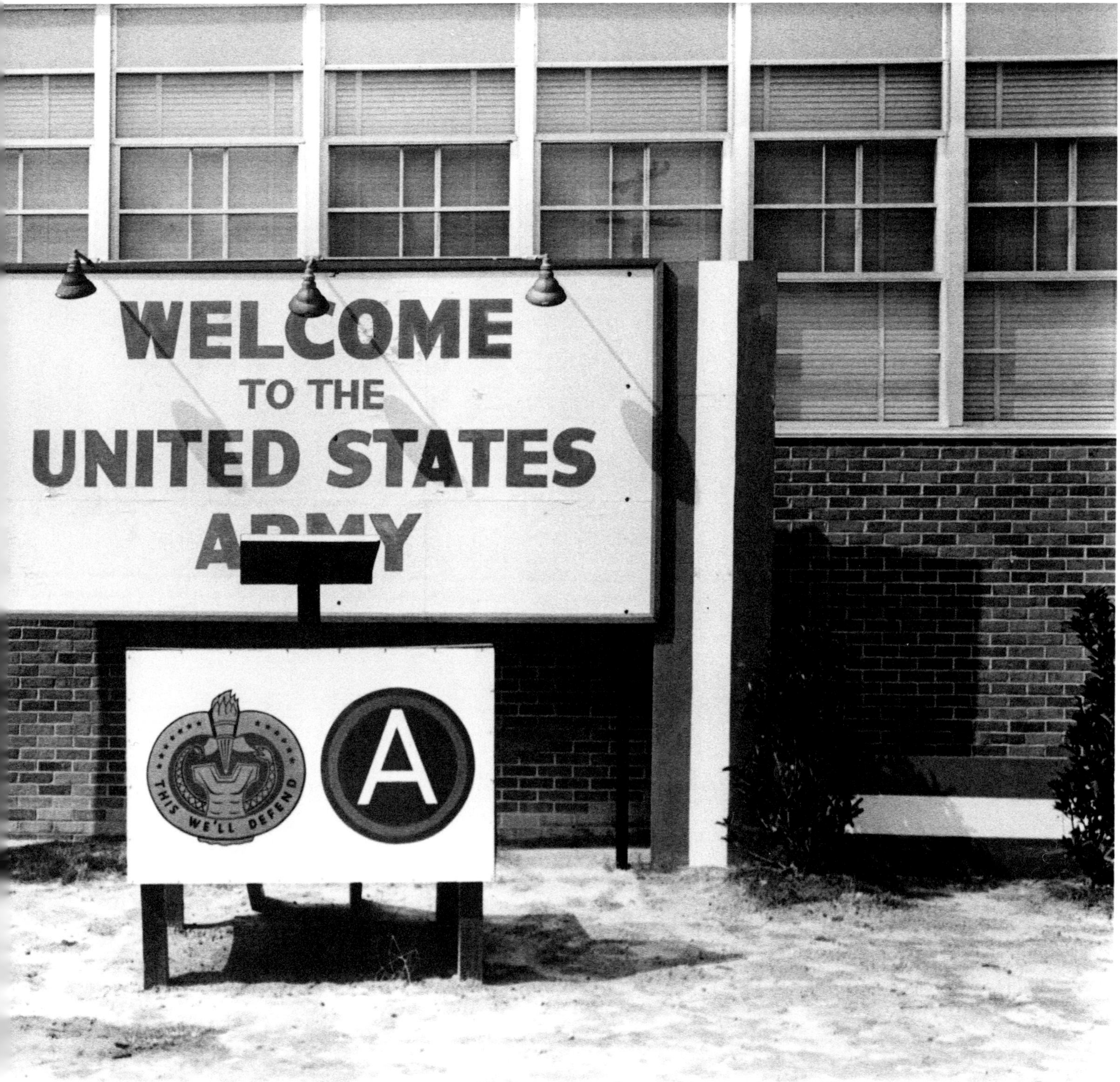
WELCOME
TO THE
UNITED STATES
THIS WE'LL DEFEND
A

INTRODUCTION

In 1940, just prior to the United States' entry into World War II, the first peacetime draft in our nation's history was enacted in response to increased world tensions. The draft was established to anticipate and fulfill wartime manpower needs.

At the end of World War II, the draft law was allowed to expire, but it was reenacted less than two years later to maintain necessary military manpower during the tense era of the Cold War with the Soviet Union. Thus, from 1948 until the draft ended in 1973, during both peacetime and periods of conflict, all American men were required to register for the draft on their eighteenth birthdays, and then either enlist in one of the armed services or be drafted into the United States Army. Approximately ten million men were drafted during this period.

Men who enlisted had the opportunity to choose branches of the service and, in many cases, assignments, but they also had a longer period of service. Draftees had no say in their army assignments.

During the presidential election of 1968, Richard Nixon promised to end the draft. His motivation was to dismantle the burgeoning anti-Vietnam War movement since, he reasoned, a youth rebellion would be less likely if young men no longer faced mandatory military service.

In October 1968, Nixon stated that a compulsory draft should not be accepted in a nation devoted to "liberty, justice and equality."[1] As a man who prided himself on his foresight in international relations, and his historical vision, Nixon liked the argument that the draft was an anachronism. Also, he continued, there was no "fair" way to operate the draft. The evolution of military tactics and strategy from hand-to-hand combat to the use of nuclear weapons made the necessity of the draft questionable and suggested the need for a professional volunteer force.[2]

This strategy may have helped Nixon win the presidency twice, but it did little to stem the tide of social upheaval that swept the country in the 1960s and 1970s.[3] Many young people were against the war in Vietnam and did not find it easy to relate to military culture. The warrior ethic, which had long been a cornerstone of Western culture, began to erode, particularly among the more affluent and educated.

One aspect of the draft that was re-introduced during this period was the lottery system—an attempt to make the draft more equitable. Lottery drawings were televised nationally. A total of 365 numbers—one for every day of the year—were placed in blue capsules and drawn by hand. During that first lottery drawing, the first date called was September 14. Thus, all males between the ages of 18 and 26, who were born on September 14, were assigned lottery number one.[4]

The draft was an American institution that managed to sustain political and public favor through two world wars before dying out under a barrage of social upheaval. Although induction authority expired in 1973, the Selective Service remains in existence today in a "stand by" mode to support the all-volunteer force in case an emergency should make it necessary for congress to authorize a resumption of the draft.[5]

A NOTE ON THE PHOTOGRAPHS:

In late 1972, I was asked by the now defunct magazine Youth to produce a photo essay on the nation's struggles to deal with the growing youth movement against the Vietnam War and, consequently, the draft.

I began with a group being inducted into the army in Philadelphia, and ended up with an extensive body of work encompassing the entire recruitment process. I followed the recruits to Ft. Jackson, South Carolina, and photographed the basic training process as well.

I was probably the first photographer to be embedded in a basic training platoon. I was given complete, uncensored access to the rituals of basic training during the time I spent there. I hope these photos convey, in unflinching detail, the rigors of basic training, juxtaposed against the vulnerability of the young soldiers.

TECHNICAL NOTE:

All photographs were taken with 35mm cameras on Kodak Tri-X film. They were hand-processed in Acufine developer, and printed on Ilford Multigrade paper before scanning.

NOTES

[1] Flynn, George Q., *The Draft 1940–1973*, (University Press of Kansas, 1993), 261.

[2] Flynn, *The Draft*, 235.

[3] Baskir, Lawrence M. & Strauss, William A., *Chance and Circumstance, The Draft, The War and The Vietnam Generation*, (Vintage Books, 1978), 132.

[4] *The Vietnam Lotteries*. https://www.sss.gov/About/History-and-records/lotter.

[5] *Background of Selective Service*. https://www.sss.gov/about.

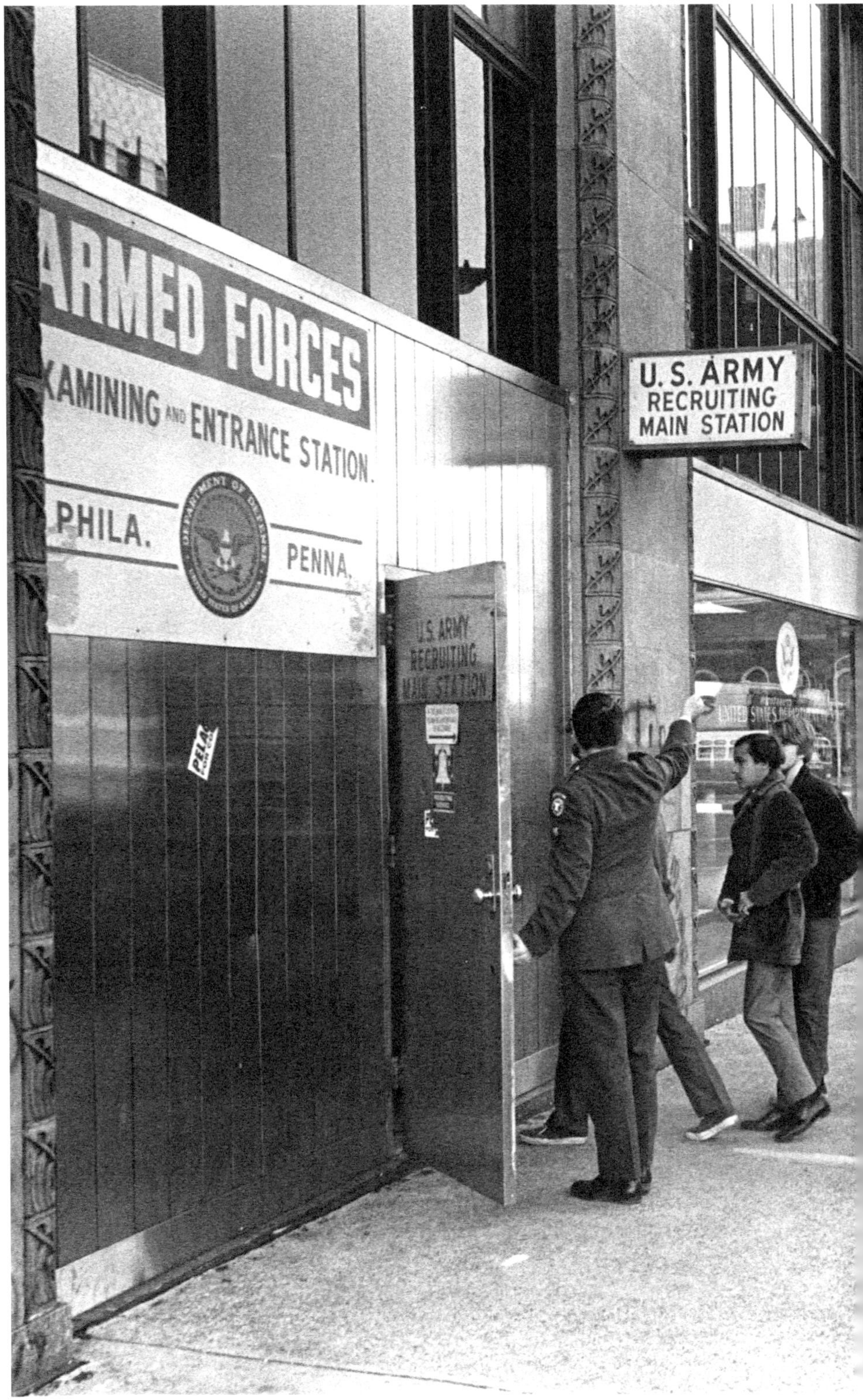
ARMED FORCES
XAMINING AND ENTRANCE STATION
PHILA.
PENNA.
U.S. ARMY
RECRUITING
MAIN STATION
U.S. ARMY
RECRUITING
MAIN STATION

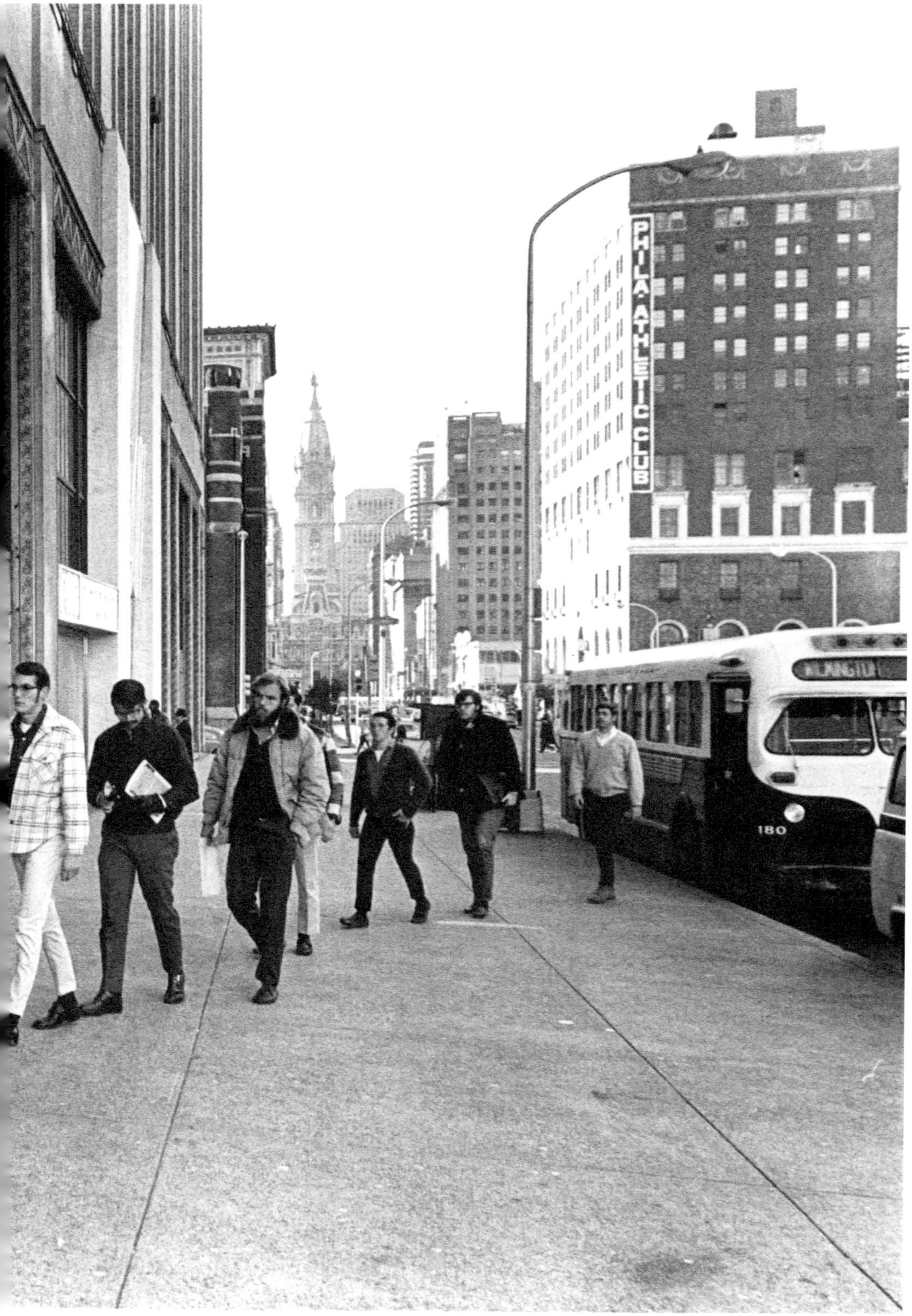
PHILA. ATHLETIC CLUB
180

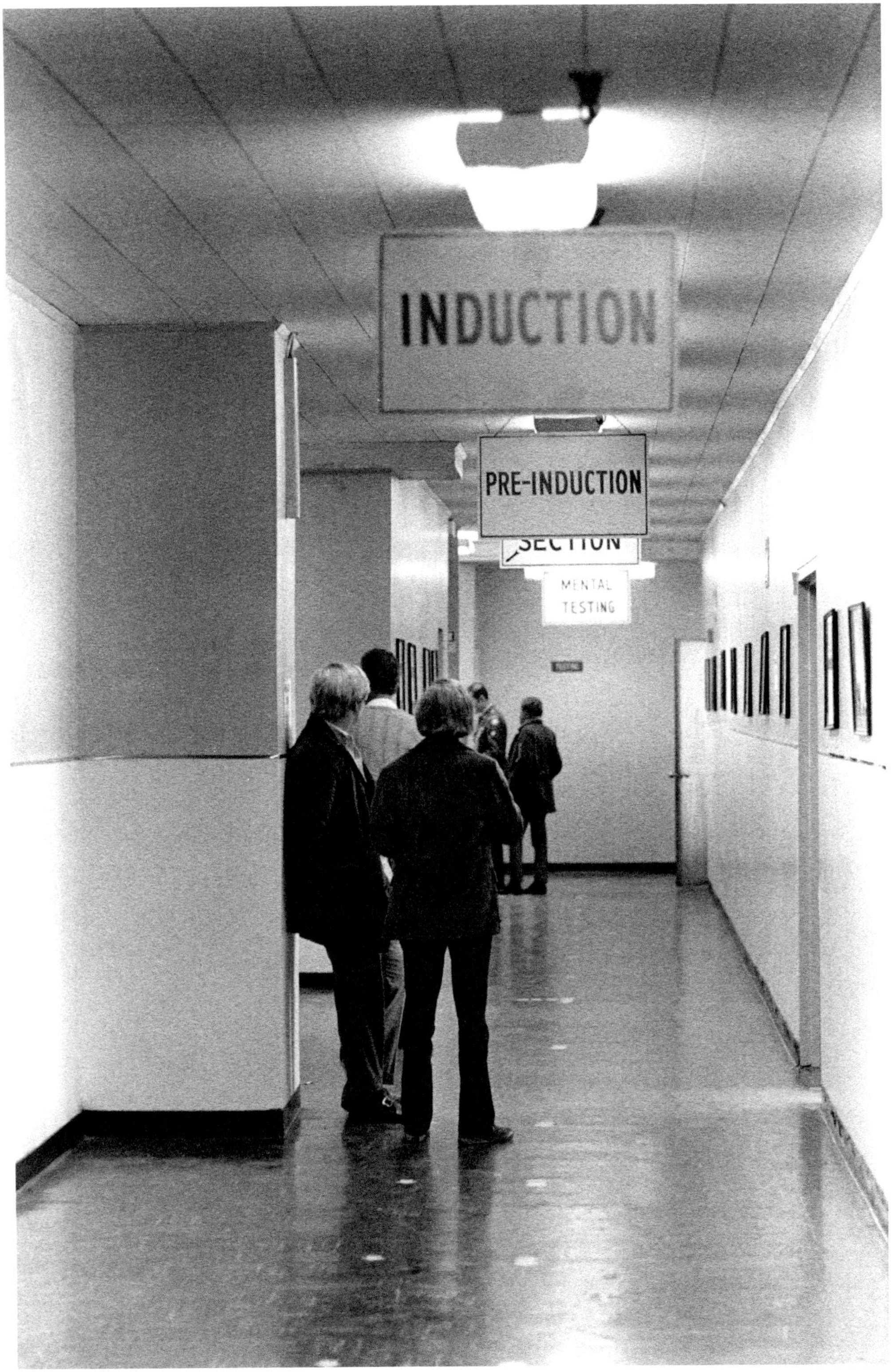
INDUCTION
PRE-INDUCTION
SECTION
MENTAL
TESTING

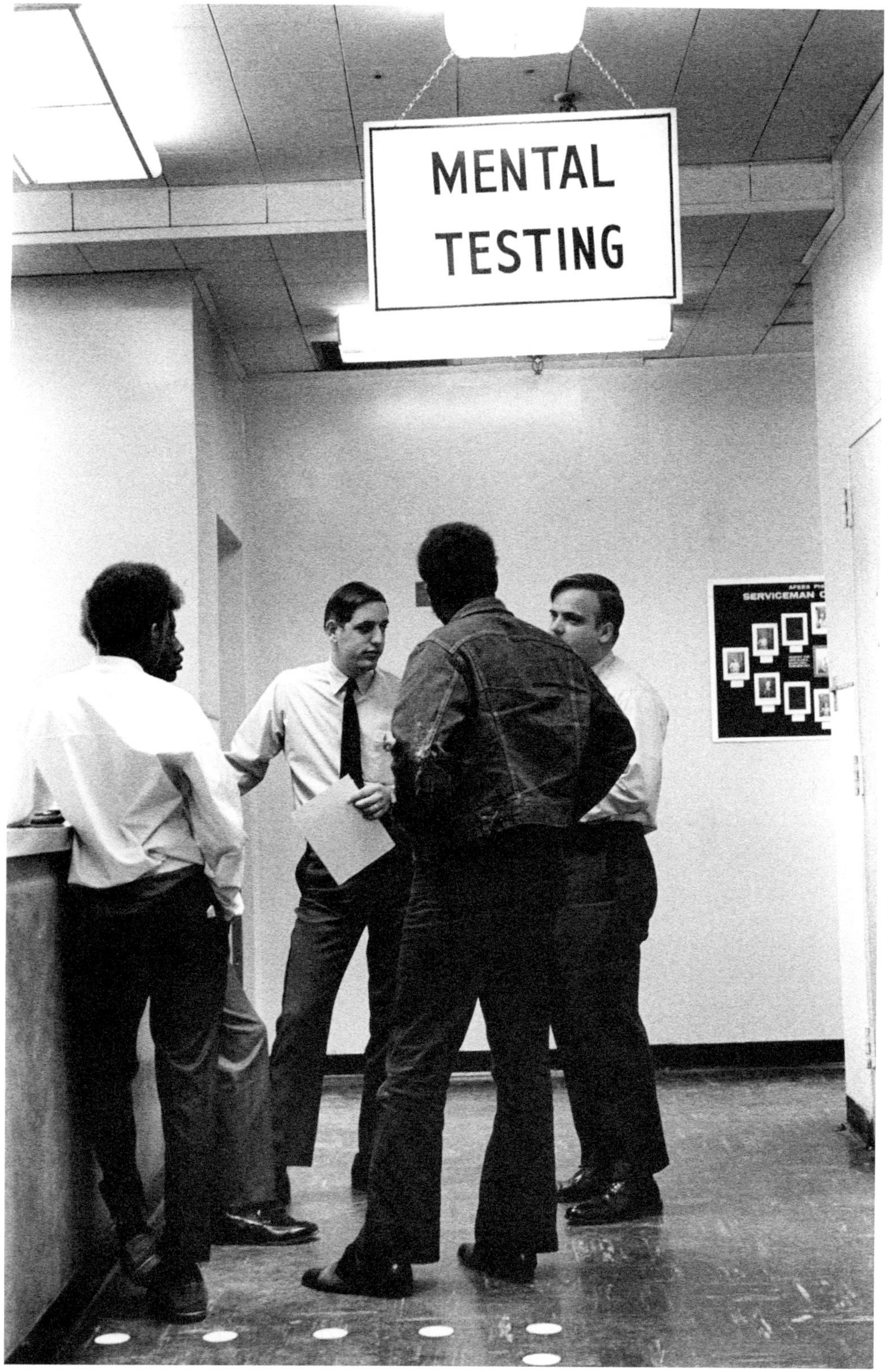
MENTAL
TESTING
SERVICEMAN

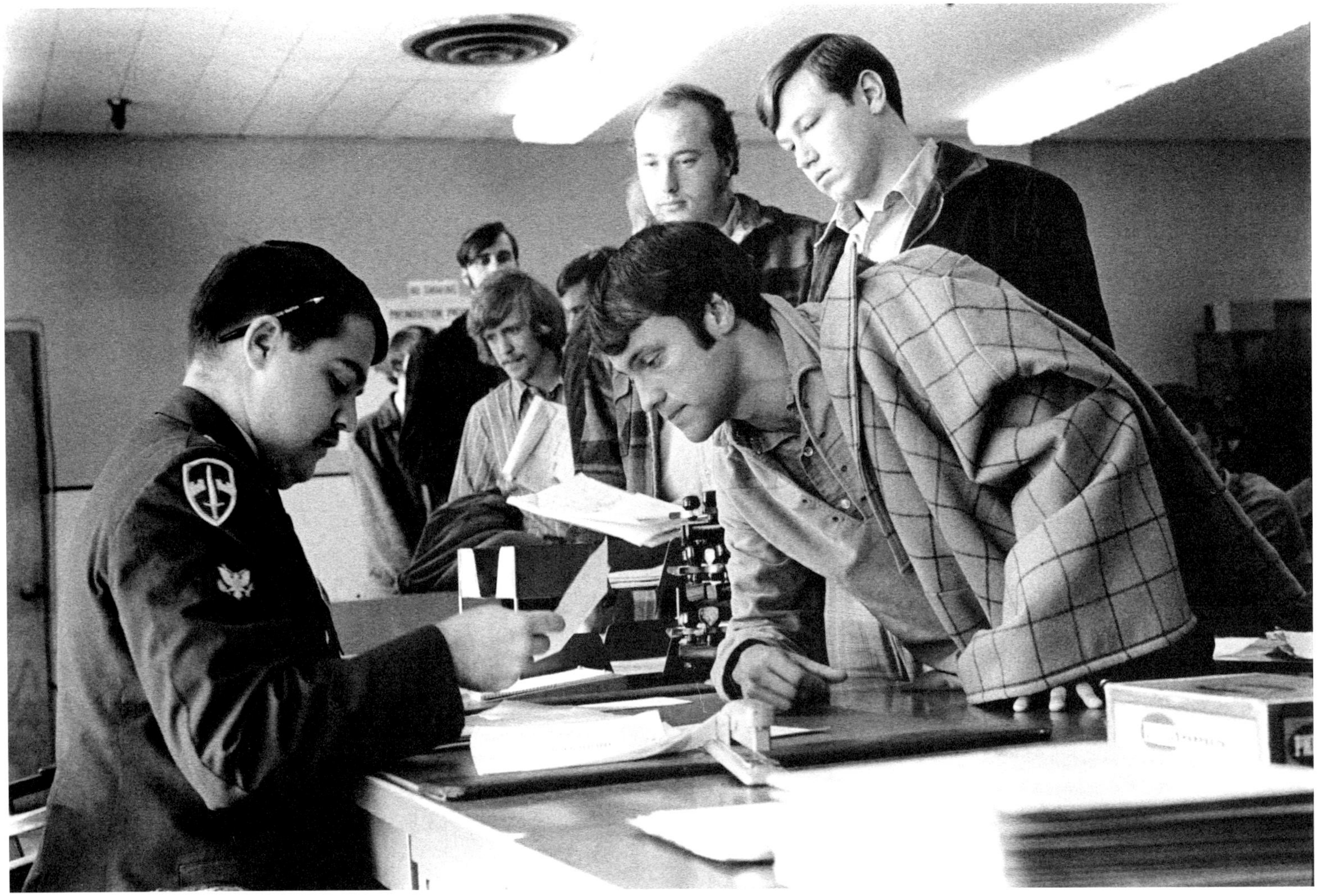

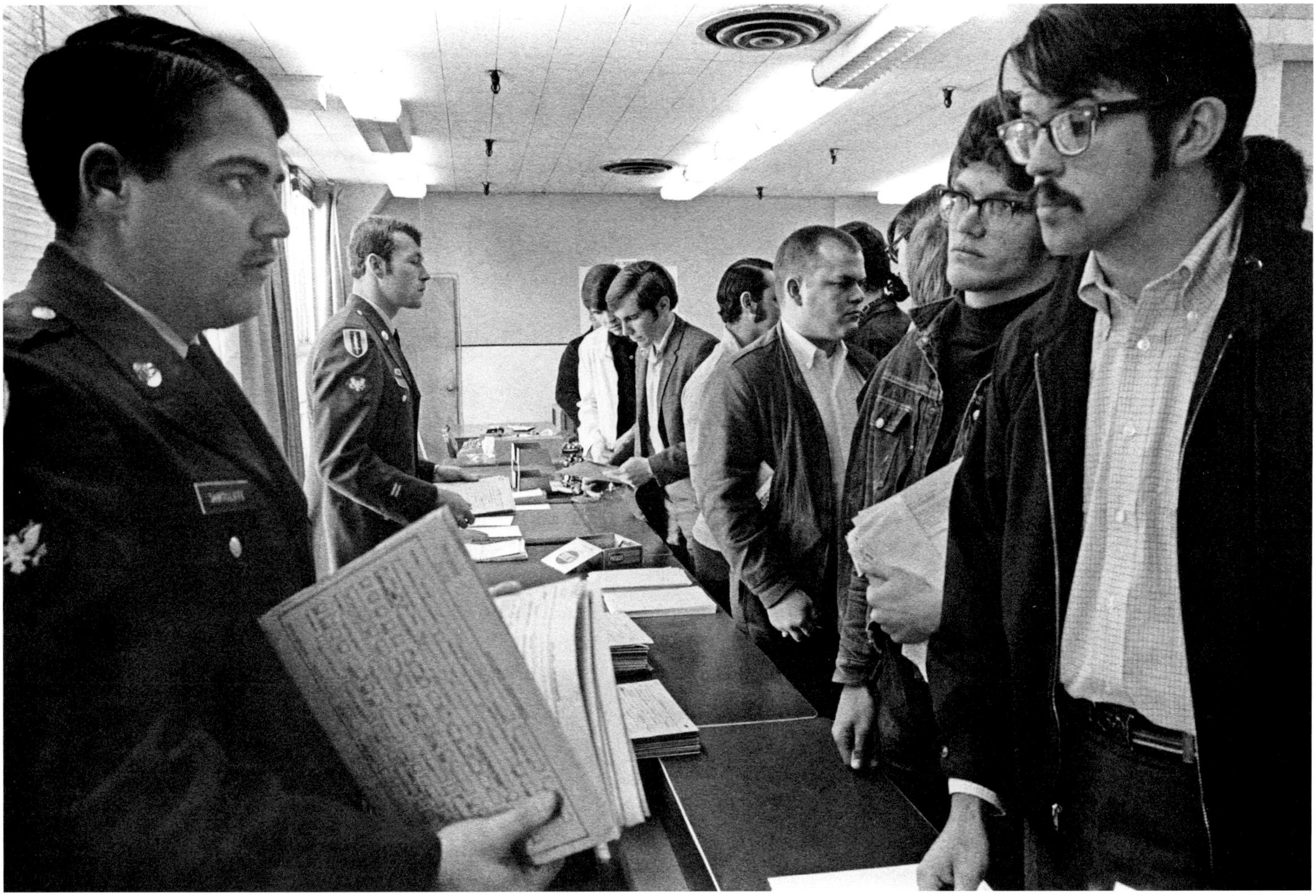

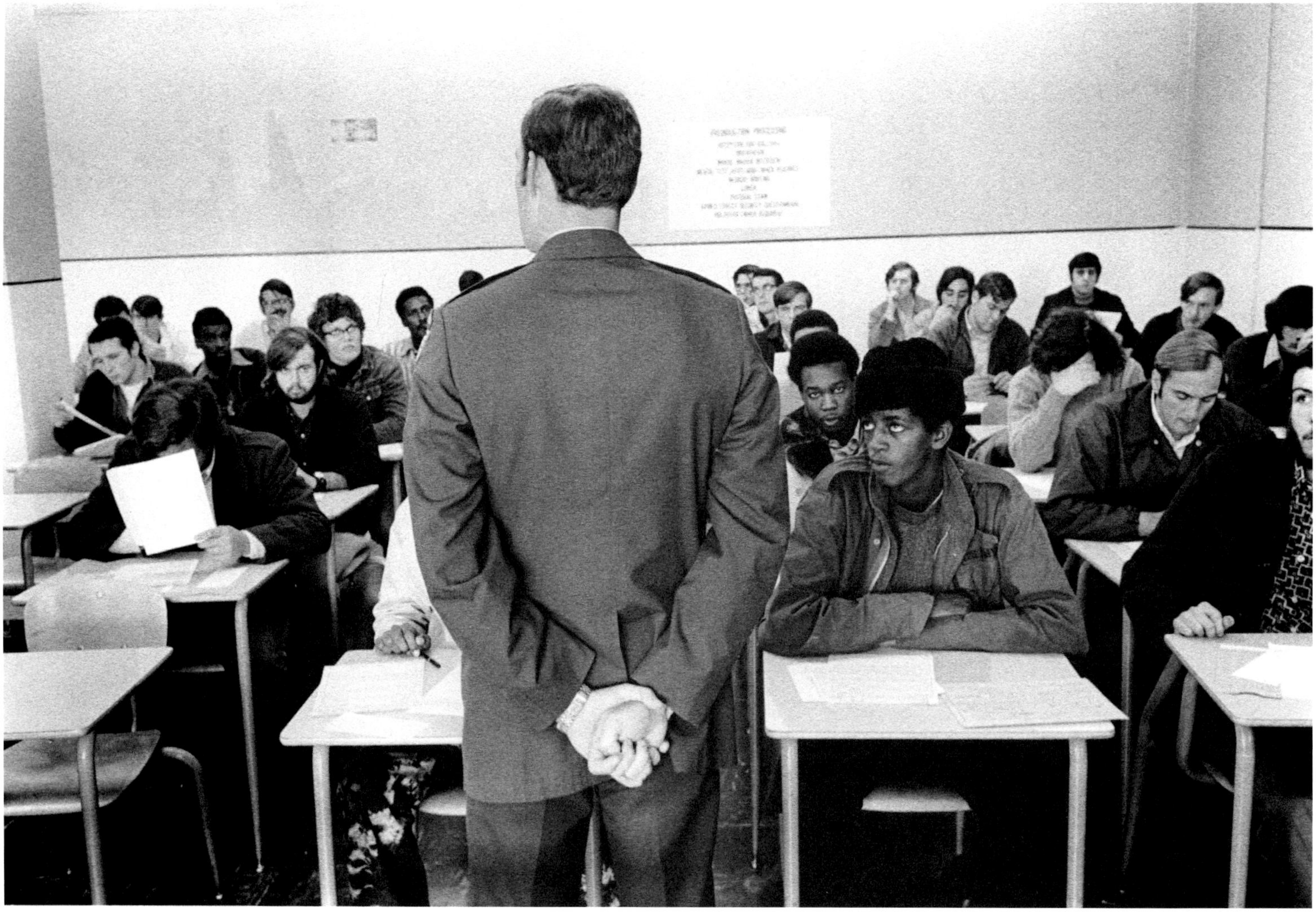

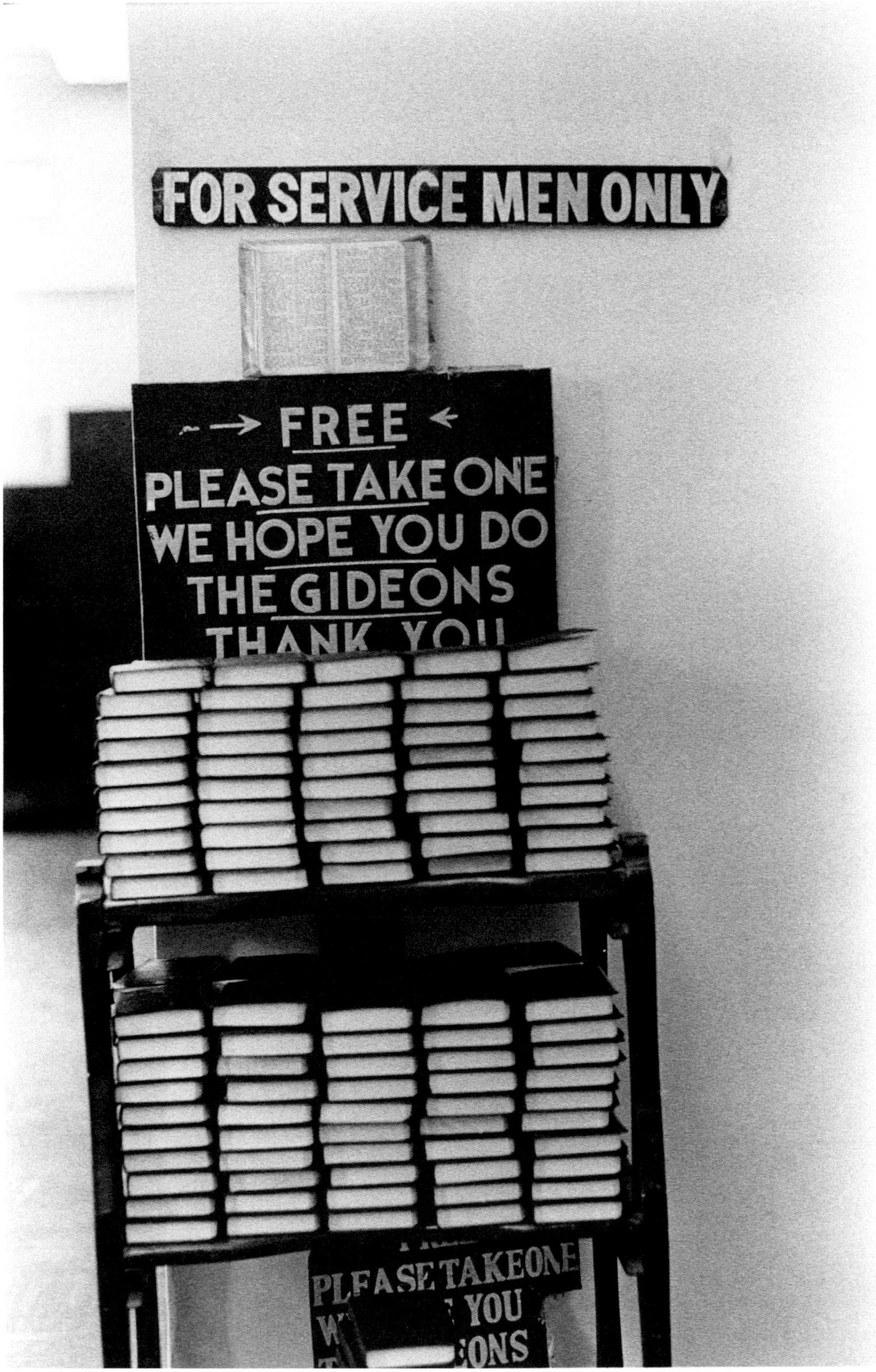
FOR SERVICE MEN ONLY
FREE
PLEASE TAKE ONE
WE HOPE YOU DO
THE GIDEONS
THANK YOU
PLEASE TAKE ONE

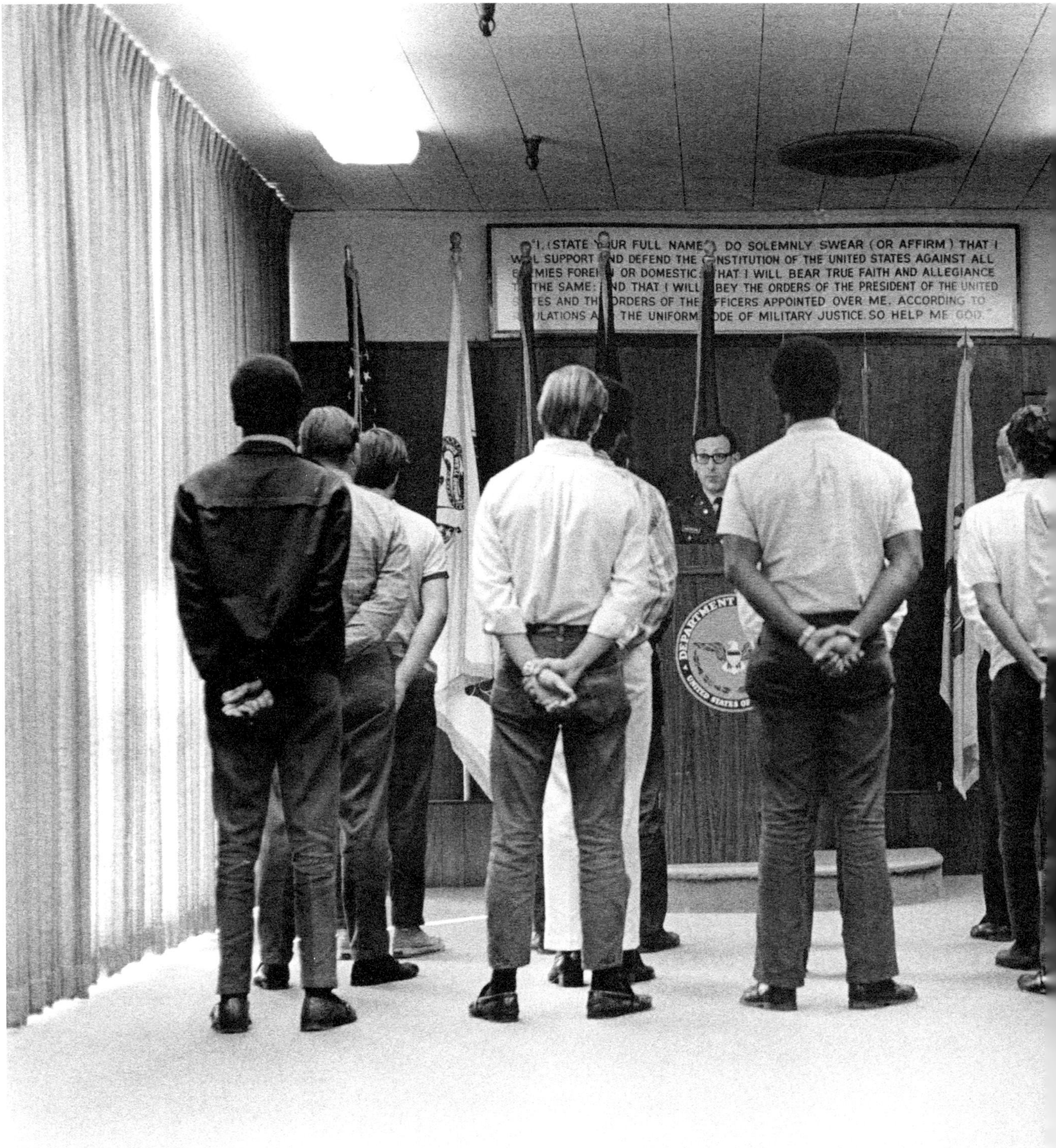
"I, (STATE UR FULL NAME DO SOLEMNLY SWEAR (OR AFFIRM) THAT I
L SUPPORT ND DEFEND THE NSTITUTION OF THE UNITED STATES AGAINST ALL
MIES FOREI OR DOMESTIC HAT I WILL BEAR TRUE FAITH AND ALLEGIANCE
THE SAME: ND THAT I WILL BEY THE ORDERS OF THE PRESIDENT OF THE UNITED
TES AND TH ORDERS OF THE FFICERS APPOINTED OVER ME, ACCORDING TO
LATIONS A THE UNIFORM ODE OF MILITARY JUSTICE SO HELP ME GOD."

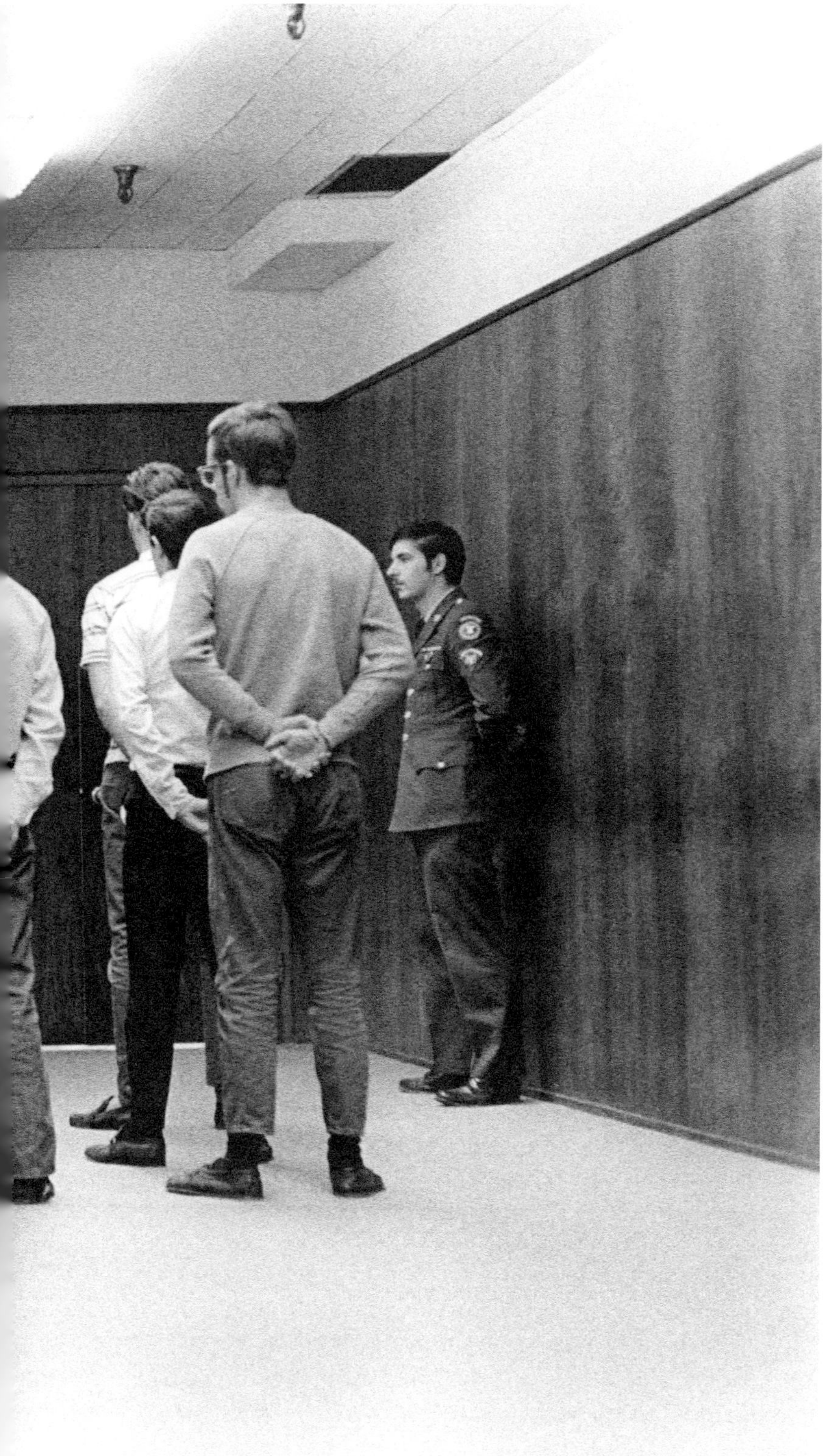

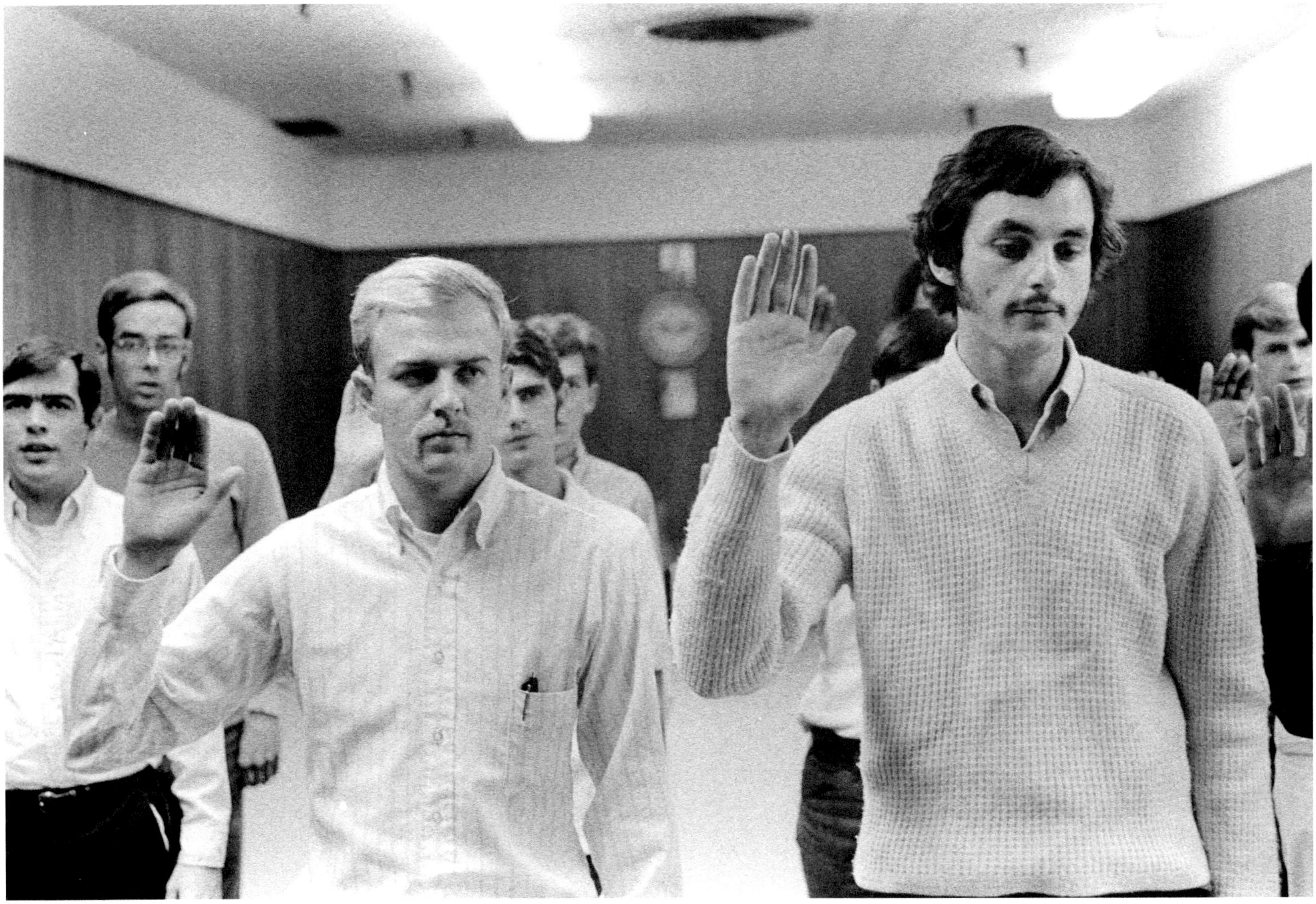

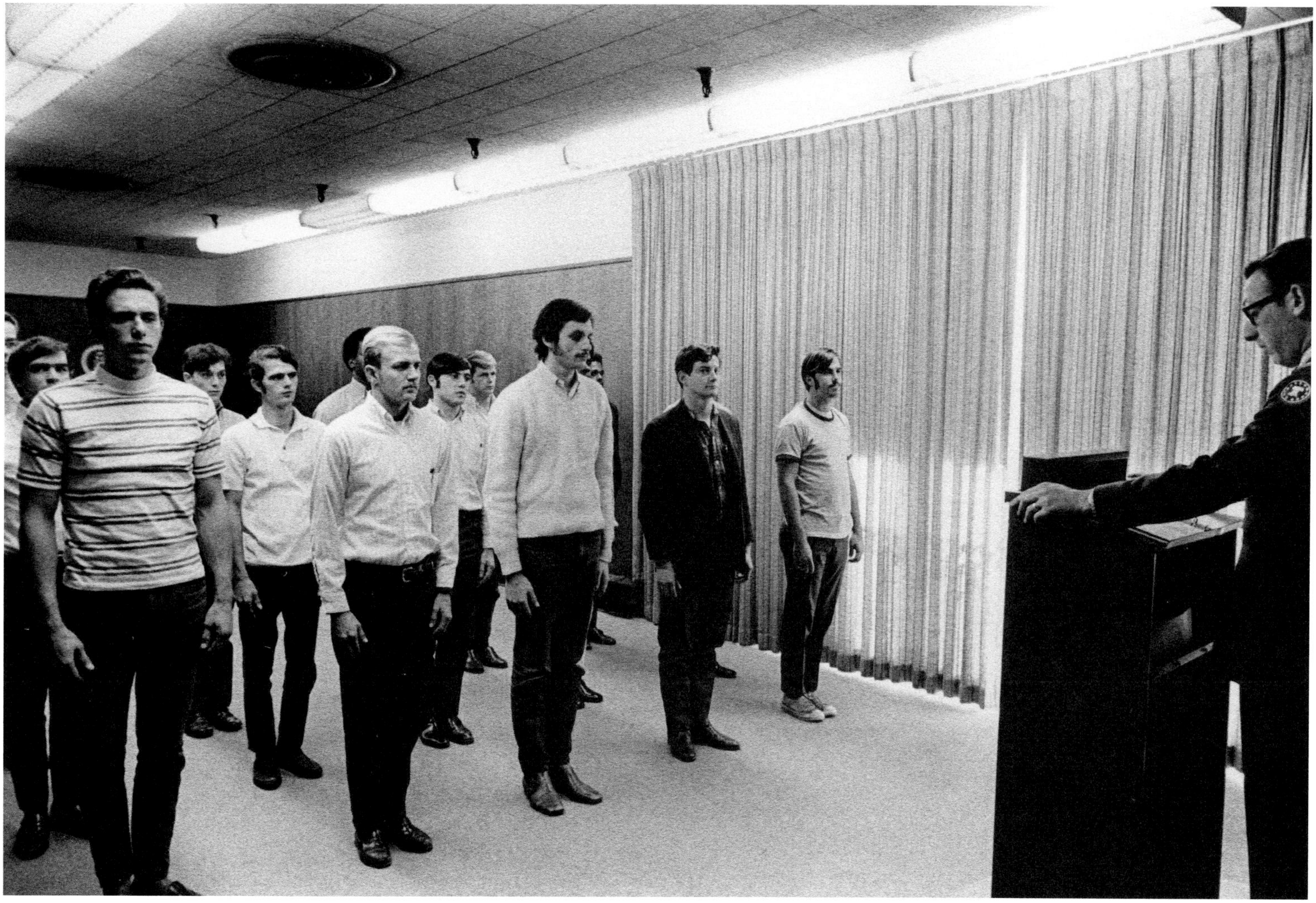

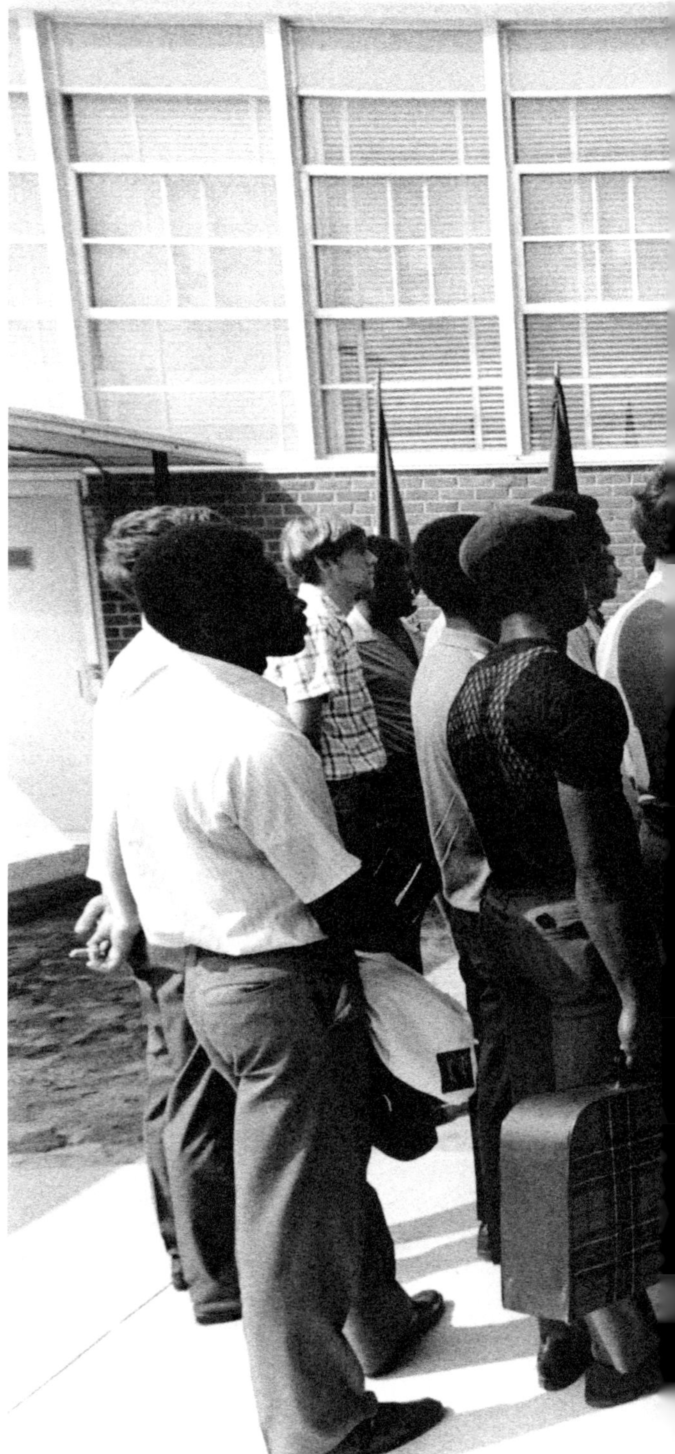

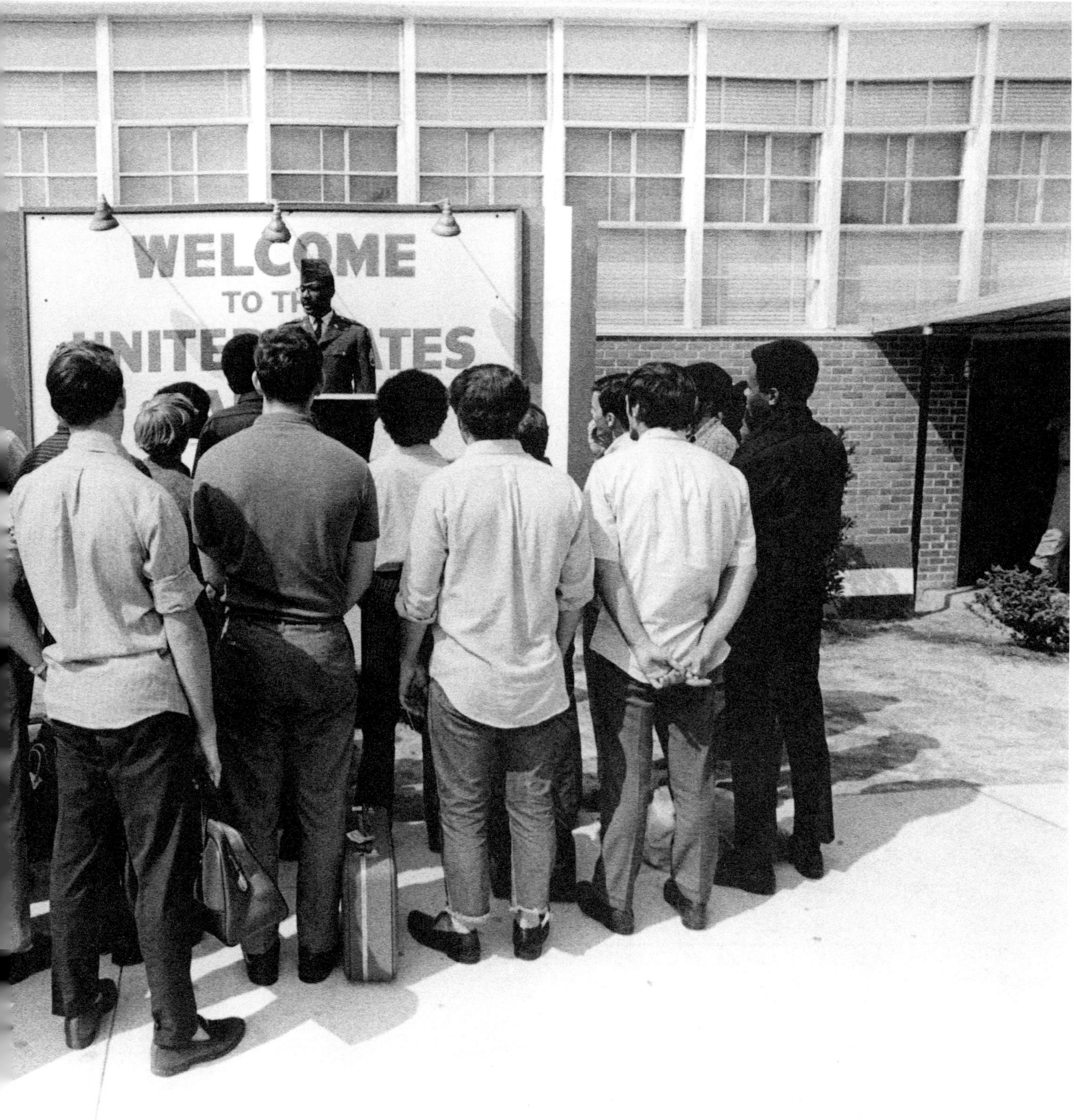
WELCOME
TO

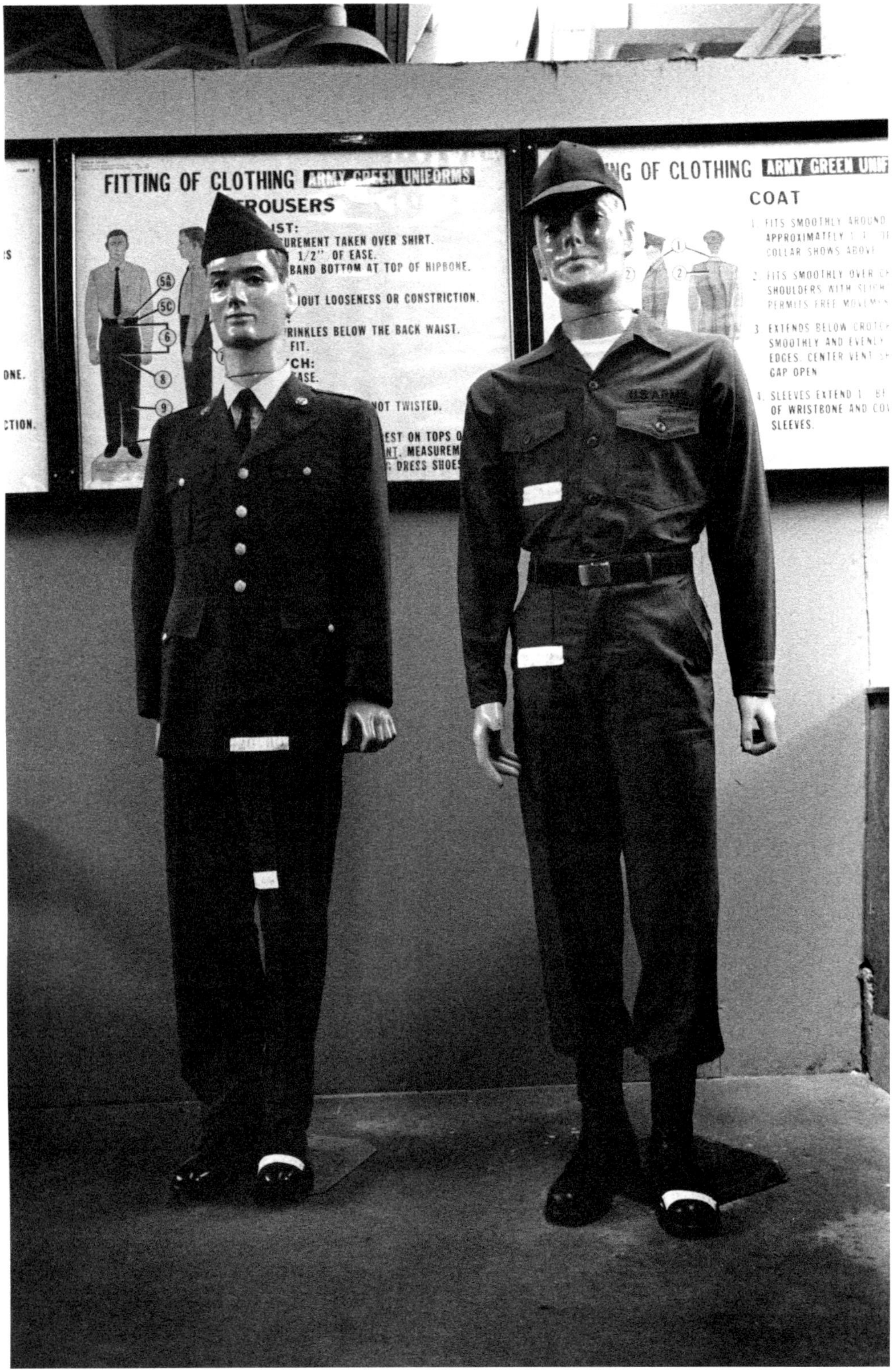
FITTING OF CLOTHING
ARMY GREEN UNIFORMS
NOT TWISTED.
COAT
SLEEVES.

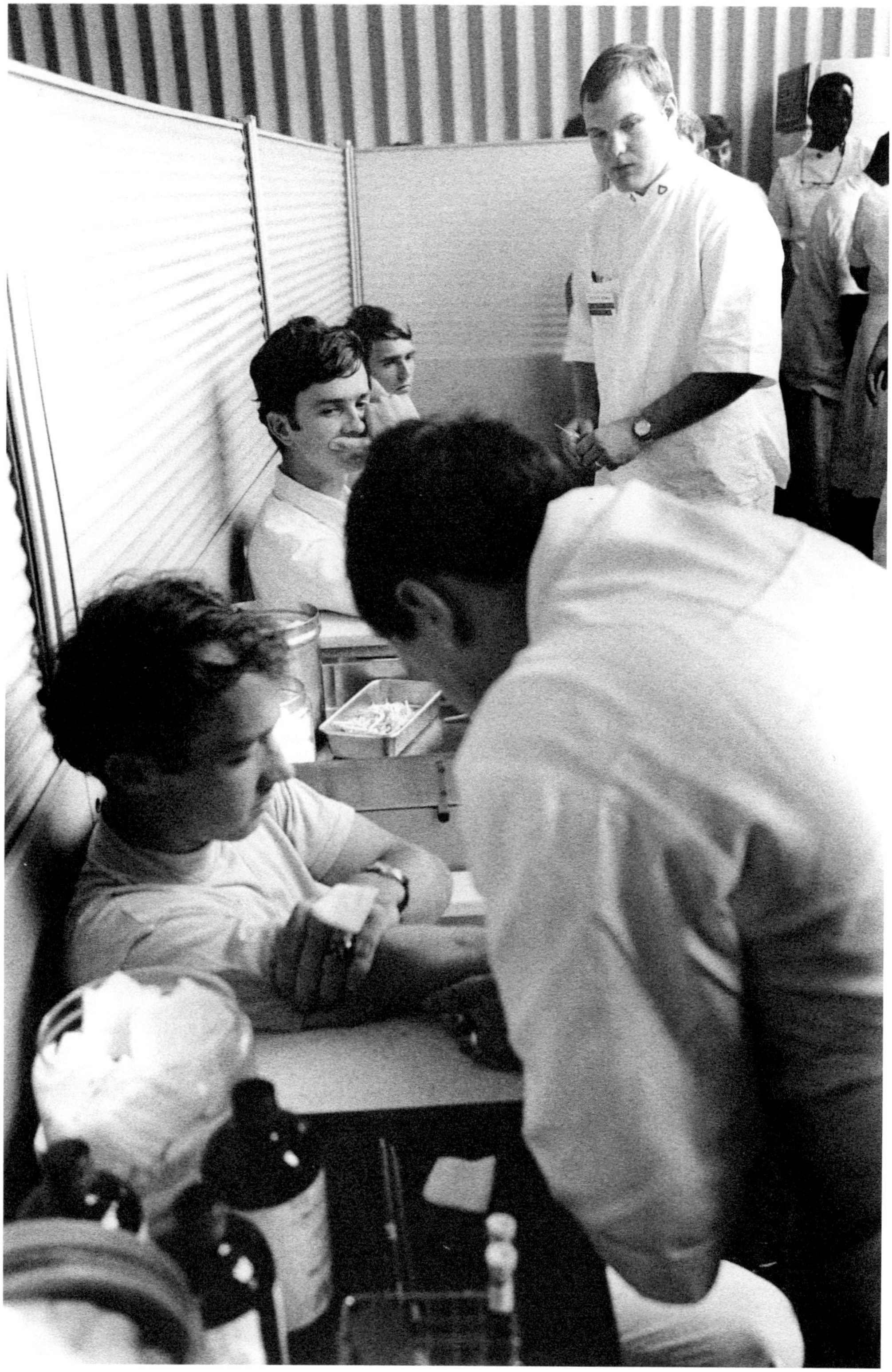

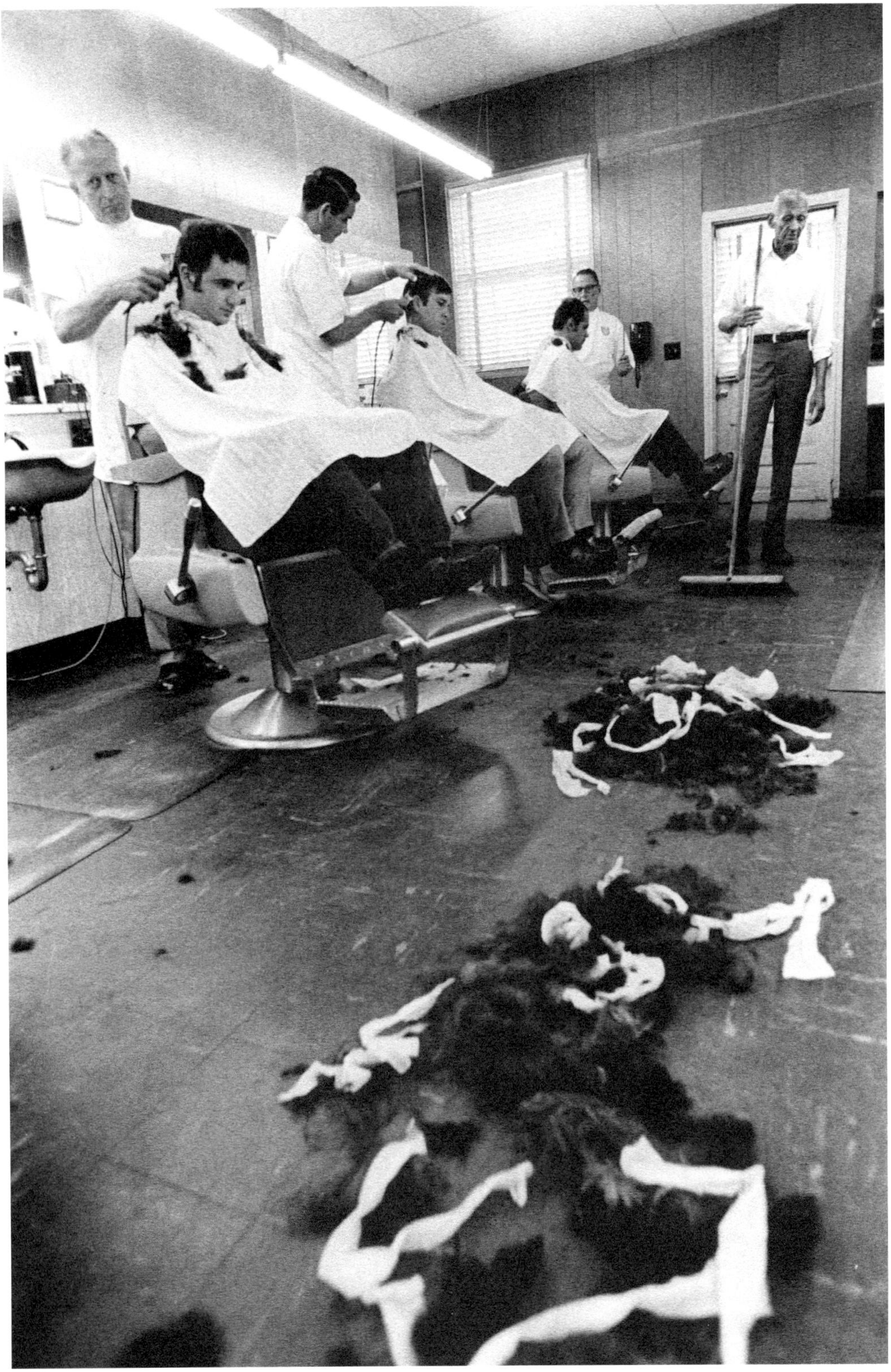

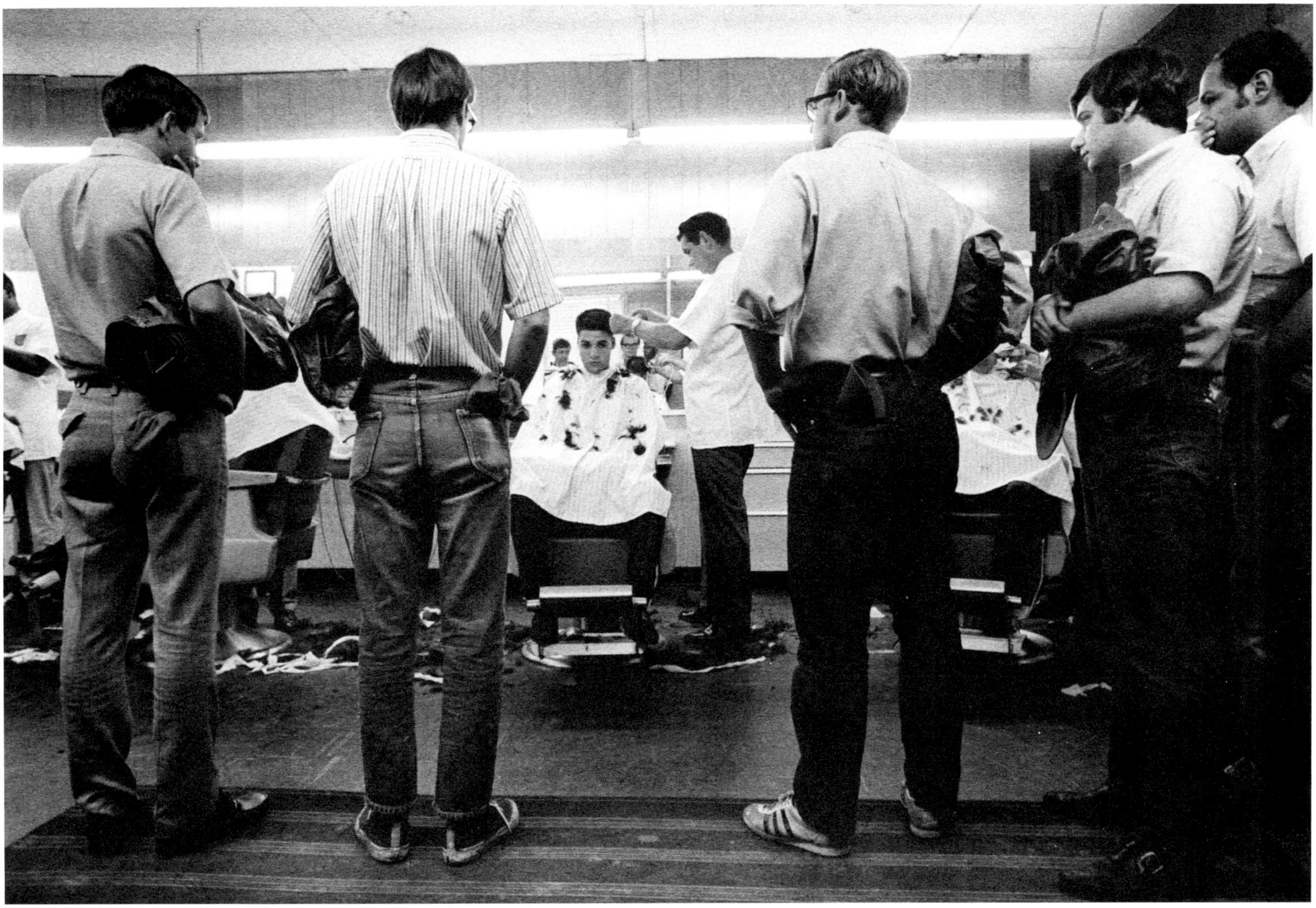

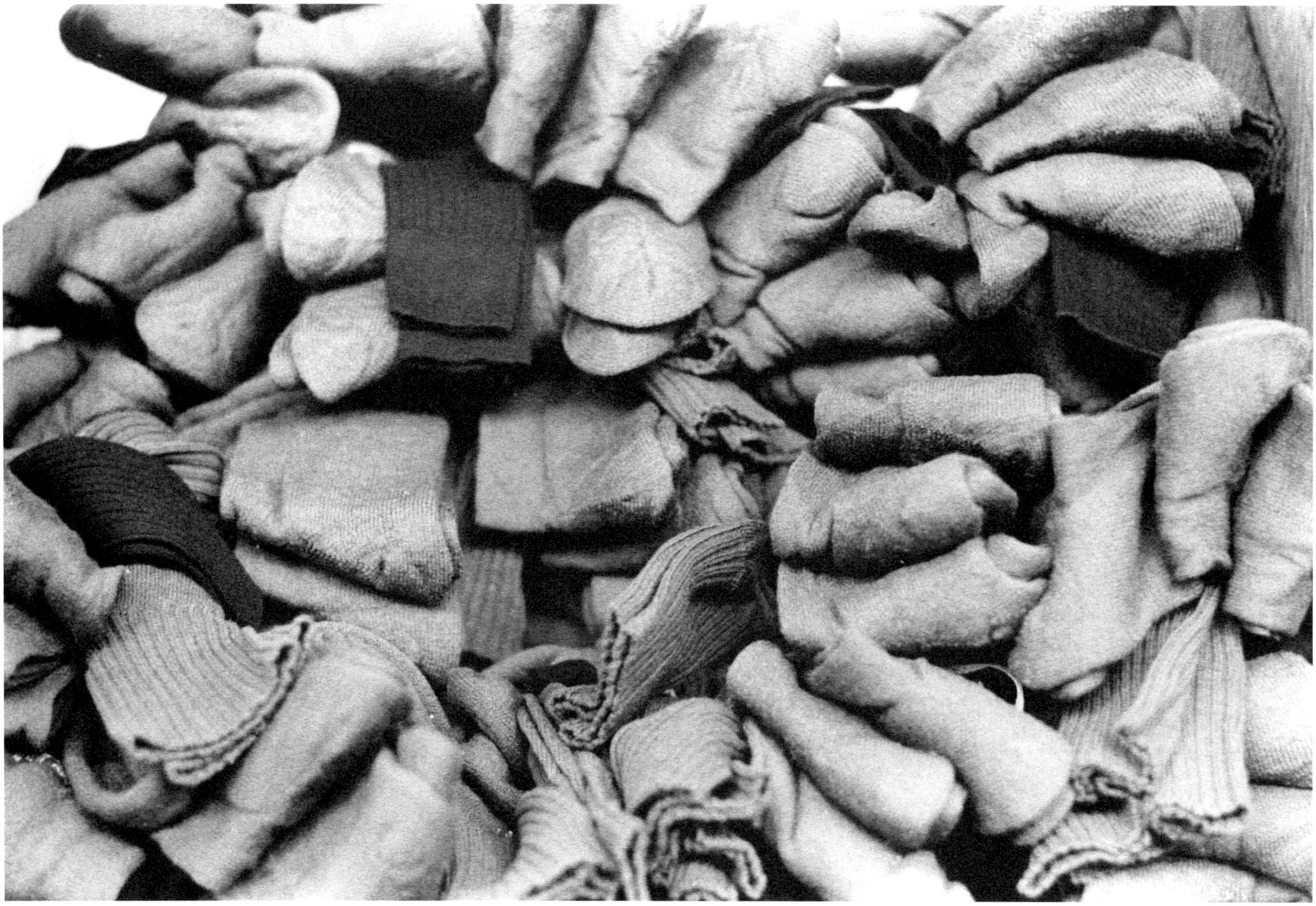

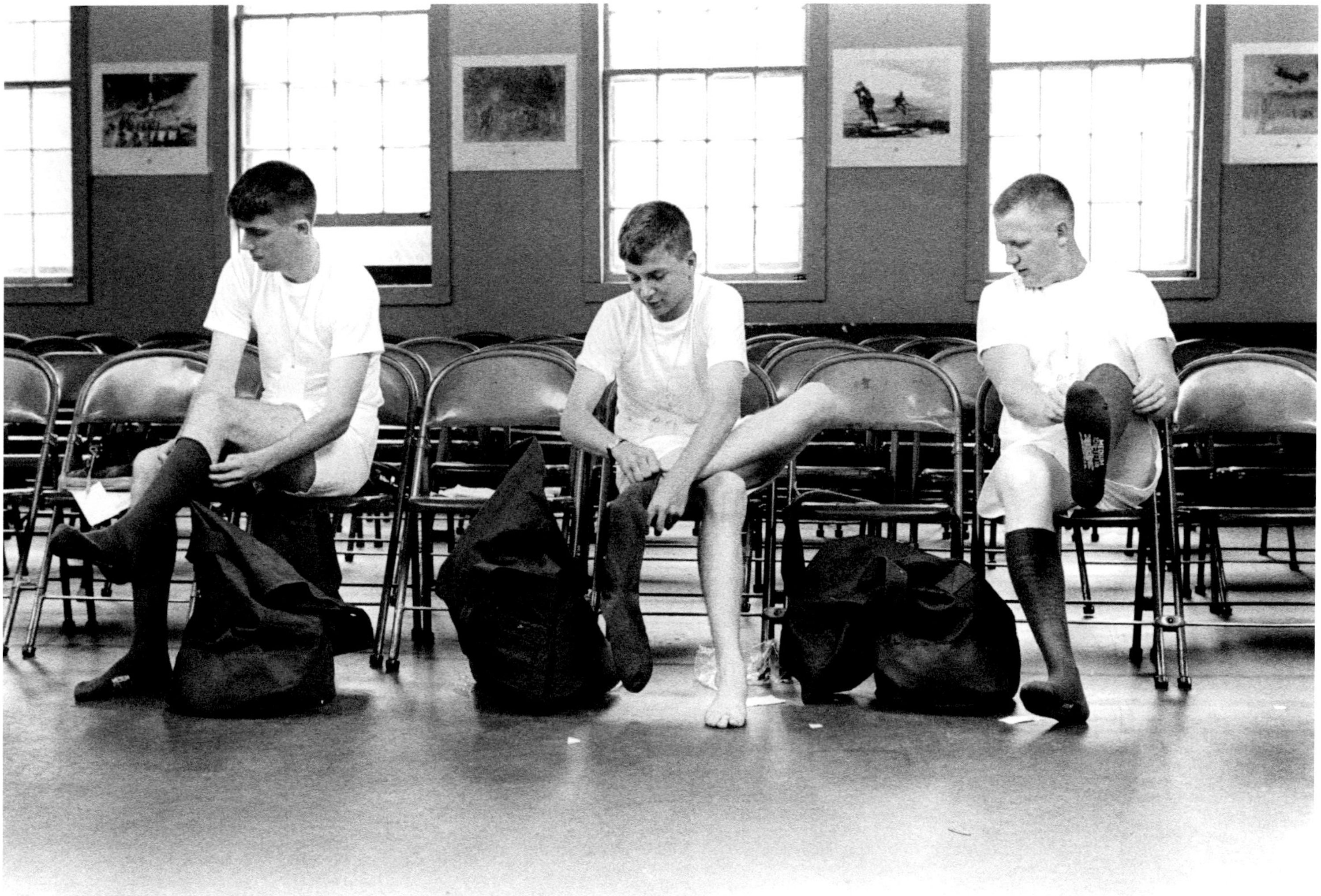

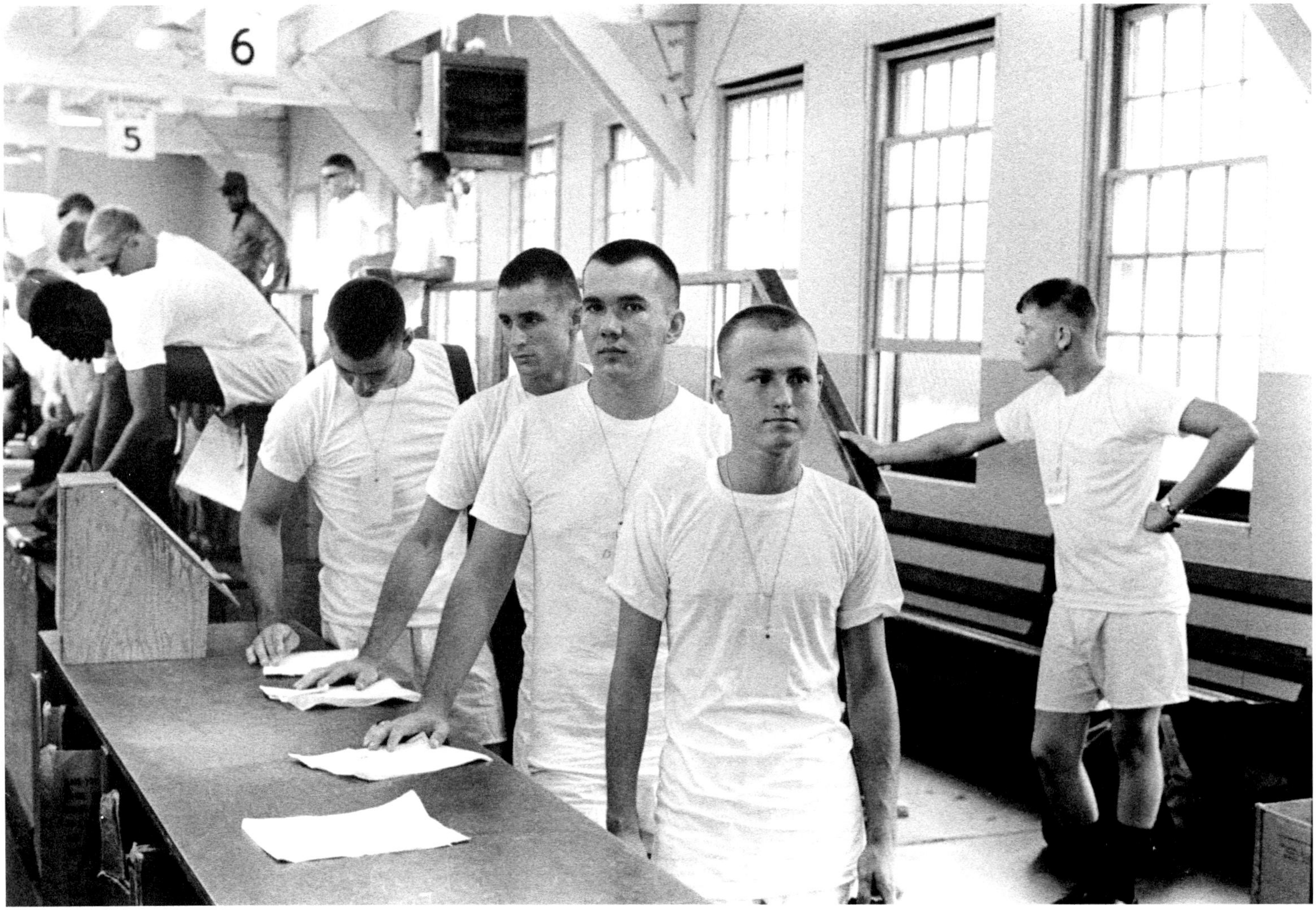
6
5

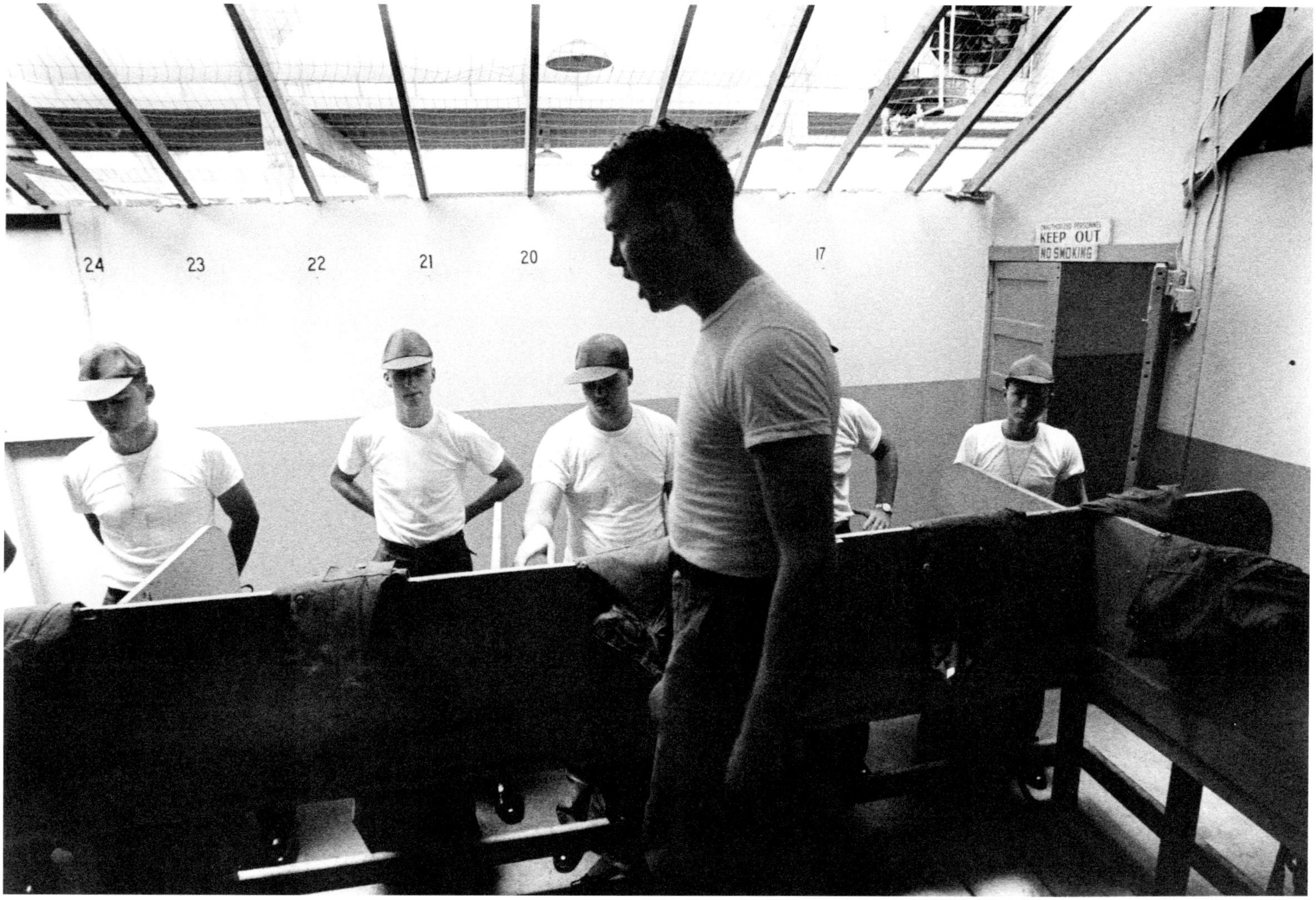
24
23
22
21
20
17
KEEP OUT
NO SMOKING

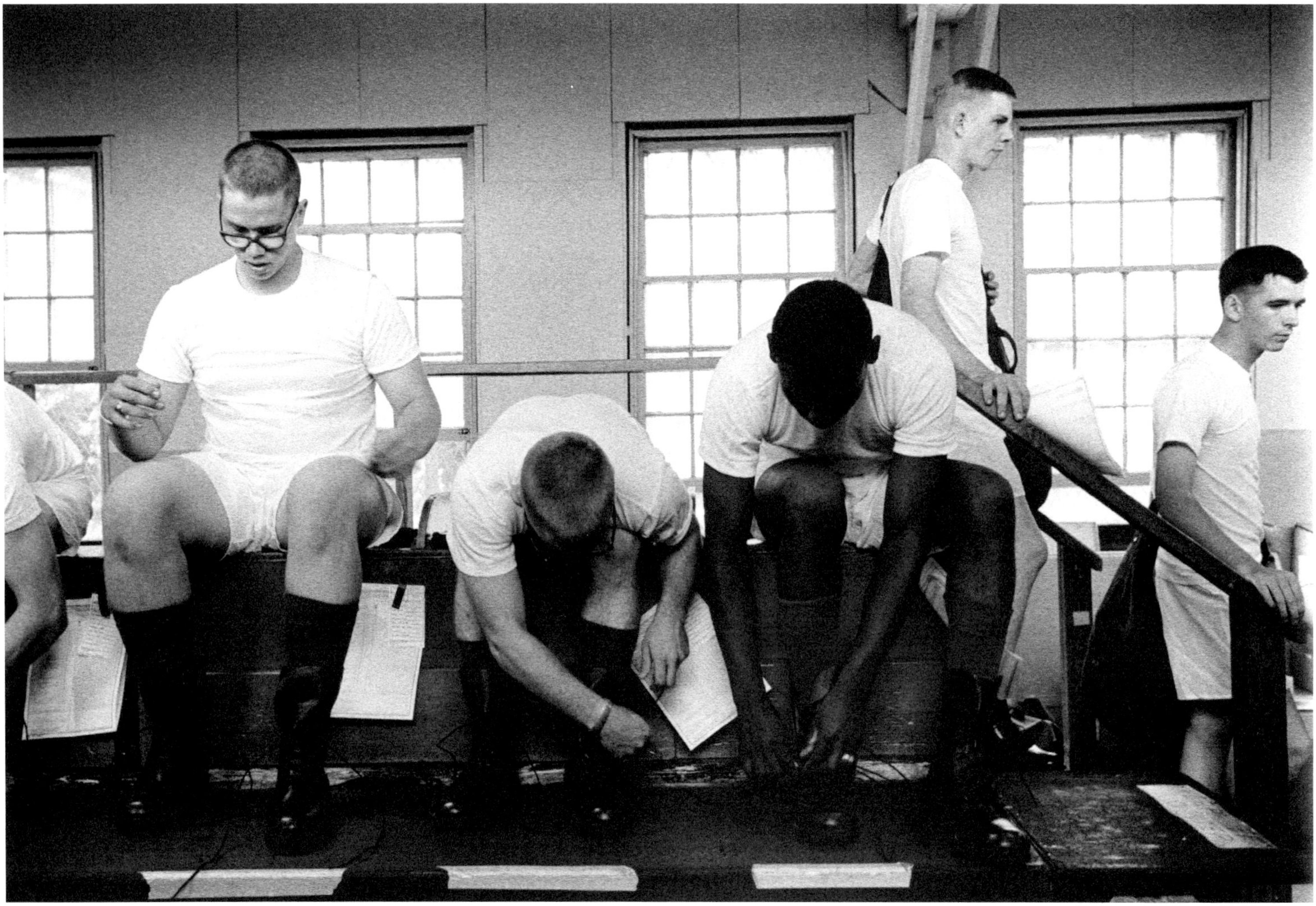

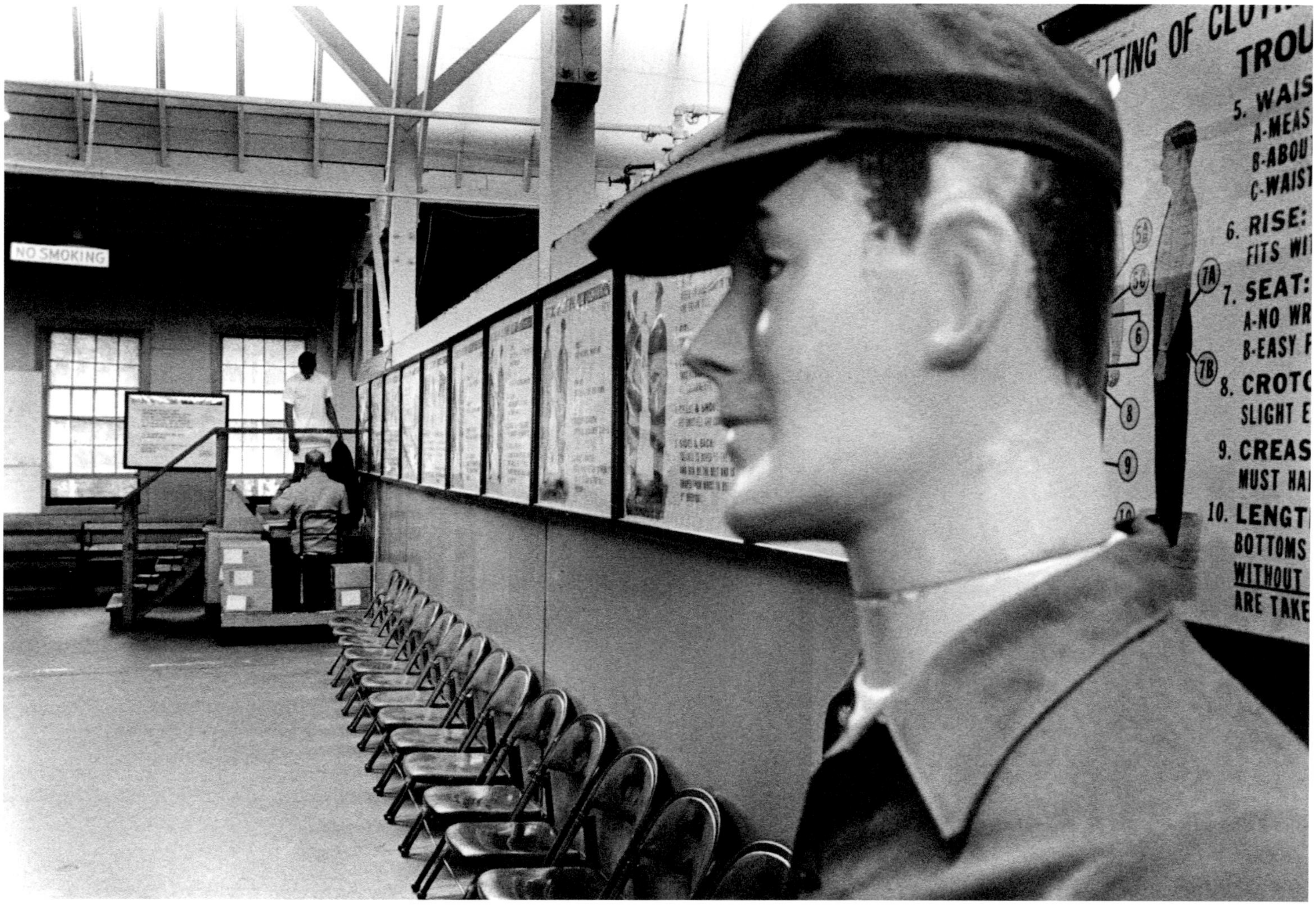
NO SMOKING
6. RISE:
7. SEAT:
BOTTOMS

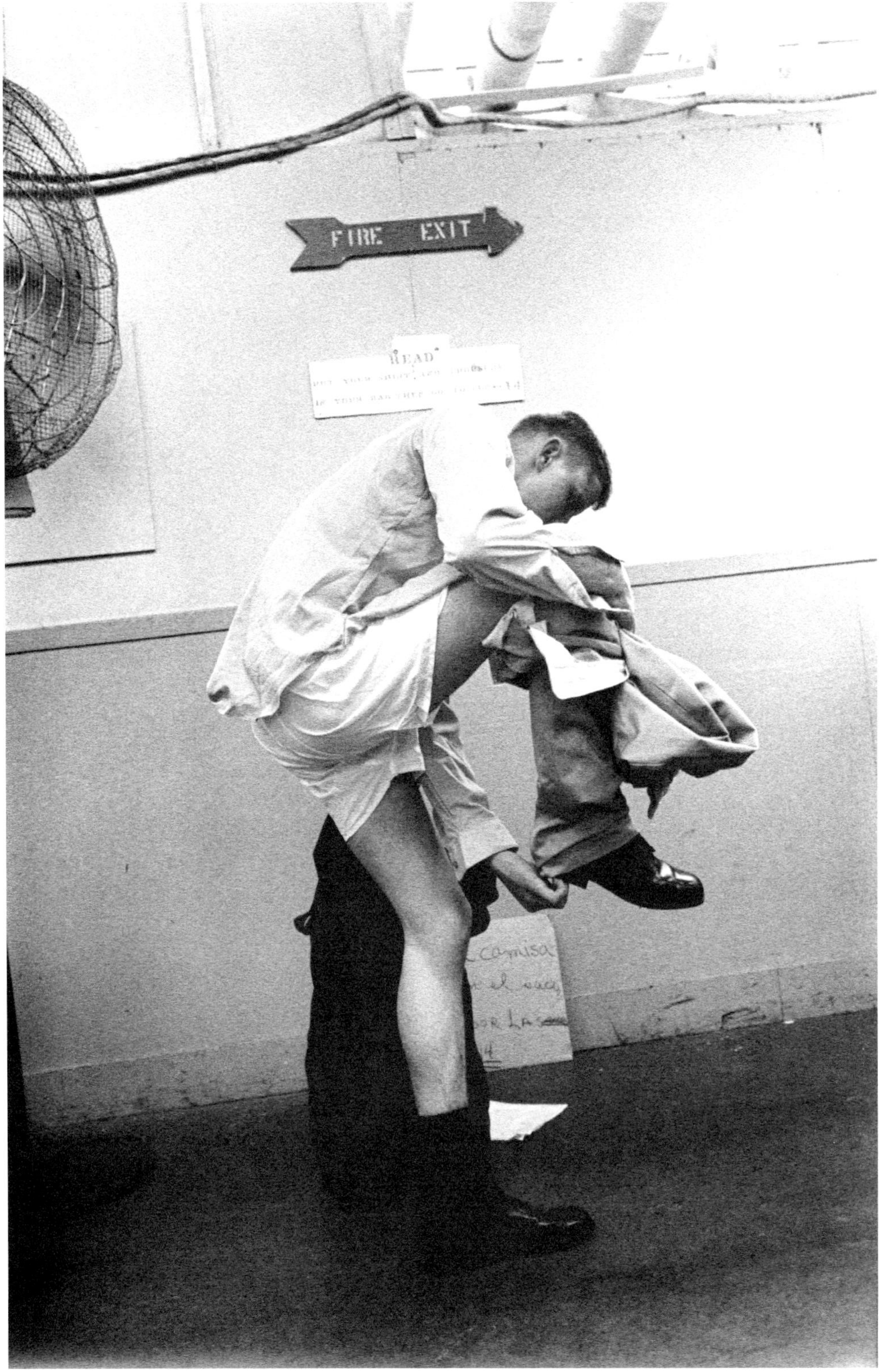
FIRE EXIT
READ

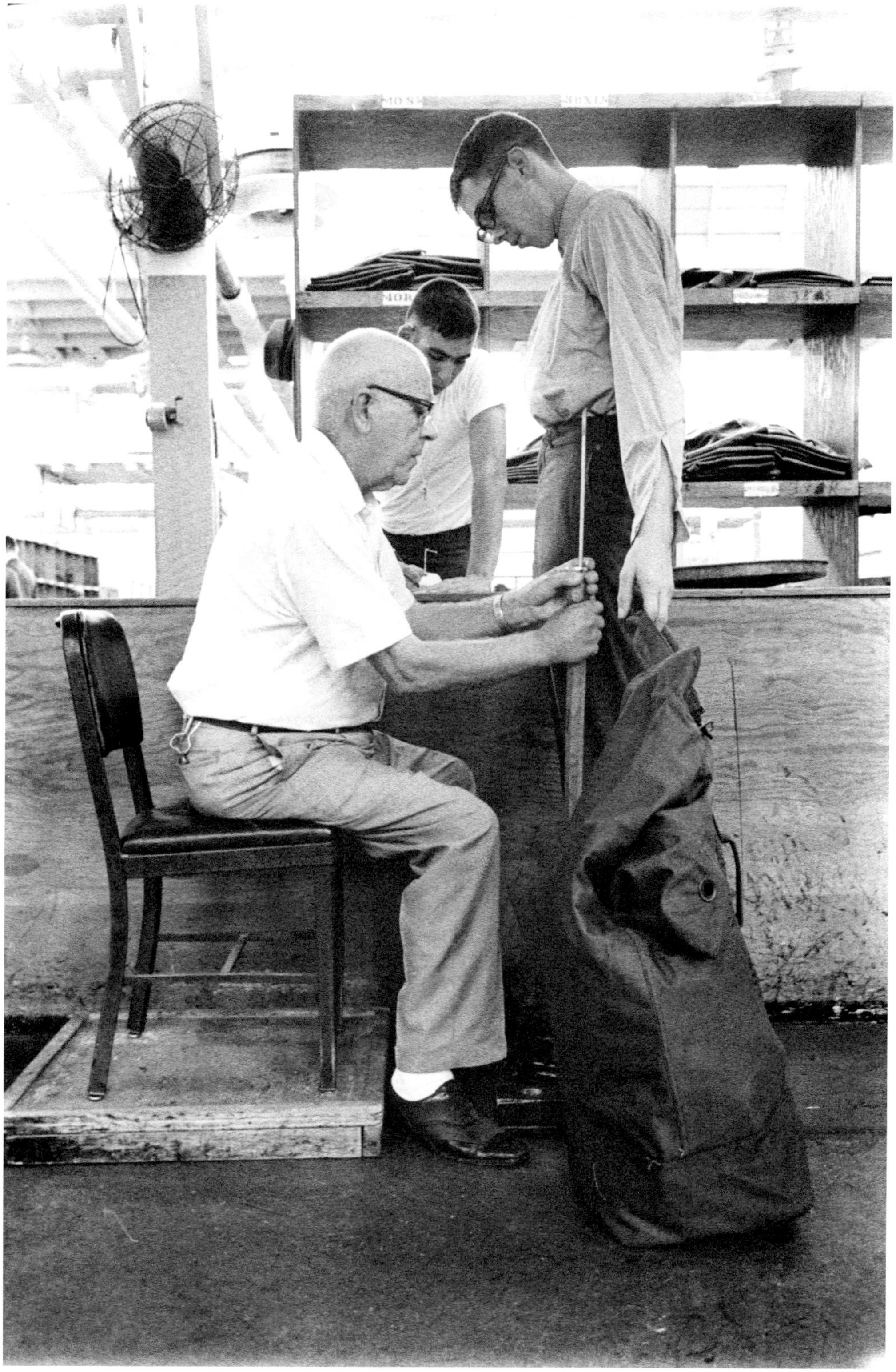

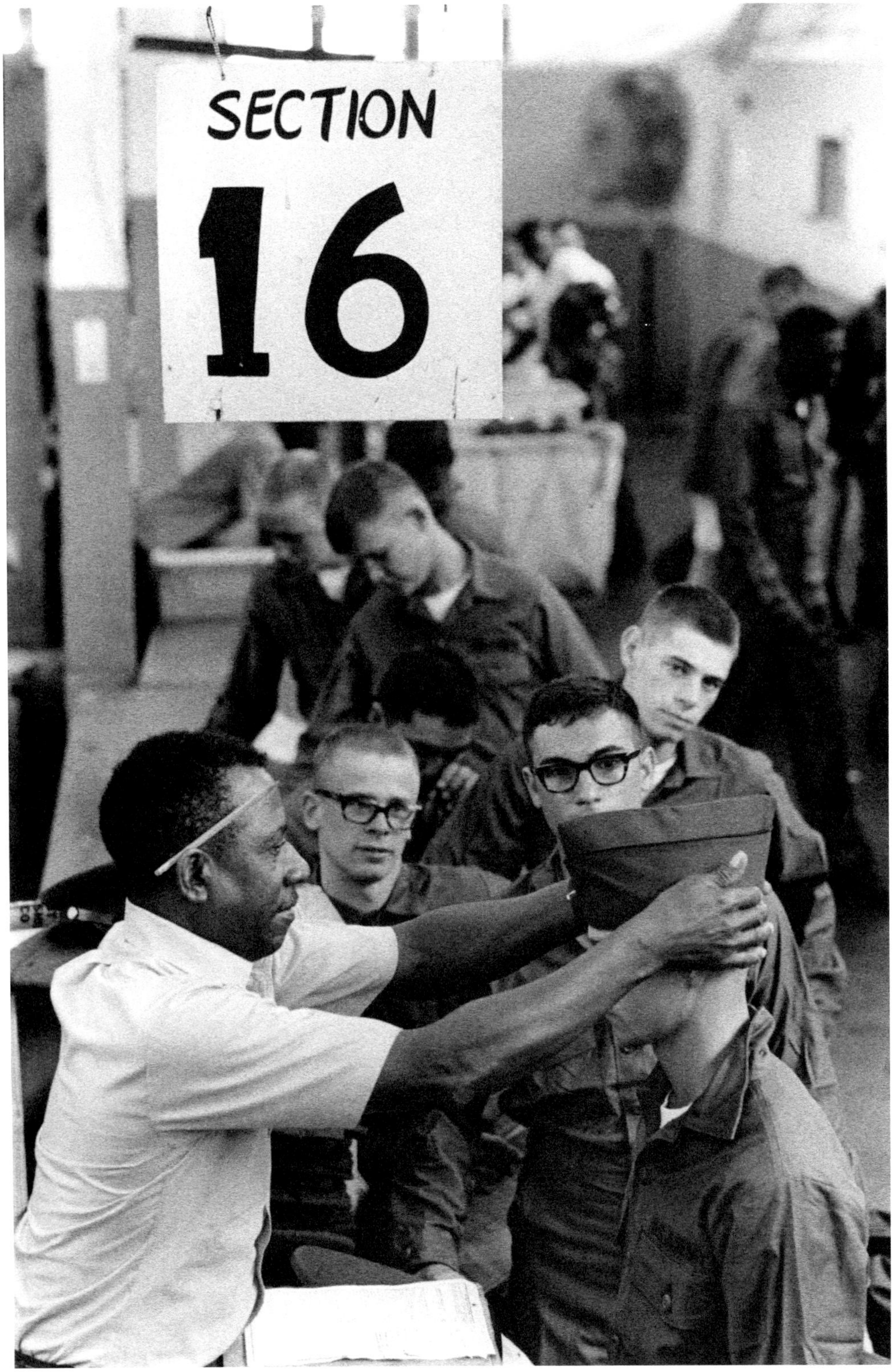
SECTION
16

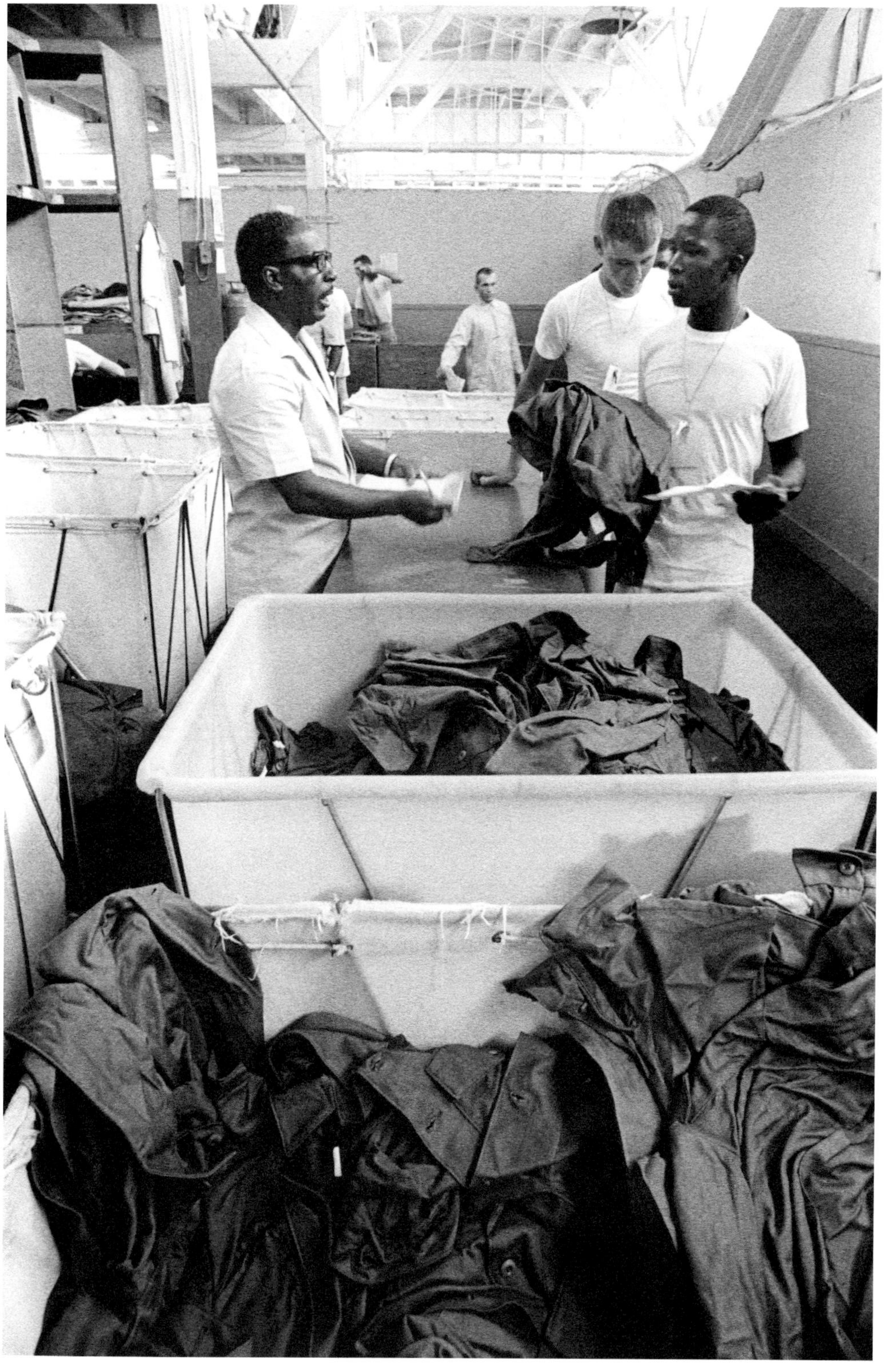

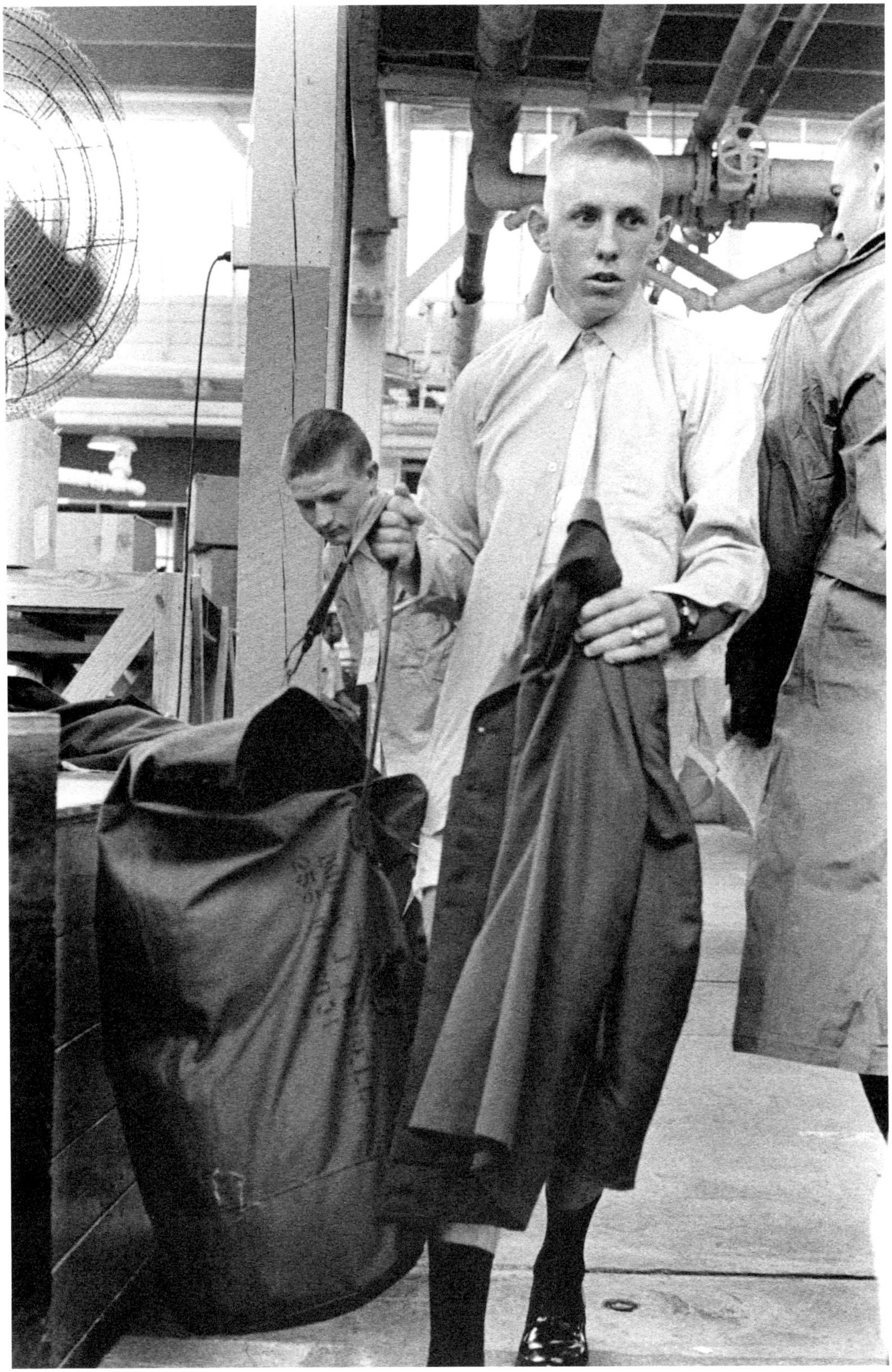

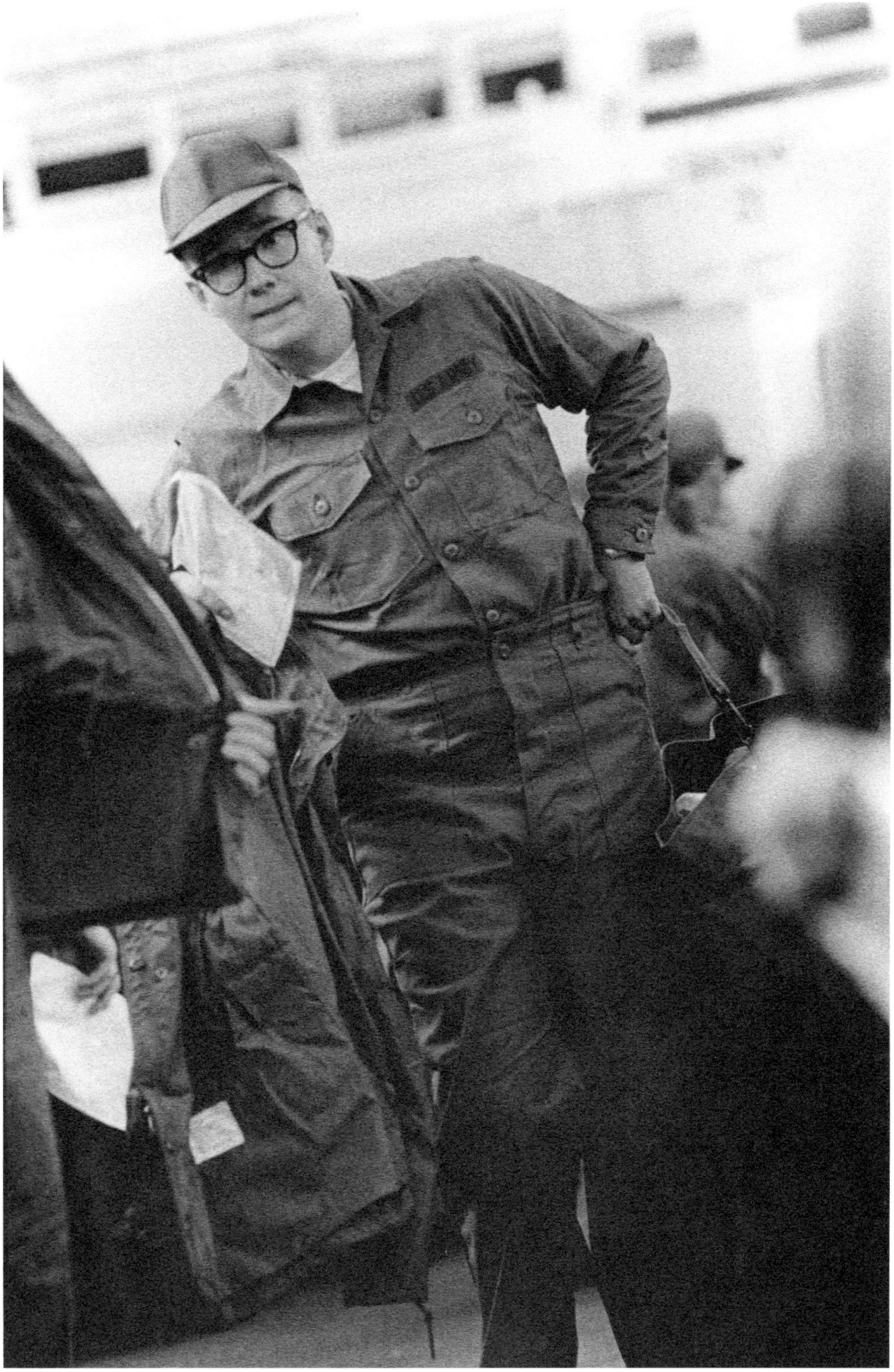

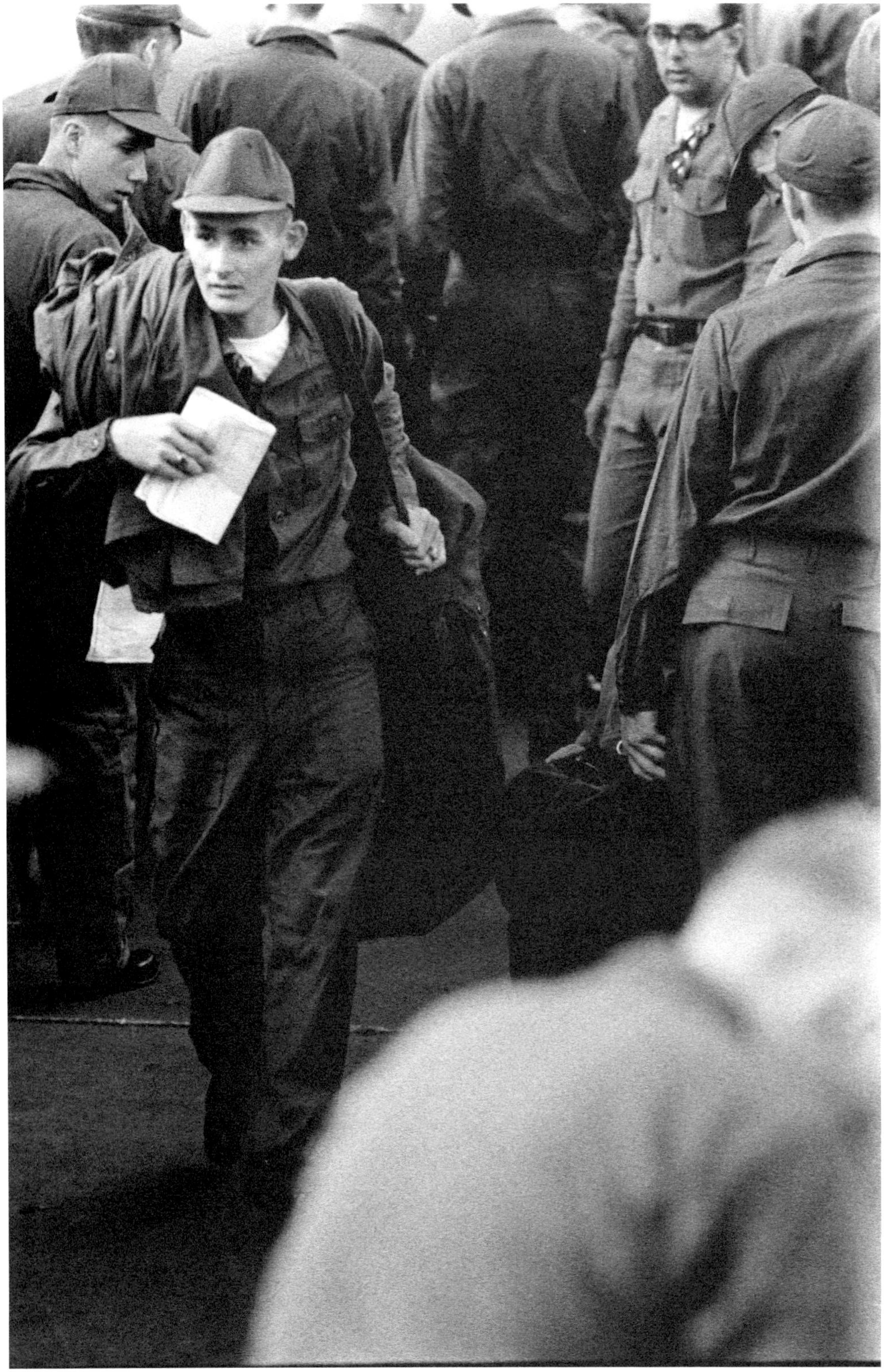

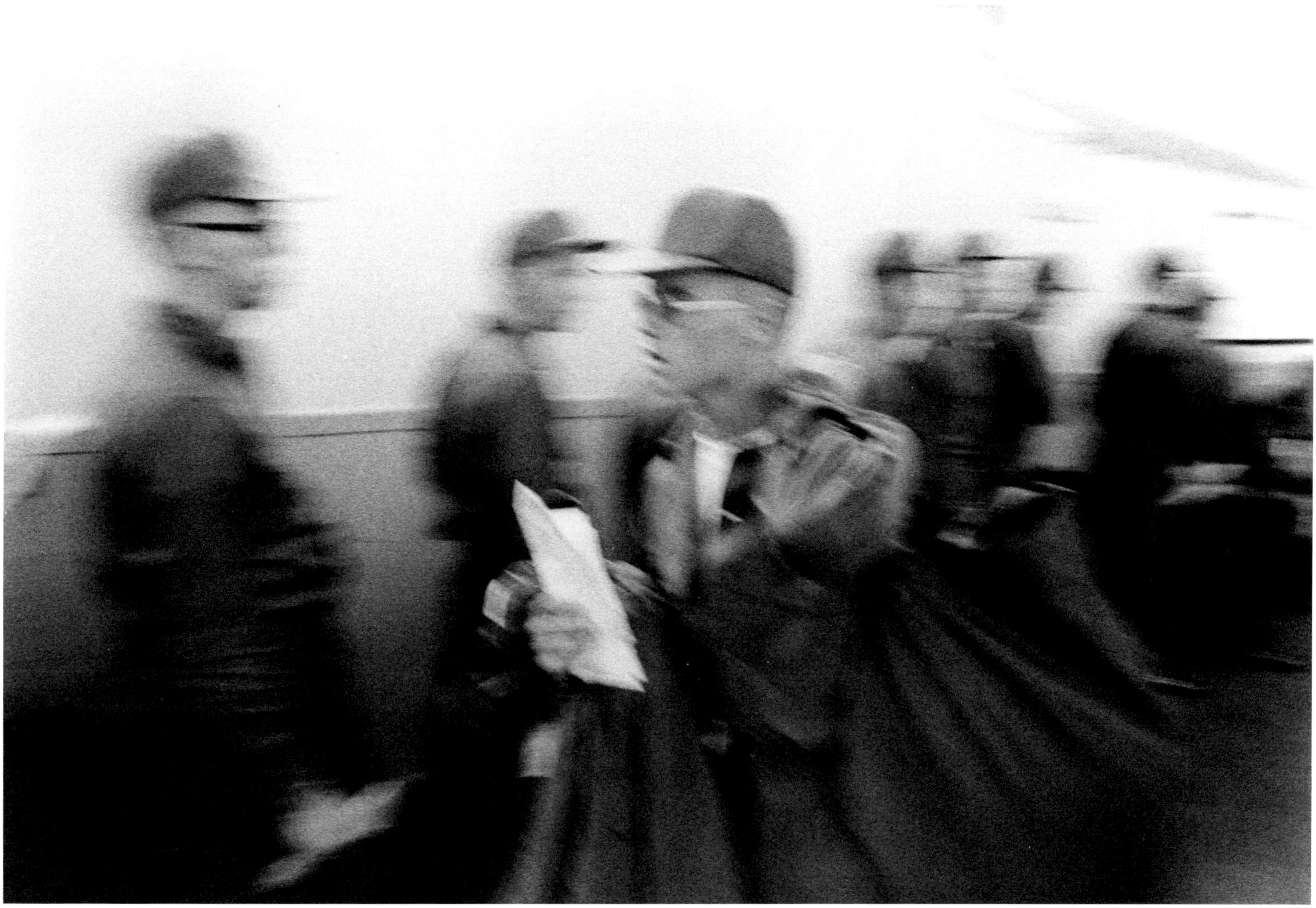

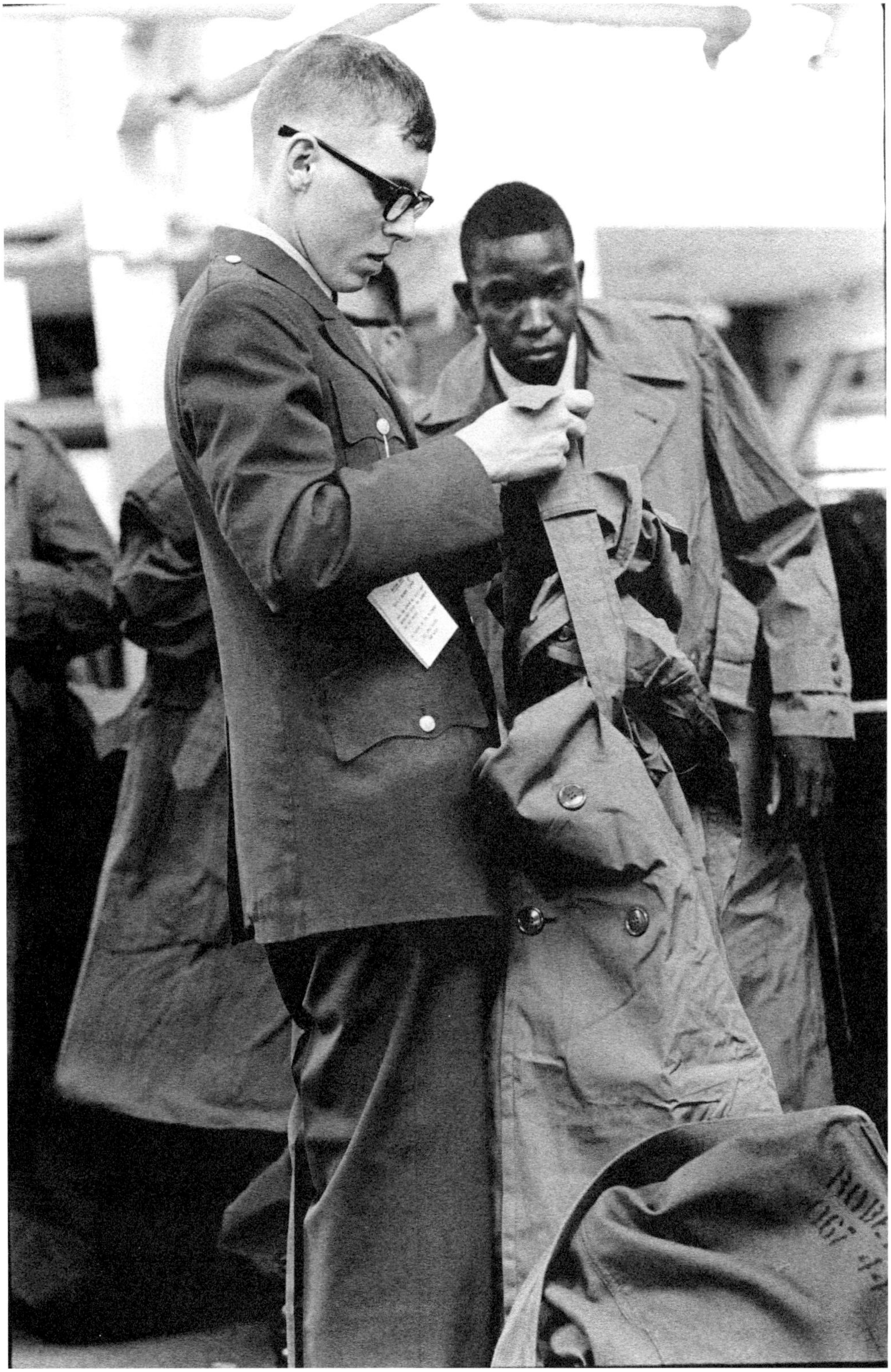

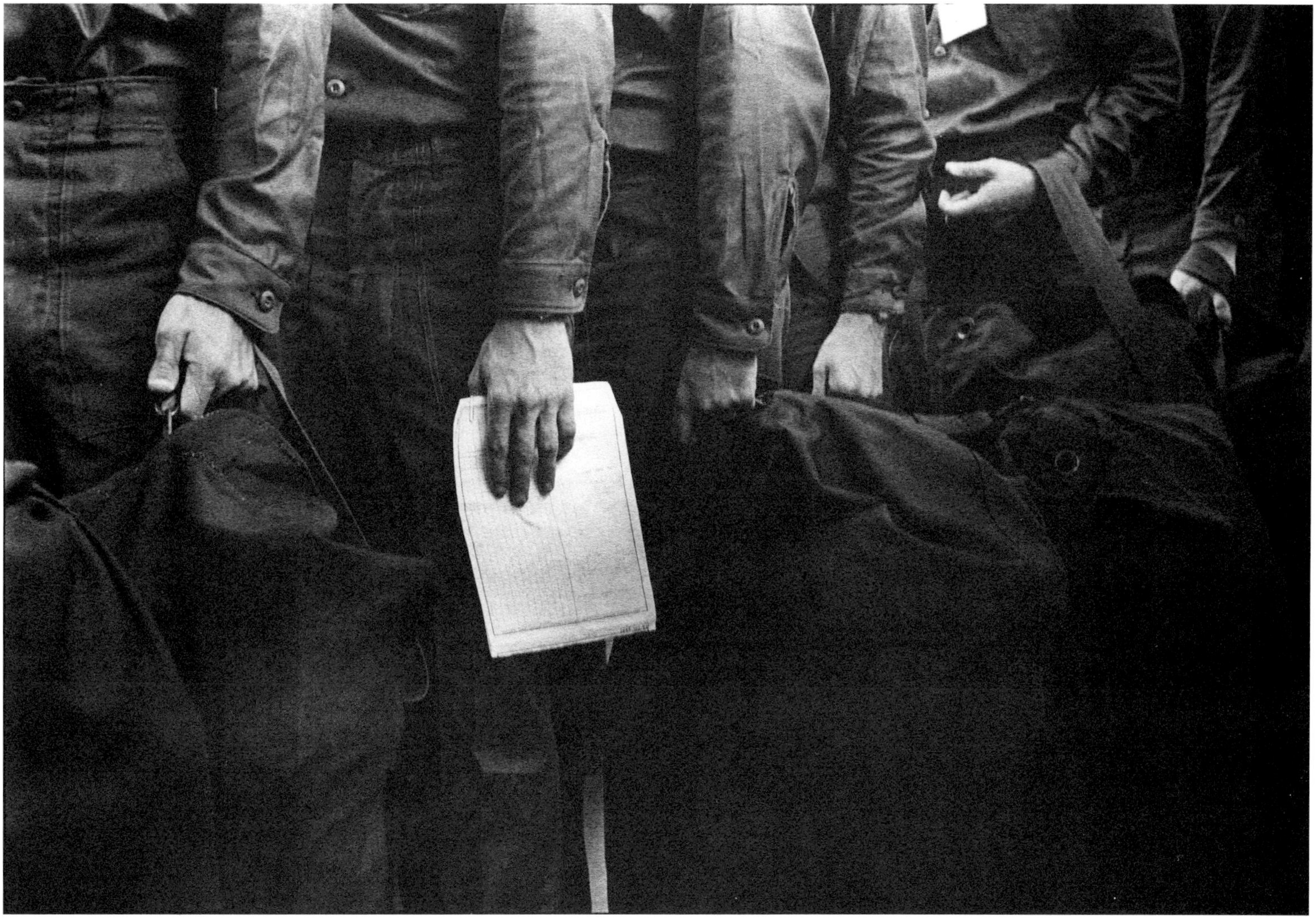

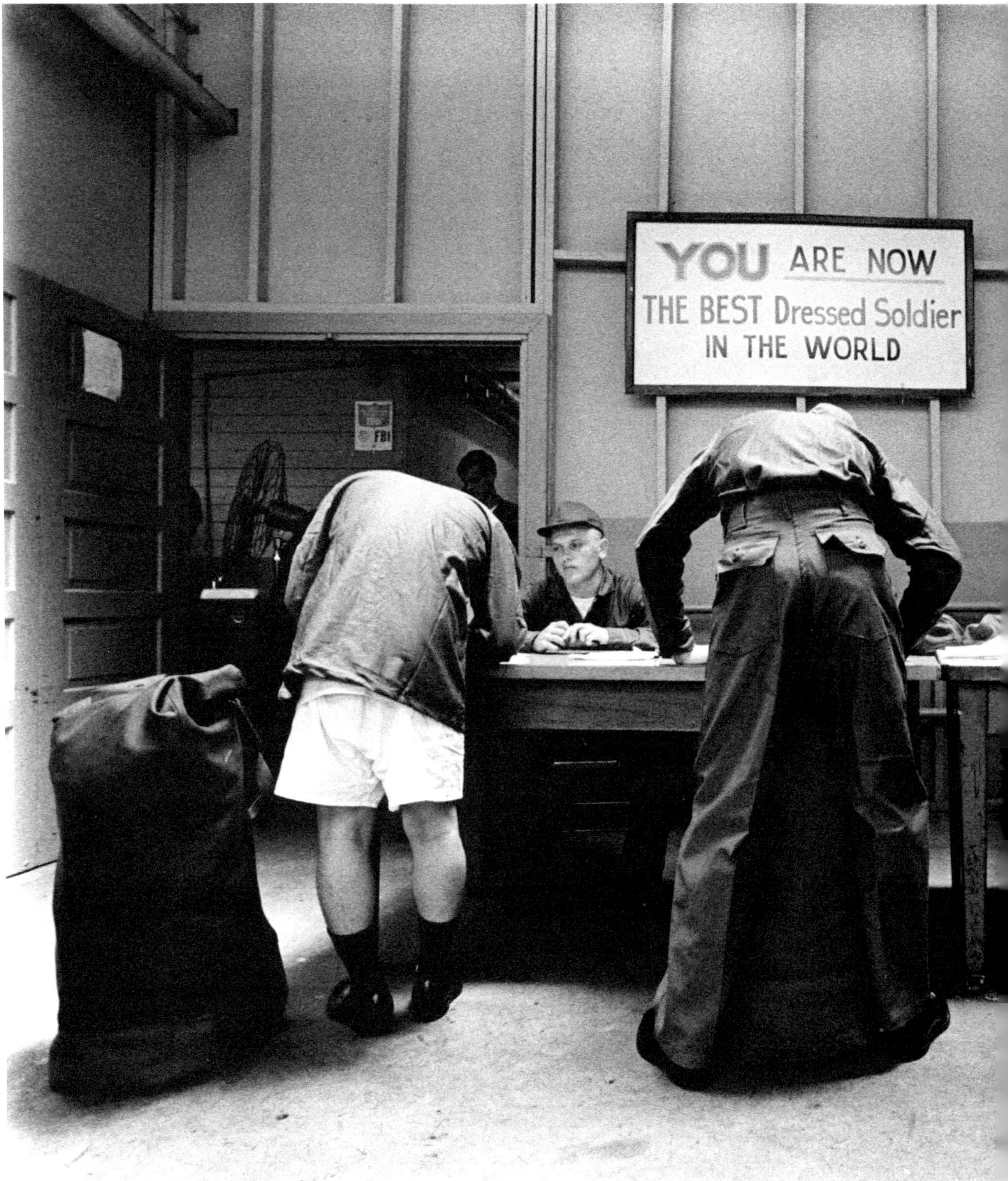
YOU ARE NOW
THE BEST Dressed Soldier
IN THE WORLD
FBI

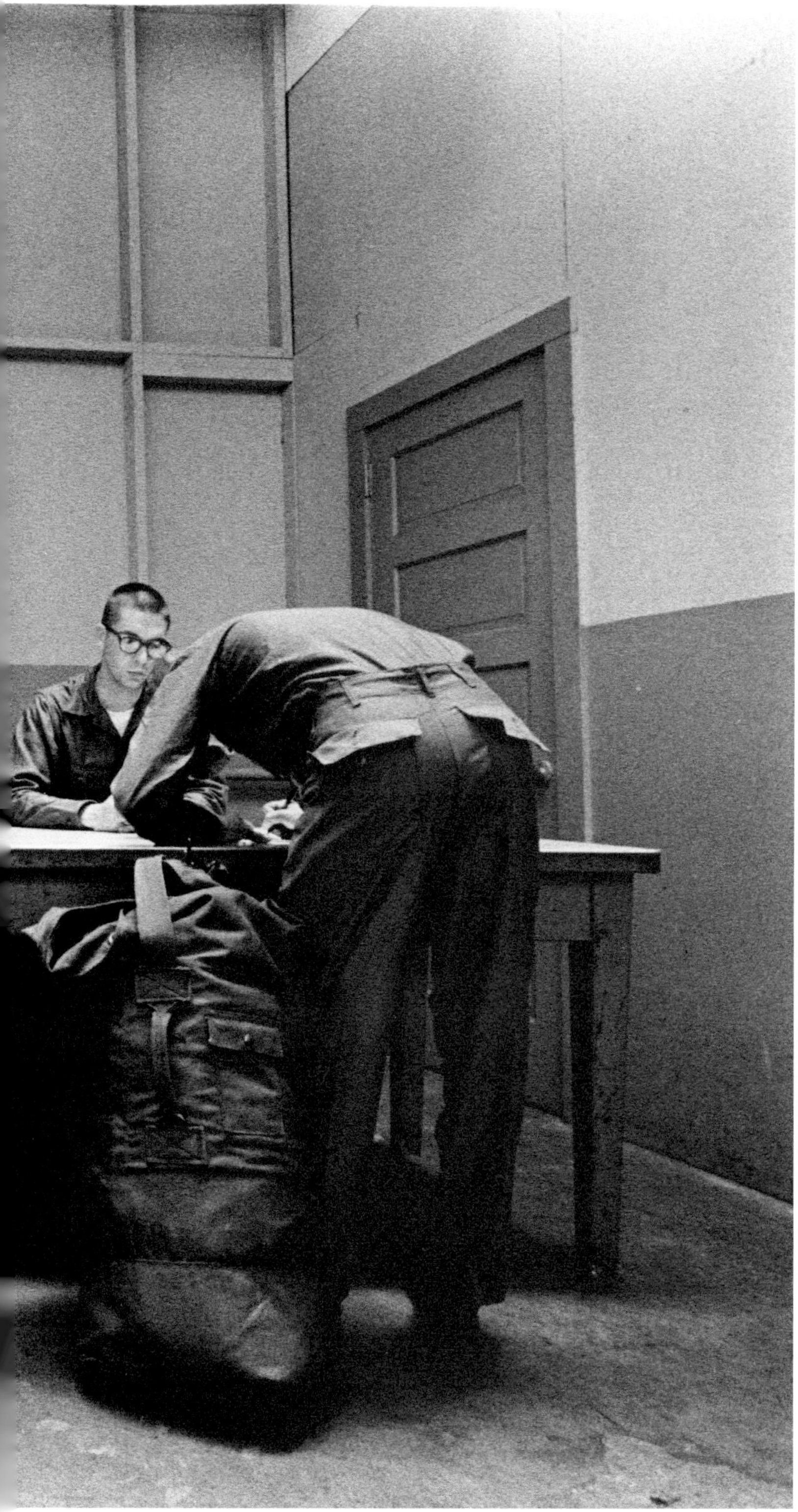

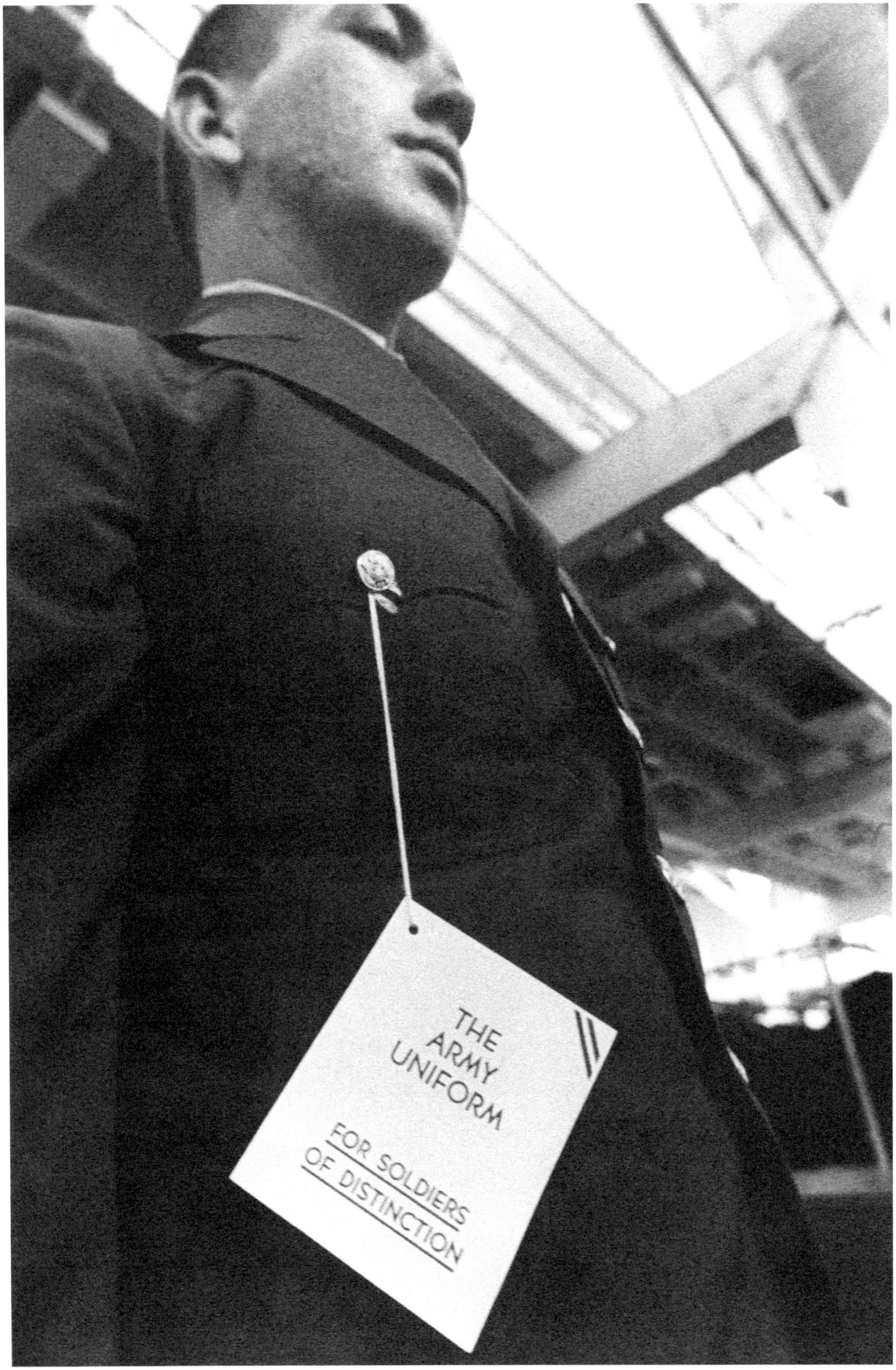
THE
ARMY
UNIFORM
FOR SOLDIERS
OF DISTINCTION

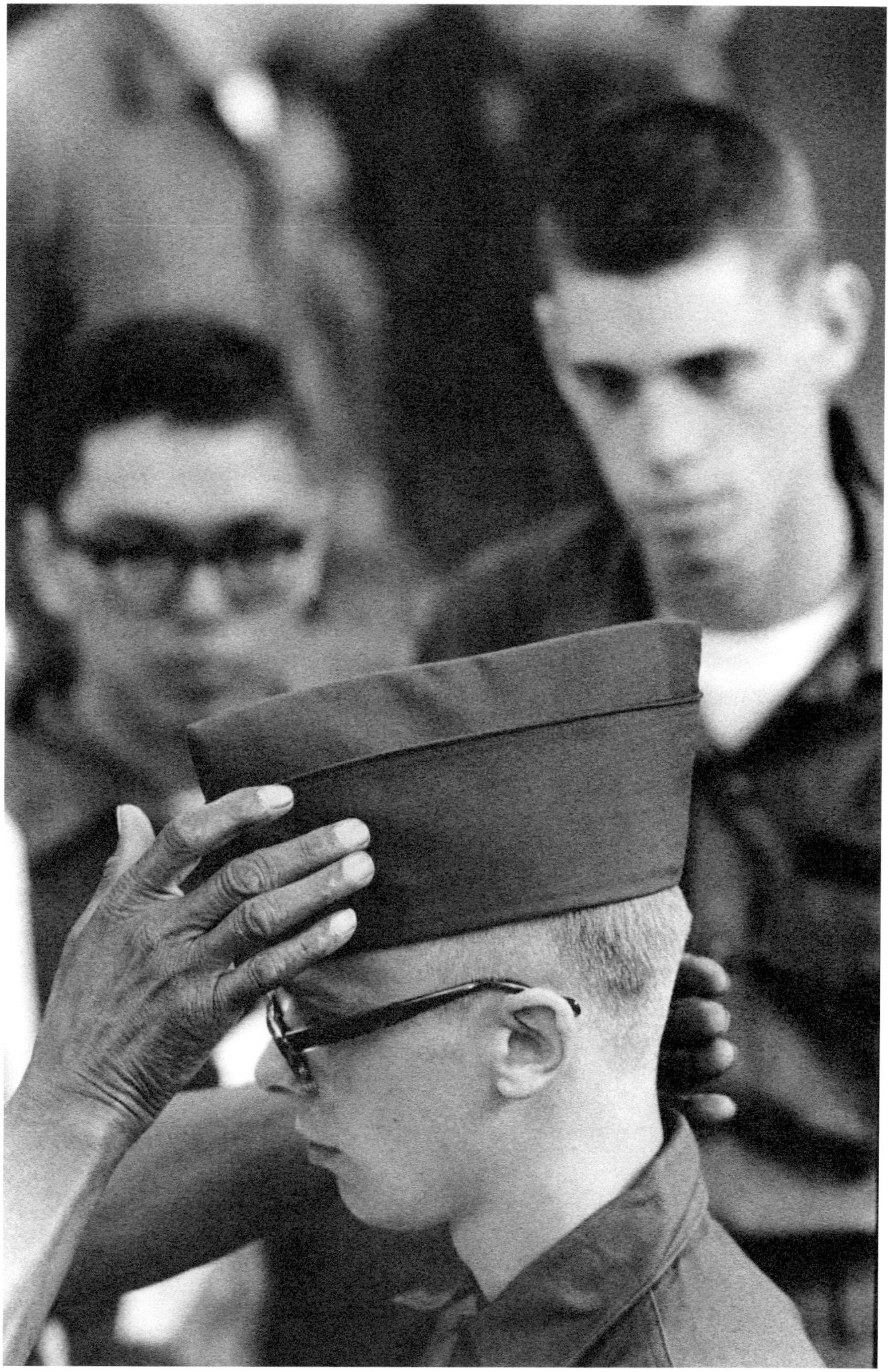

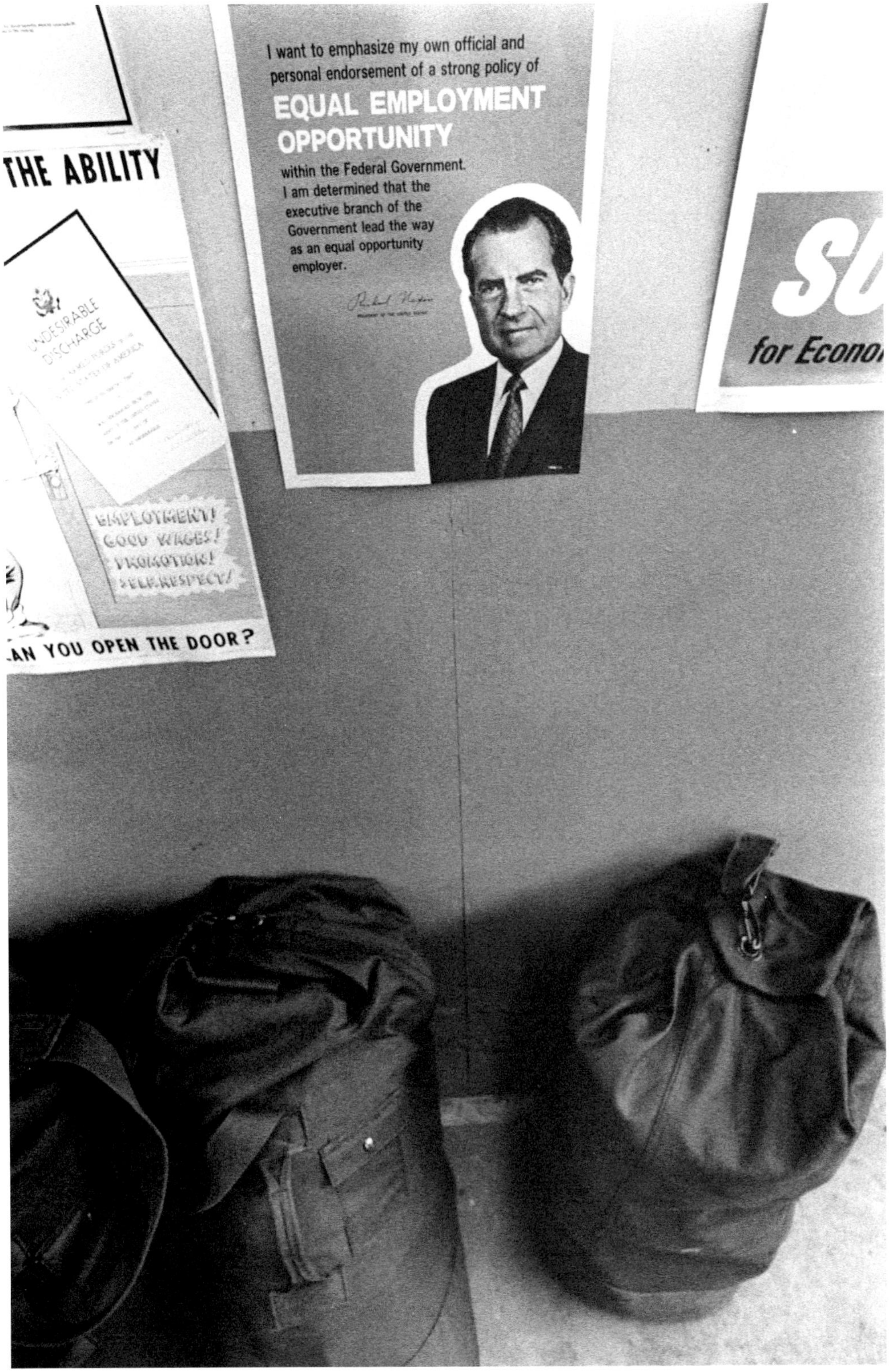
I want to emphasize my own official and personal endorsement of a strong policy of
EQUAL EMPLOYMENT OPPORTUNITY
within the Federal Government. I am determined that the executive branch of the Government lead the way as an equal opportunity employer.
THE ABILITY
UNDESIRABLE DISCHARGE
EMPLOYMENT! GOOD WAGES! PROMOTION! SELF-RESPECT!
AN YOU OPEN THE DOOR?
for Econo

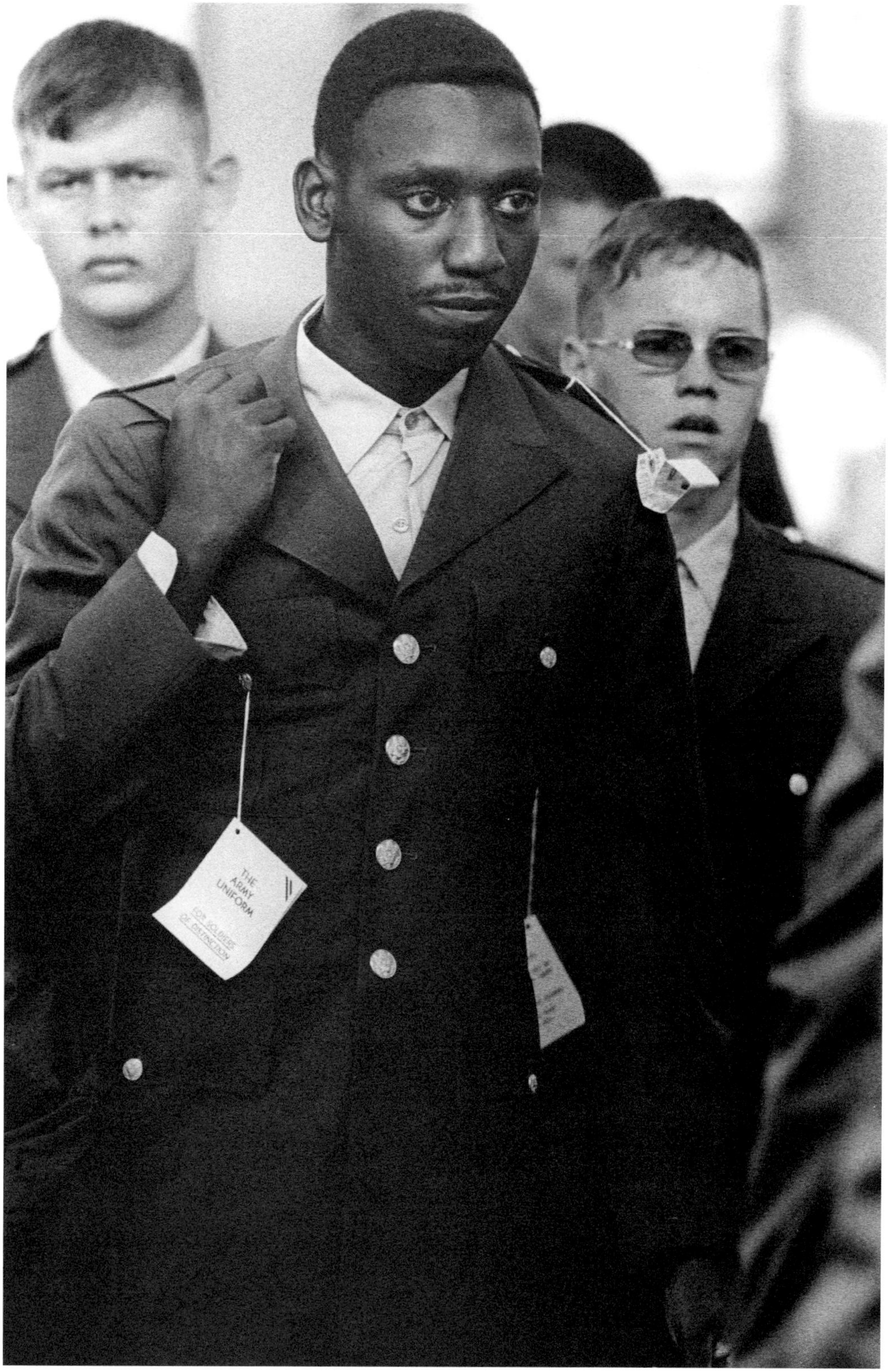
THE ARMY UNIFORM
FOR SOLDIERS OF DISTINCTION

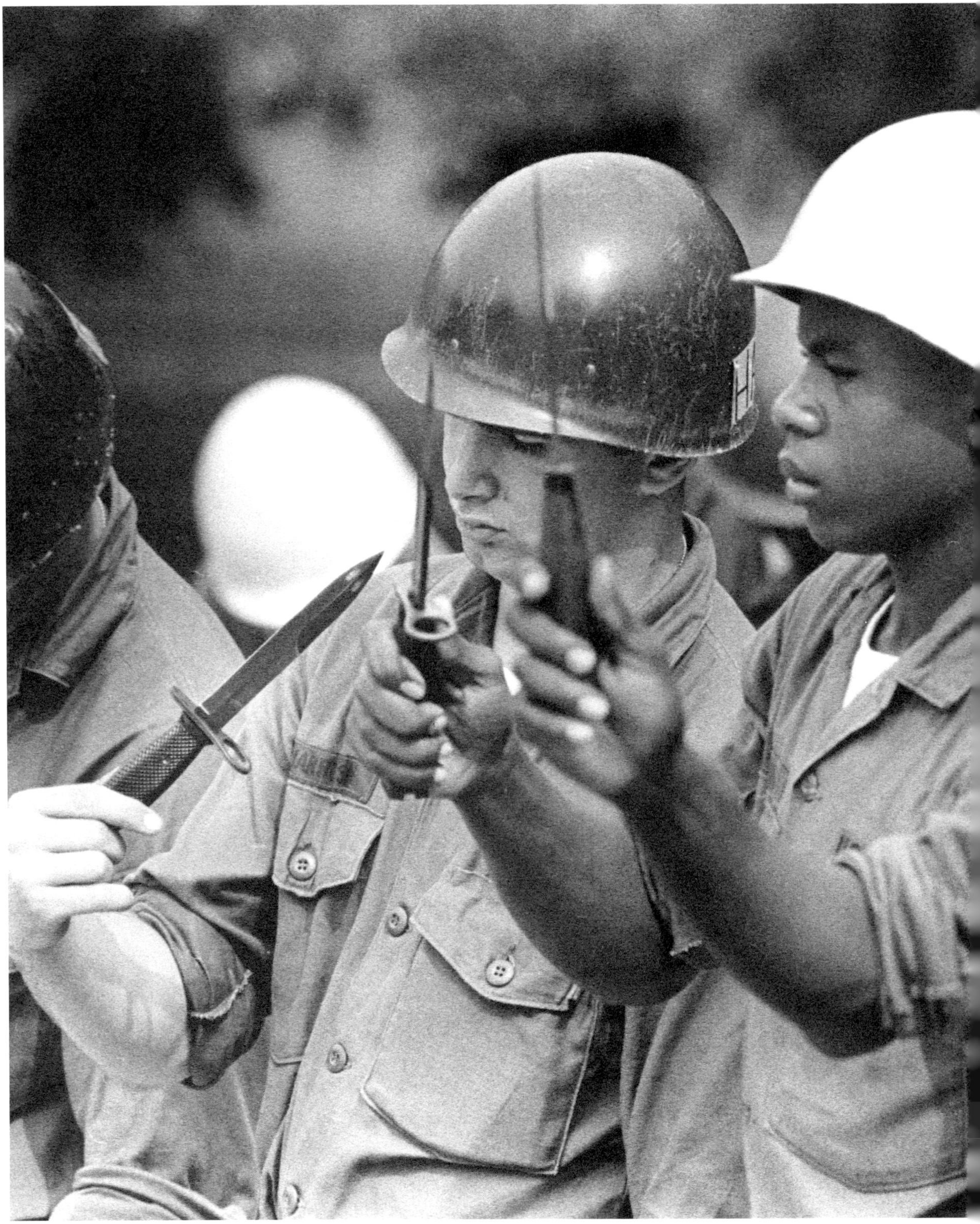

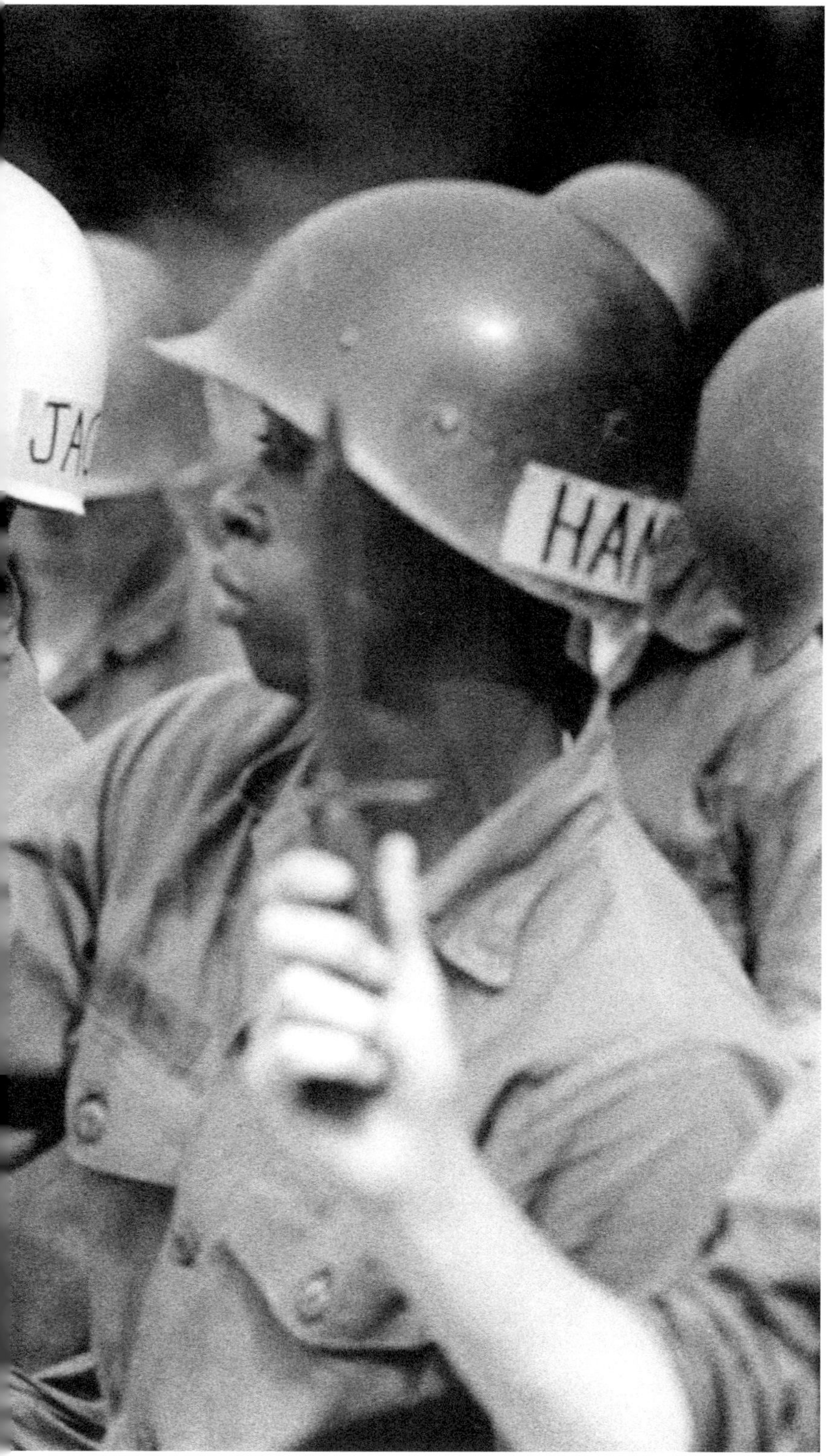
JA
HA

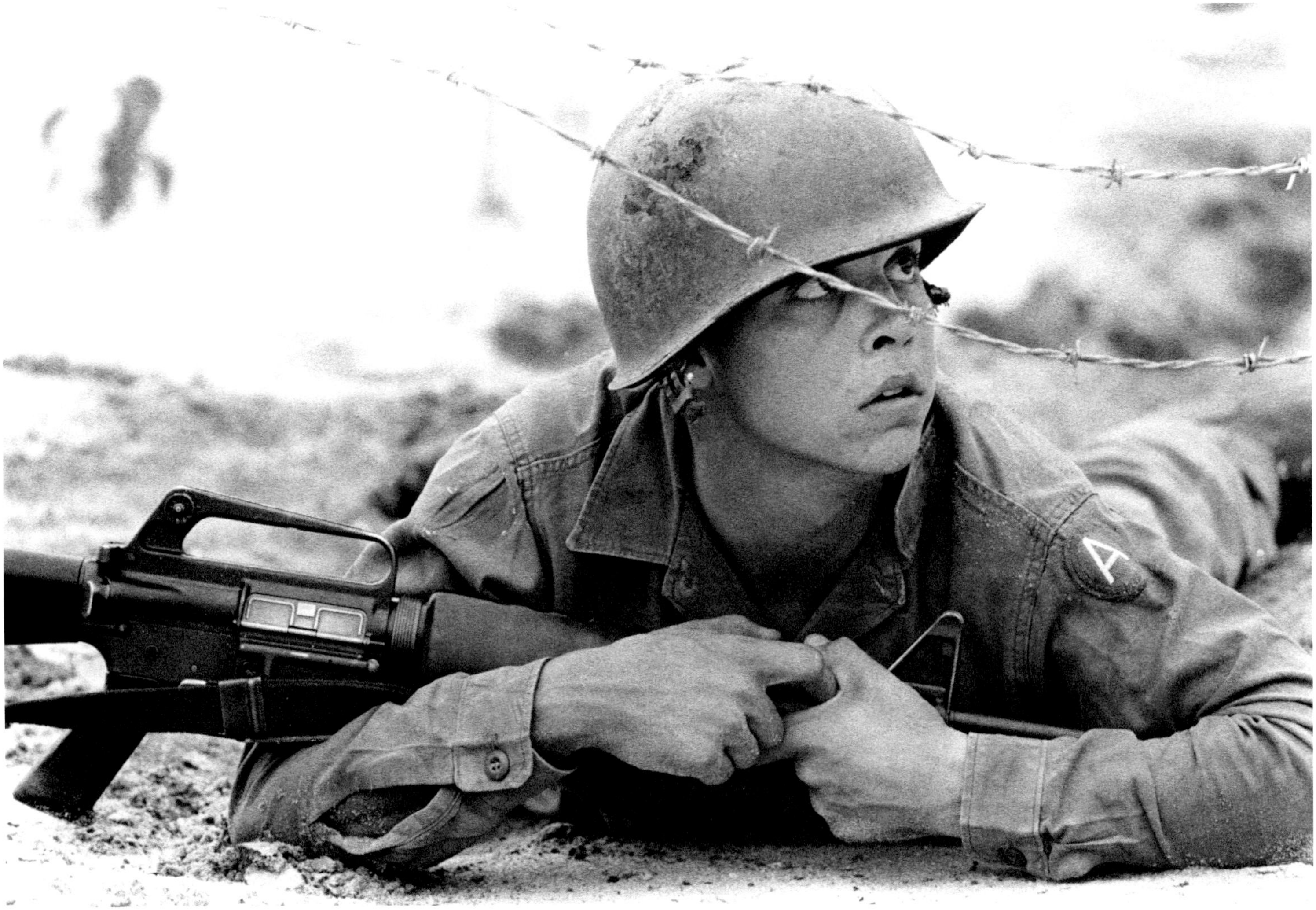

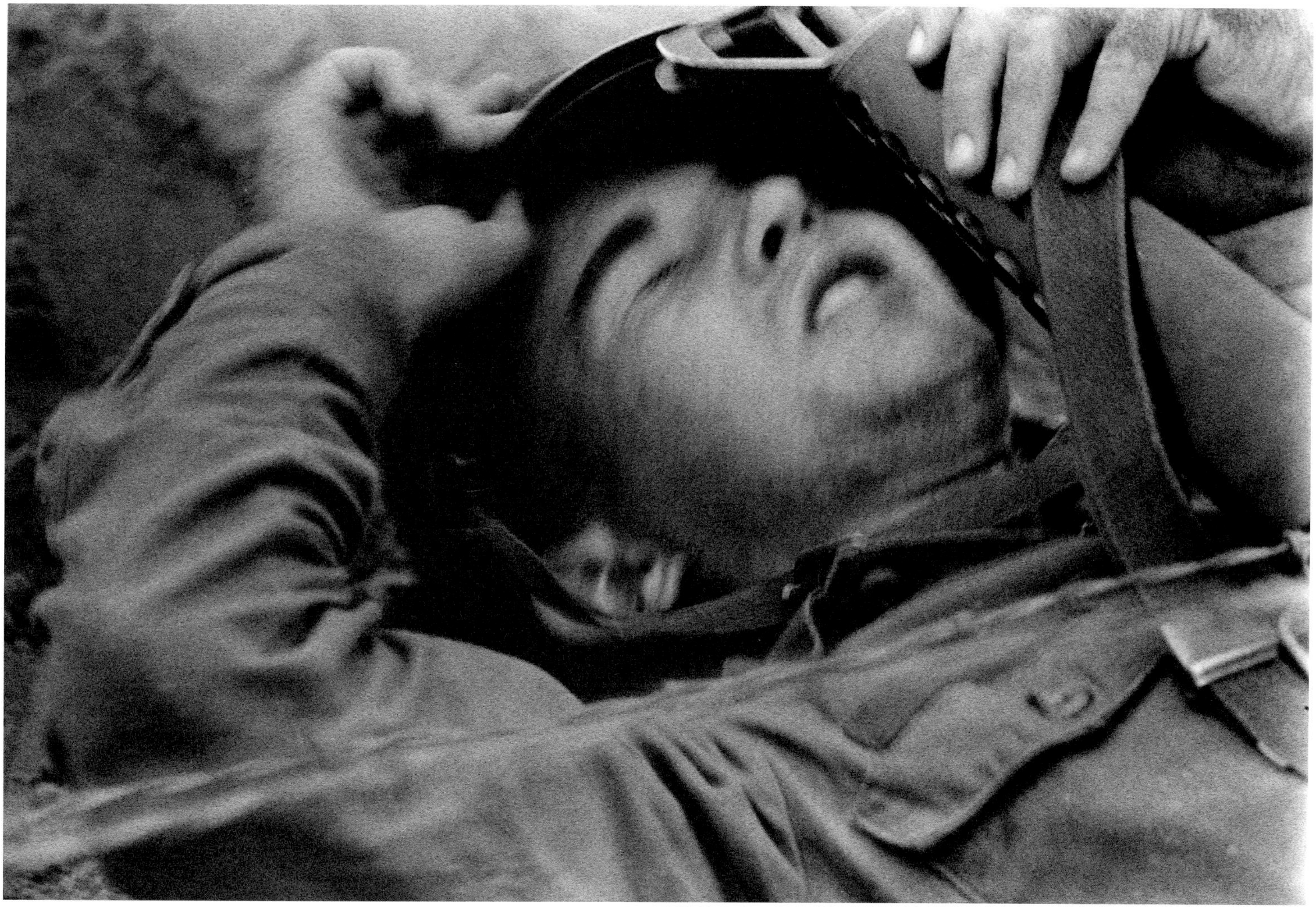

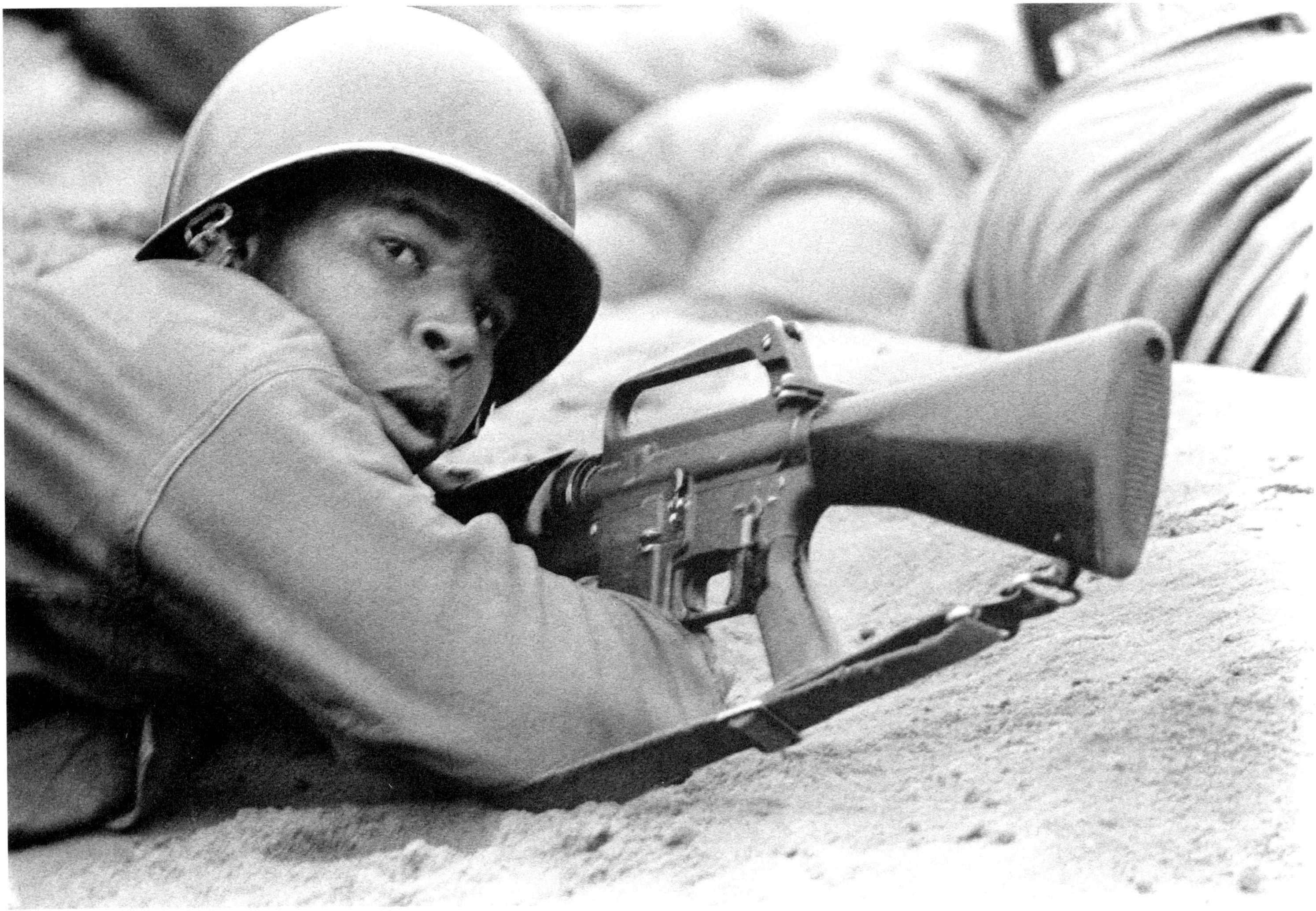

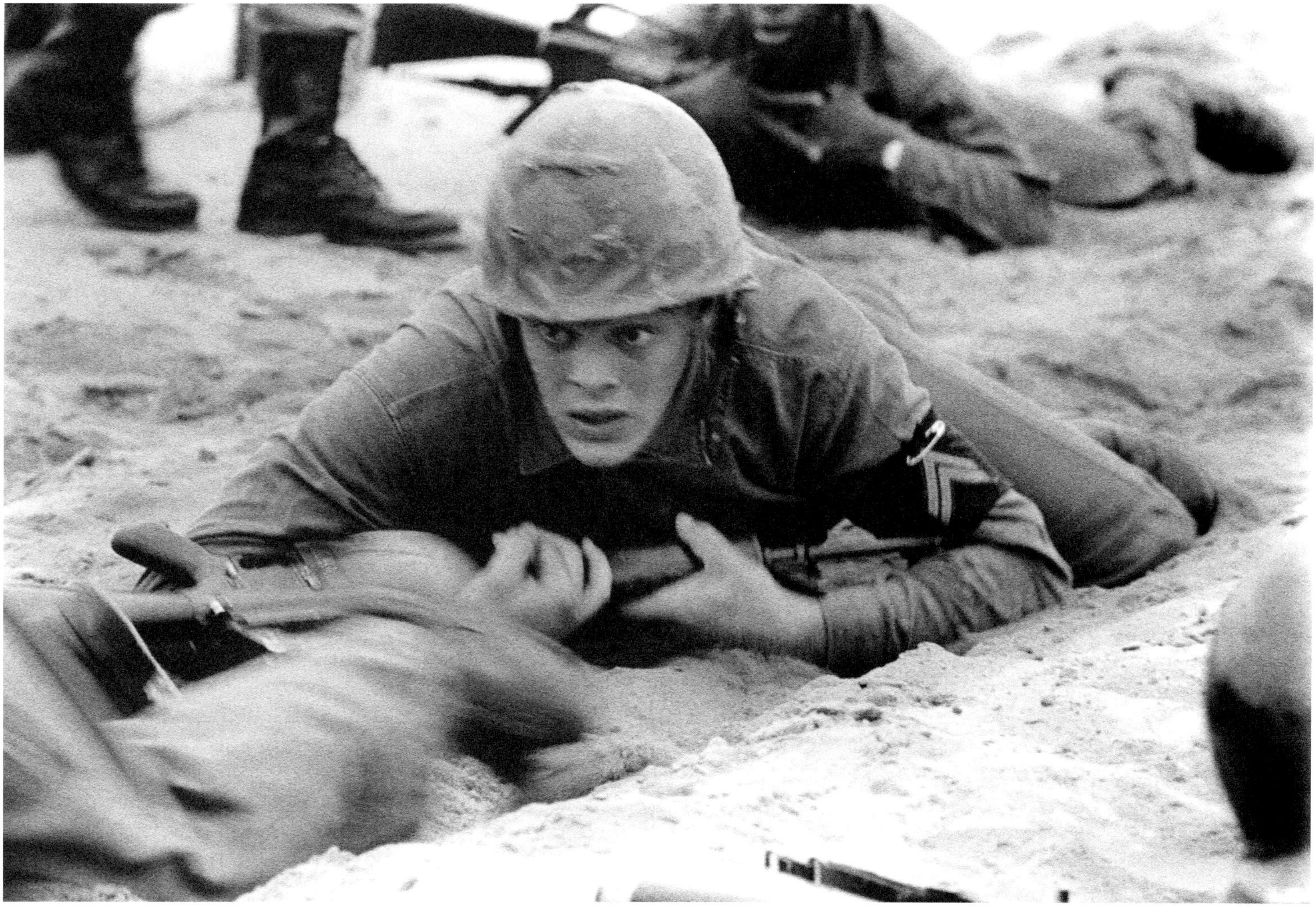

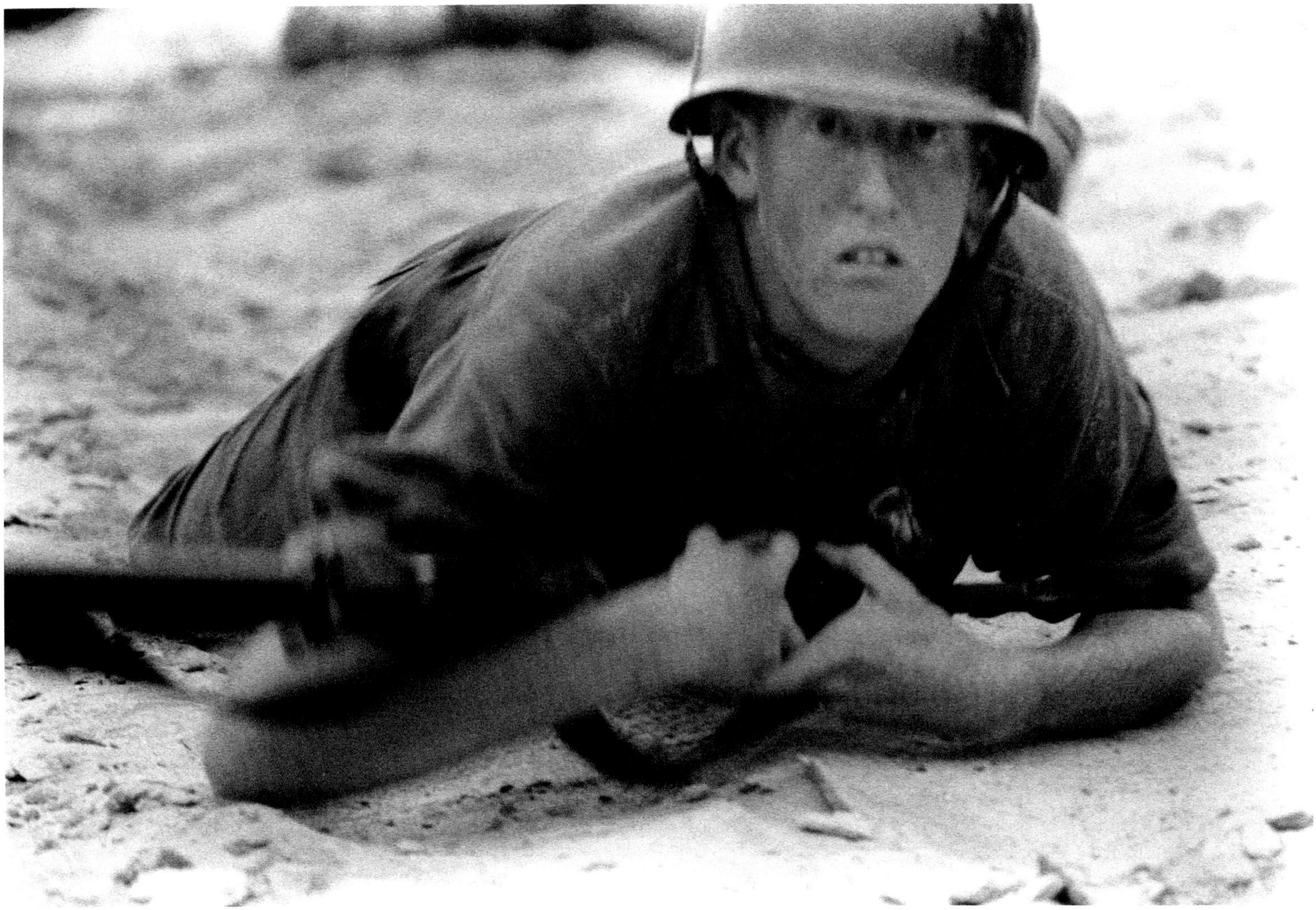

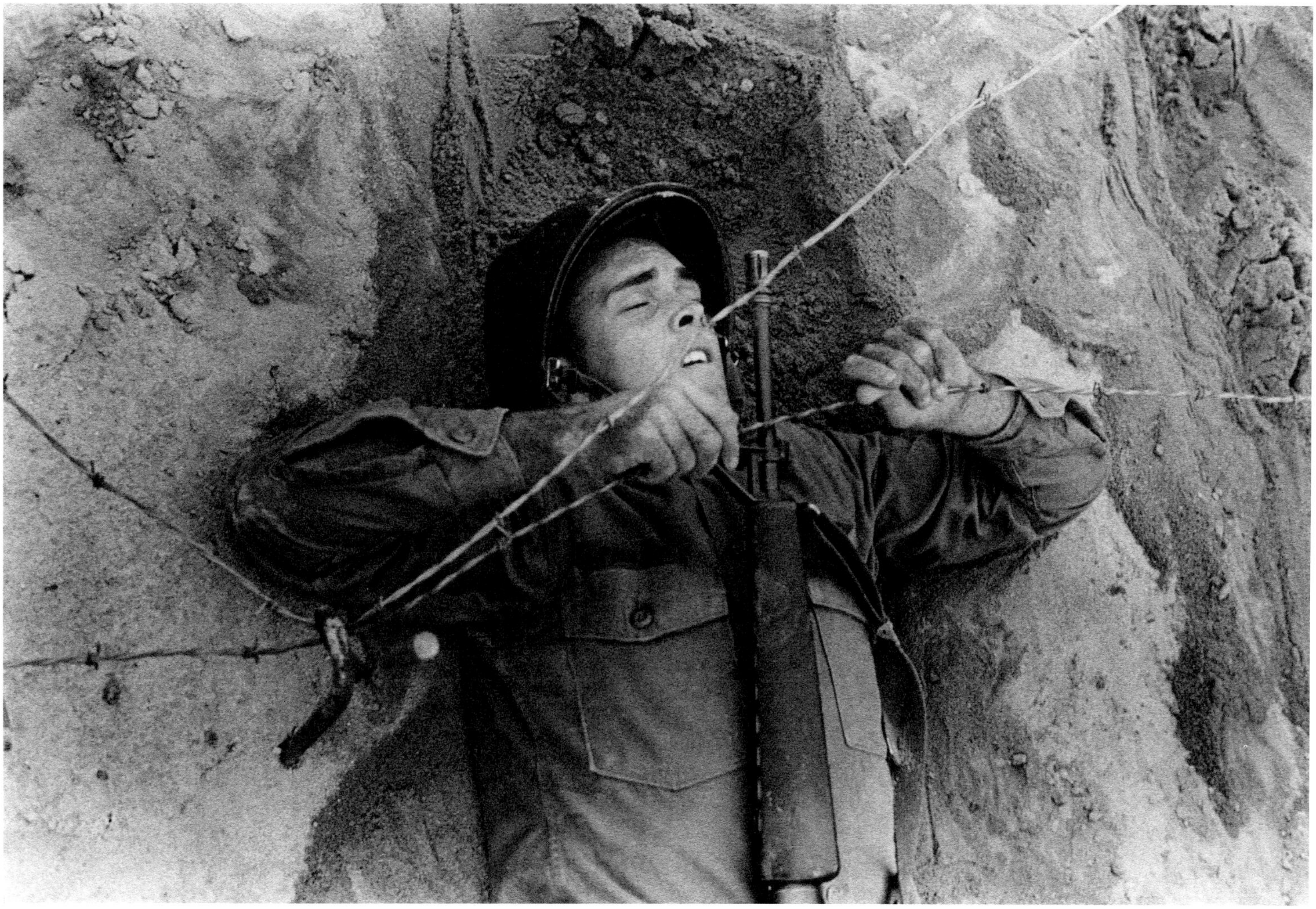

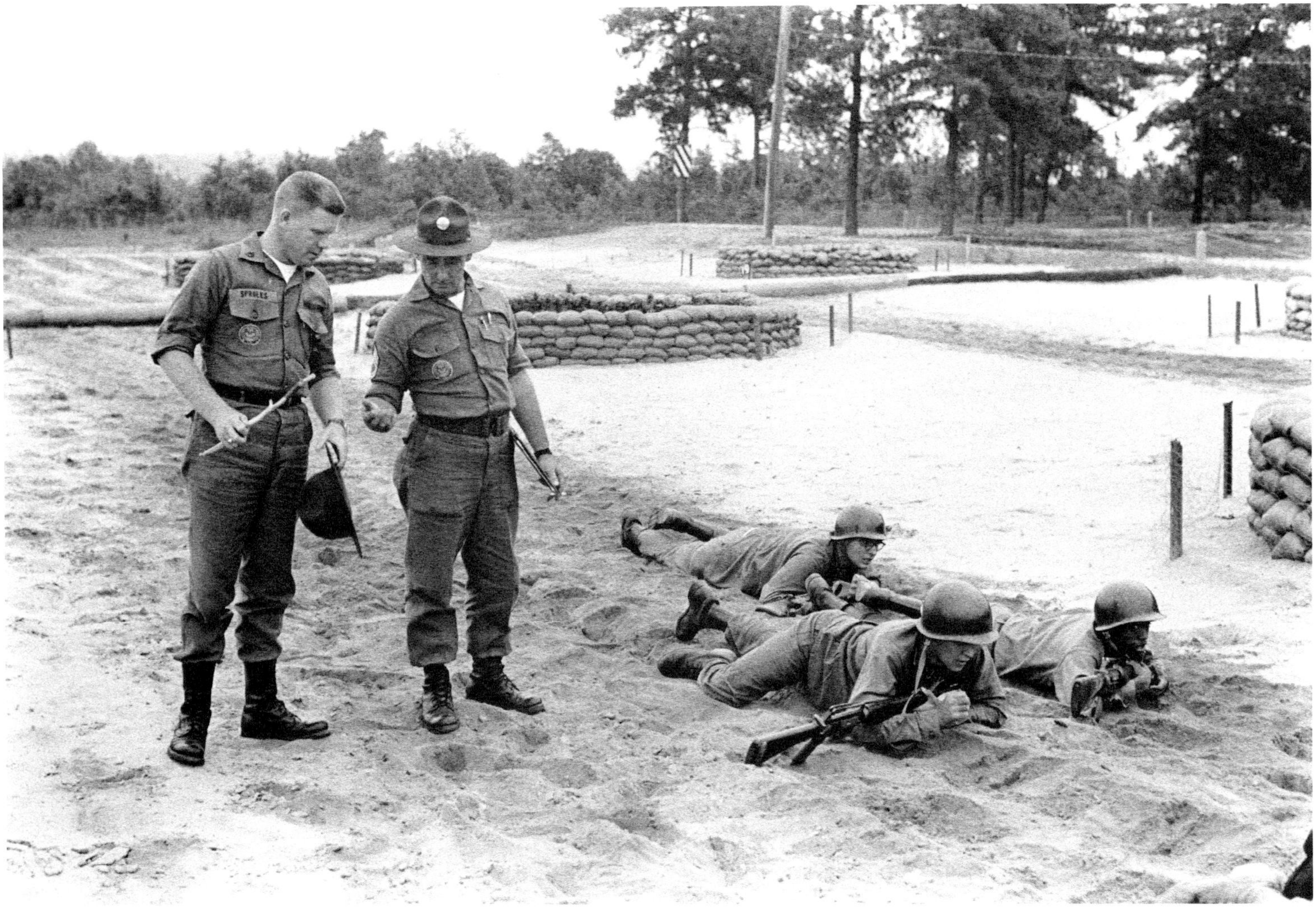
SPROLES

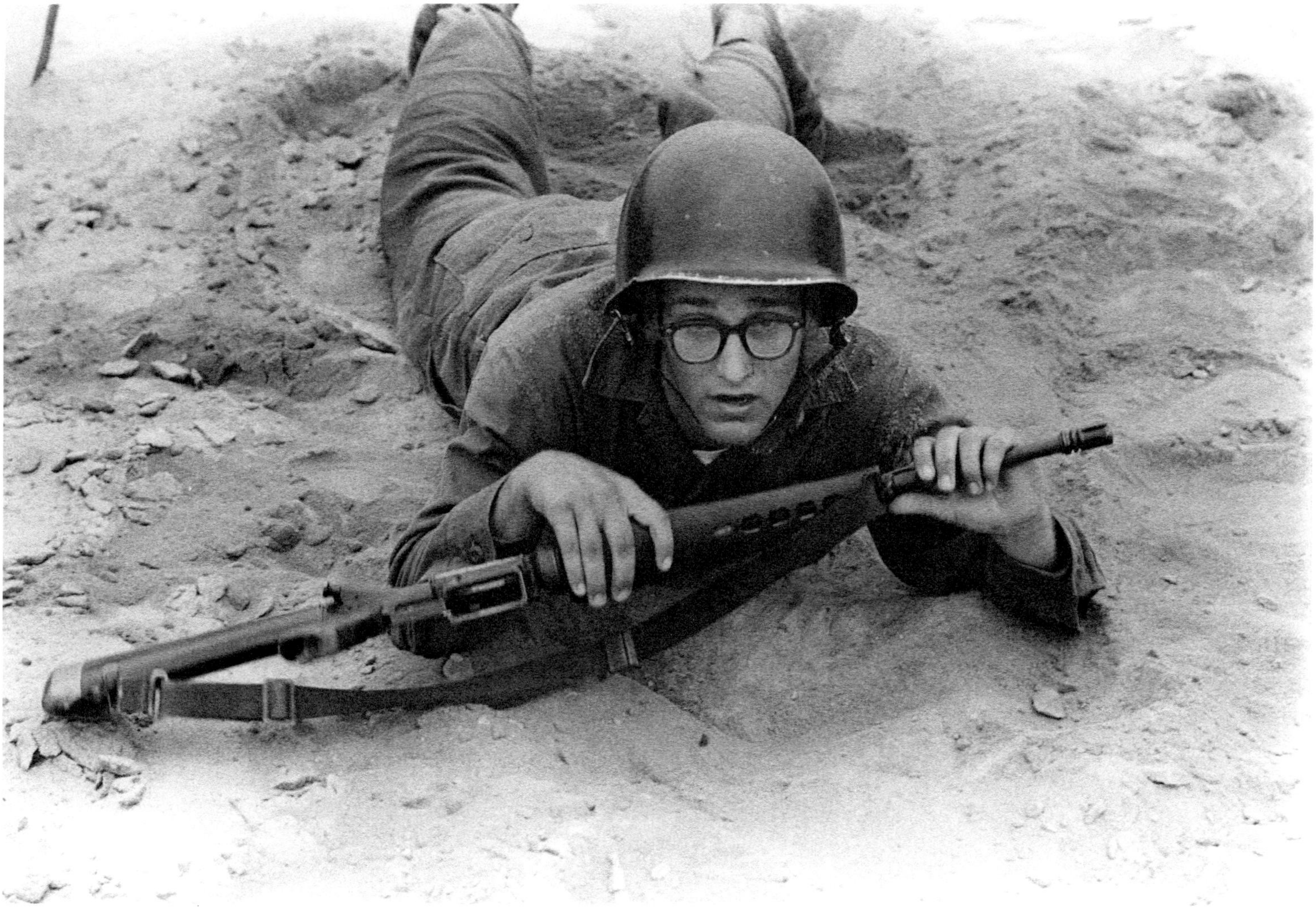

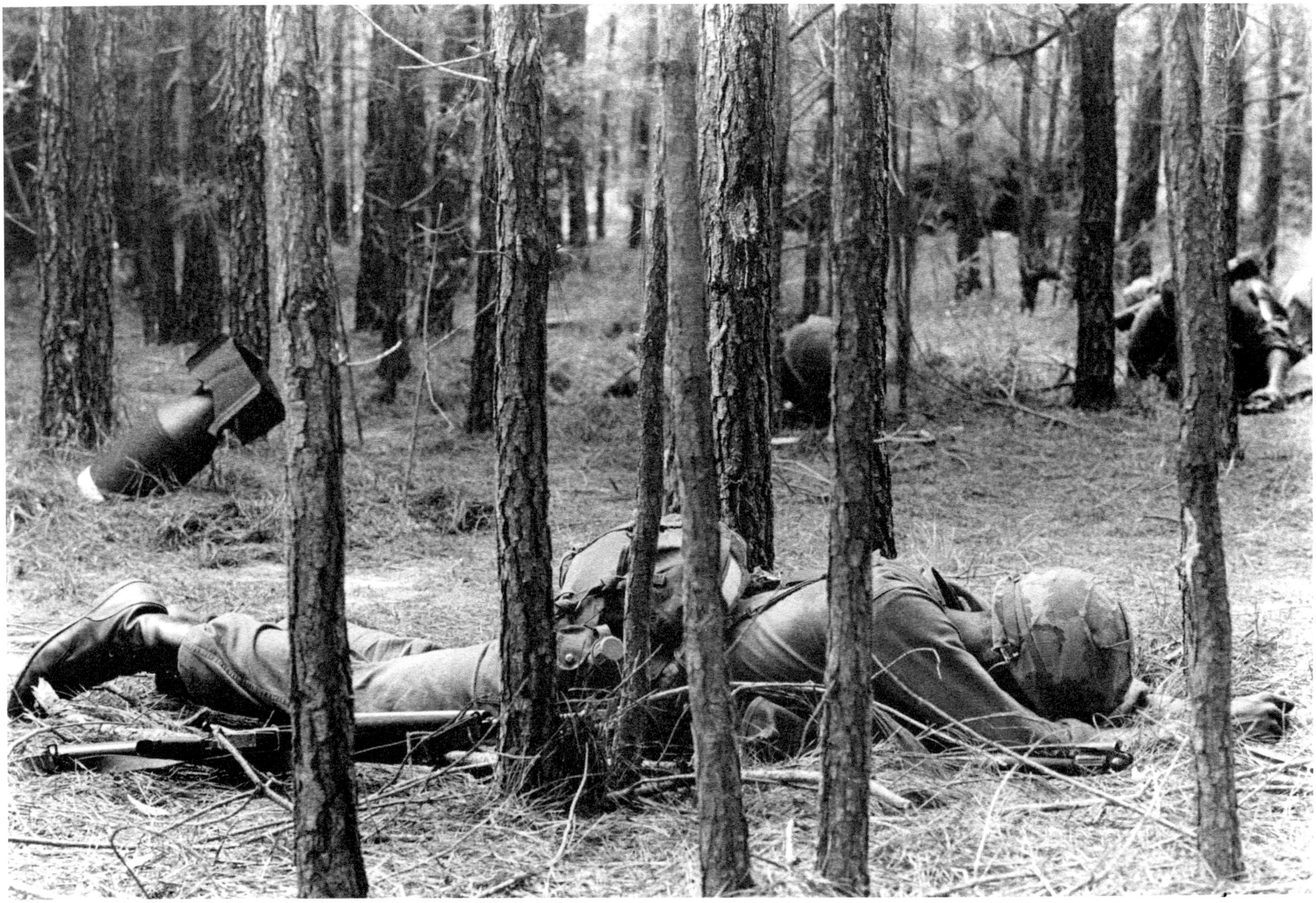

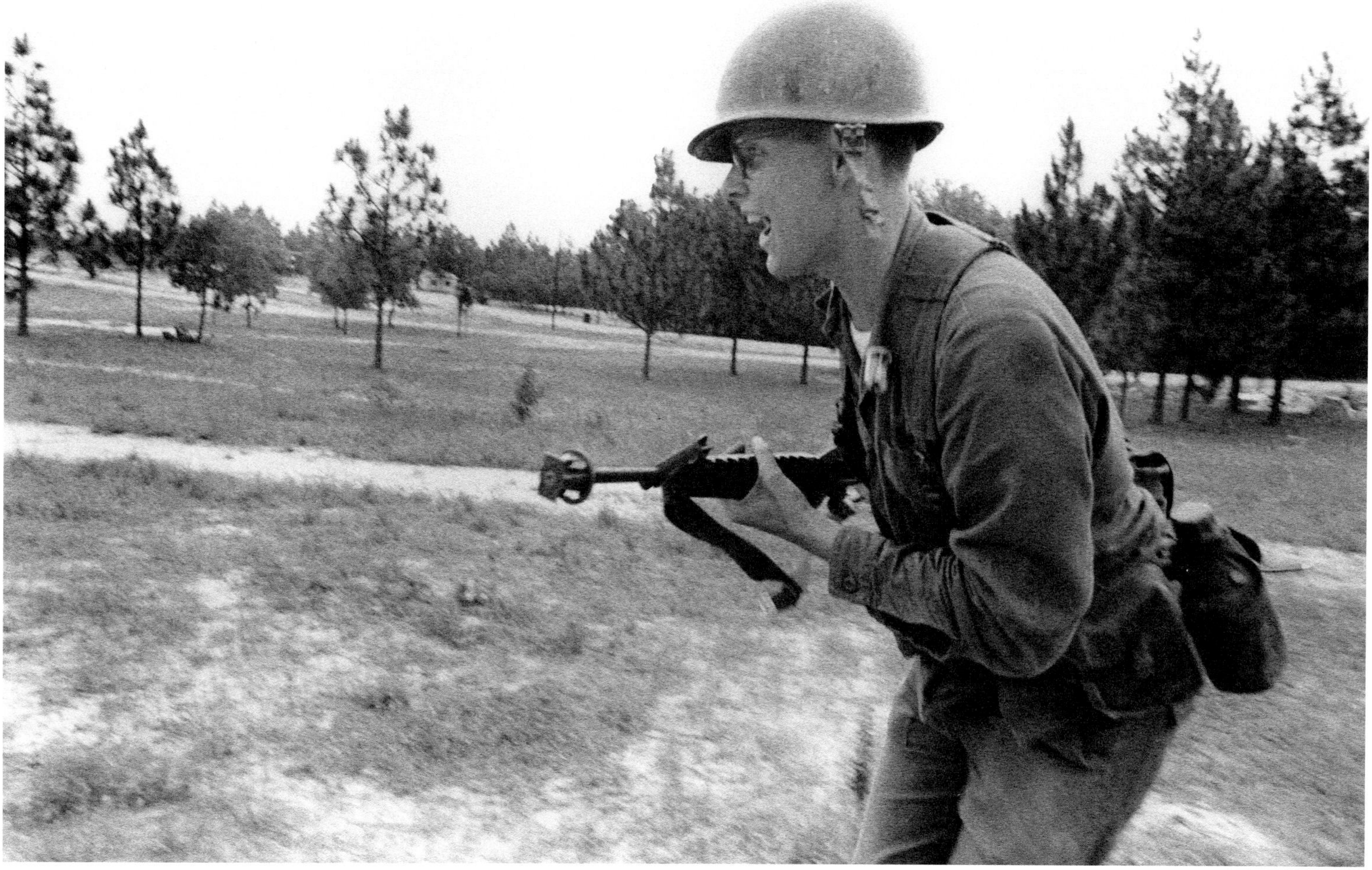

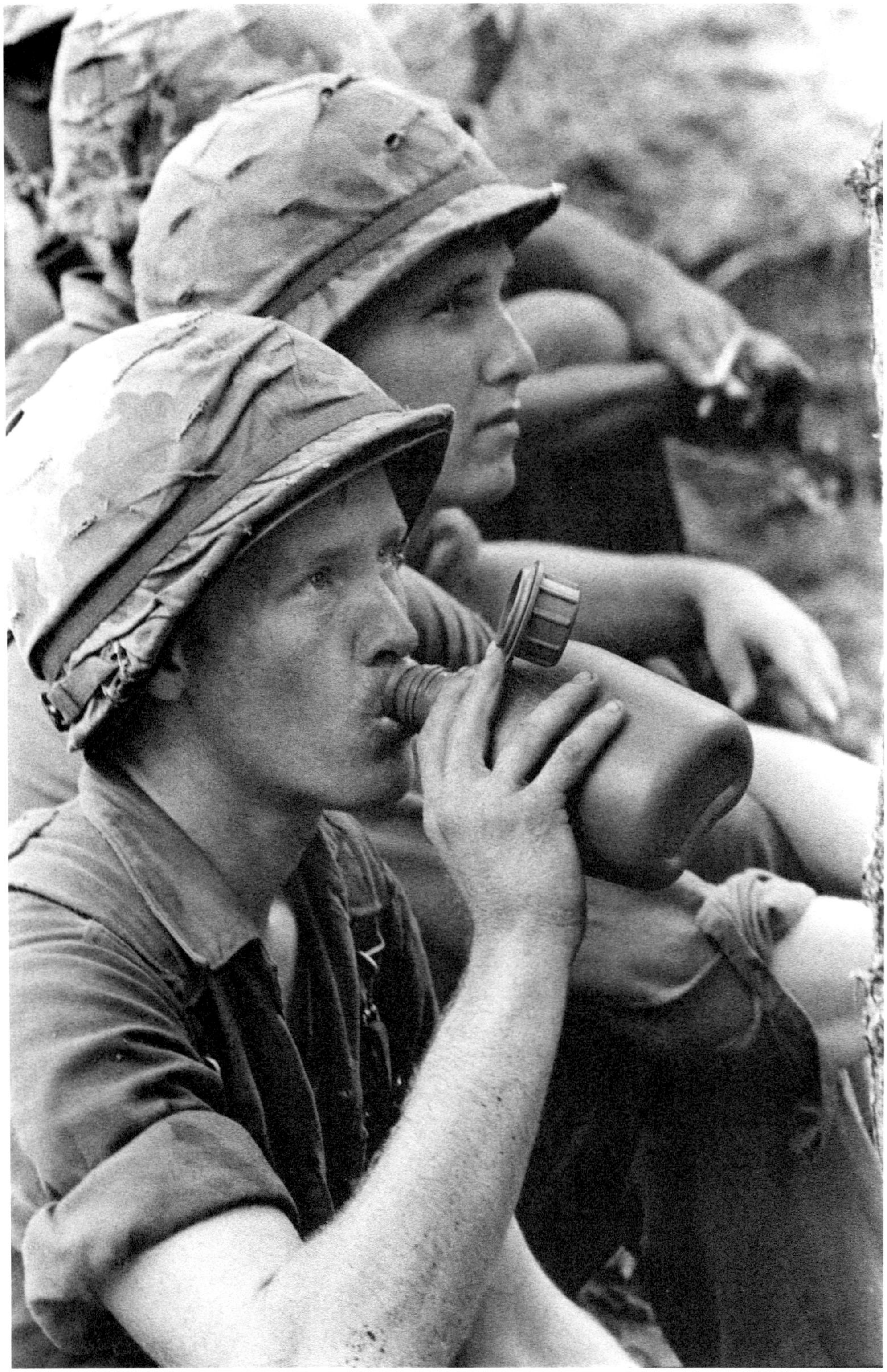

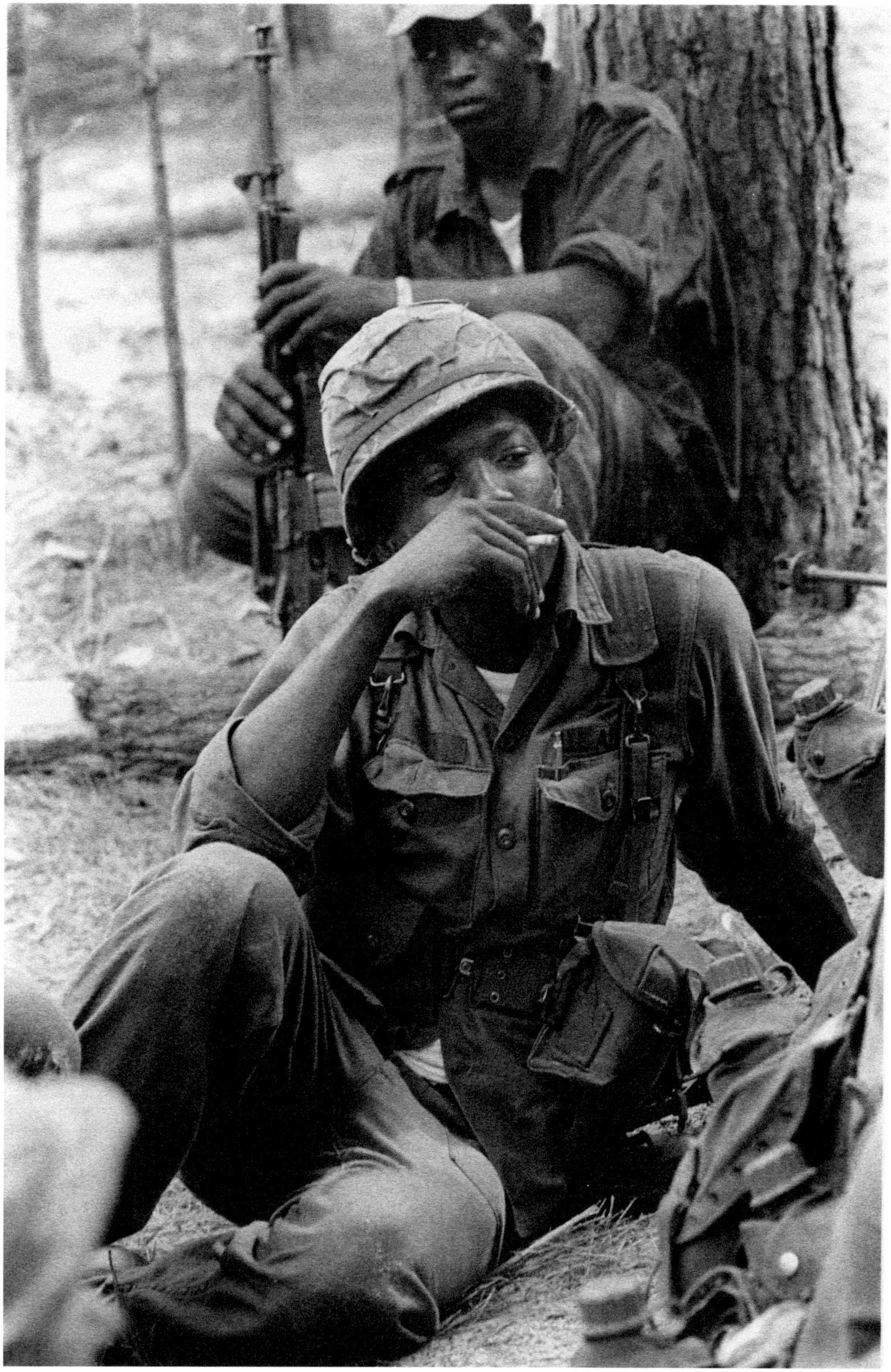

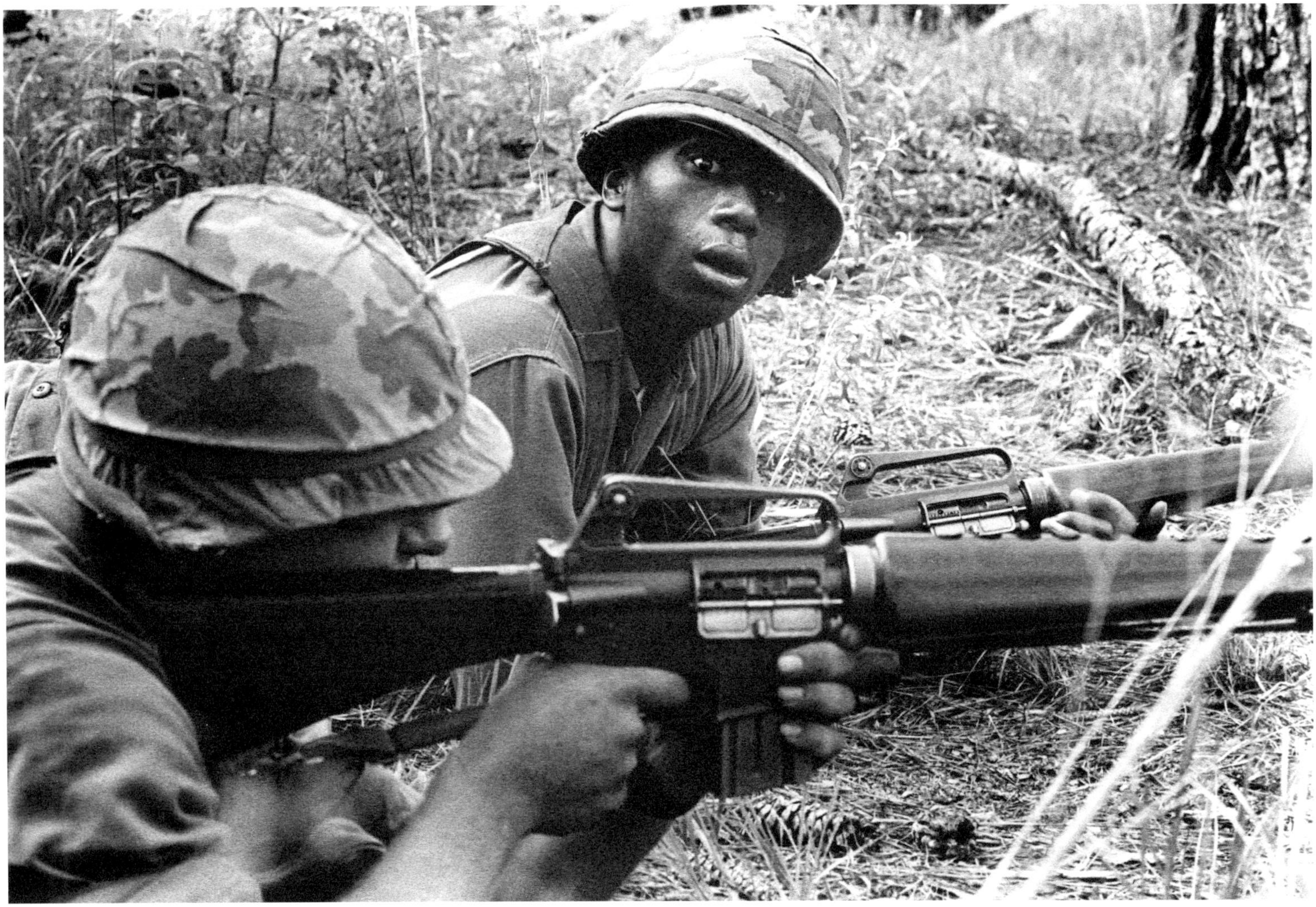

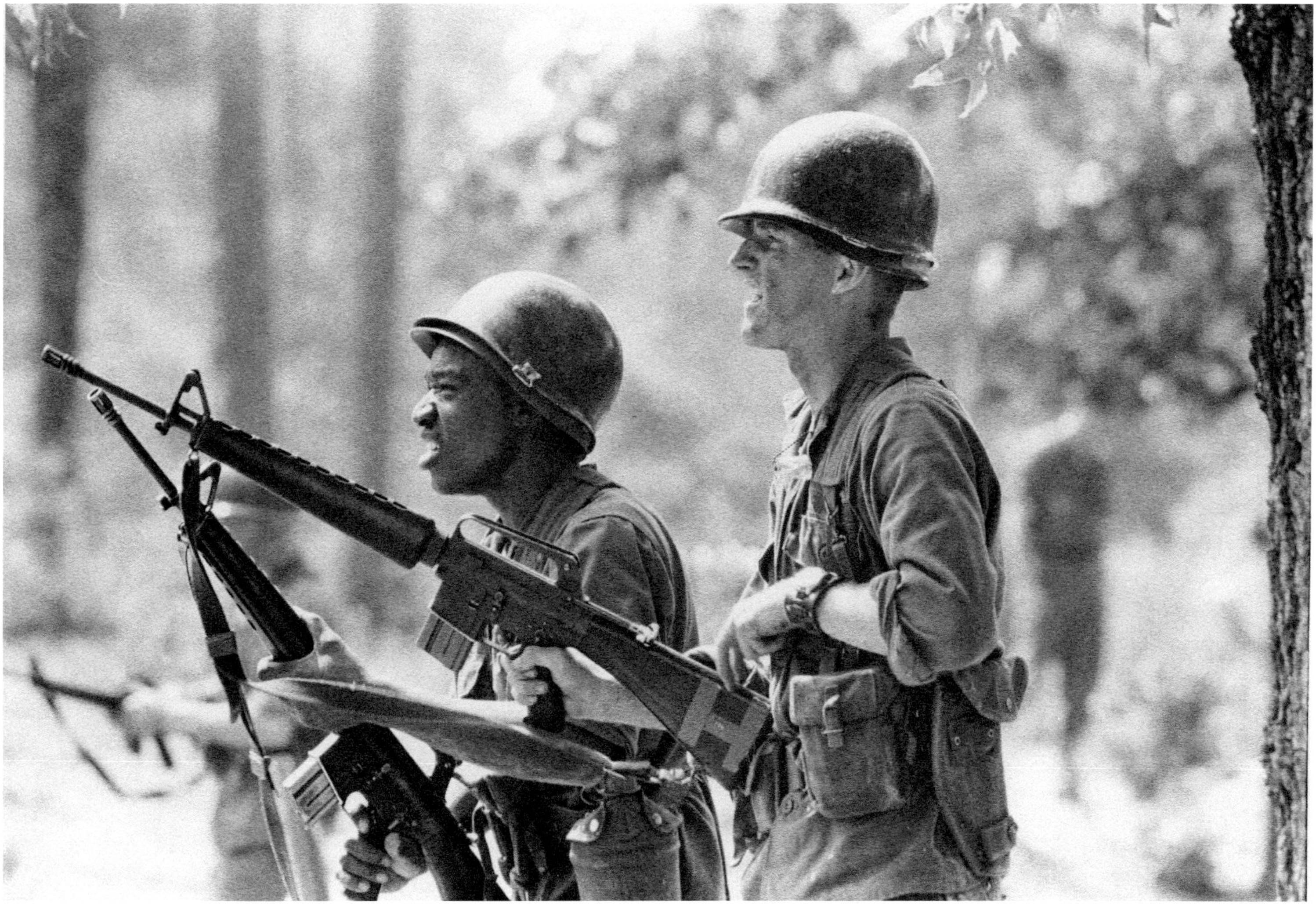

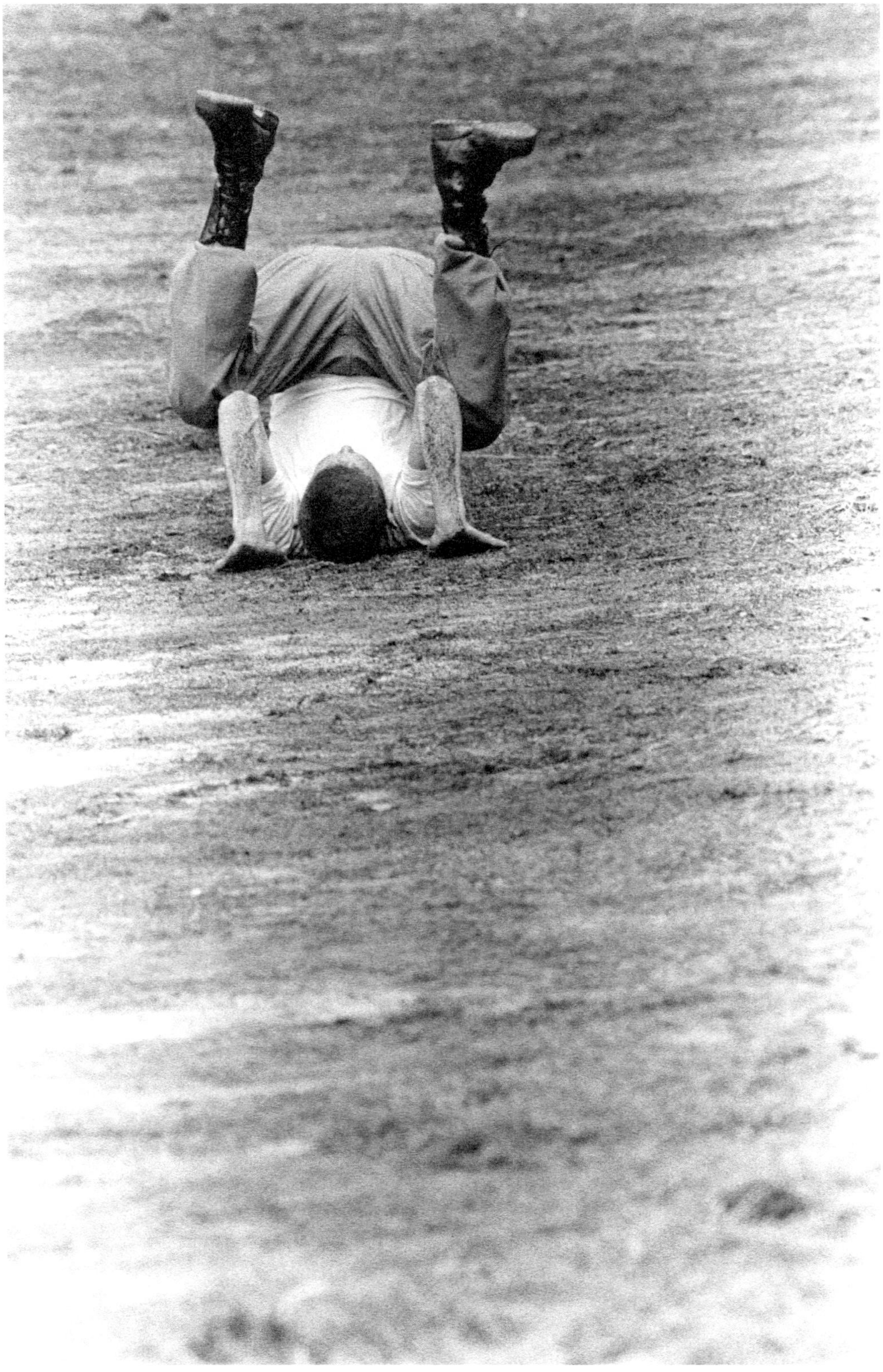

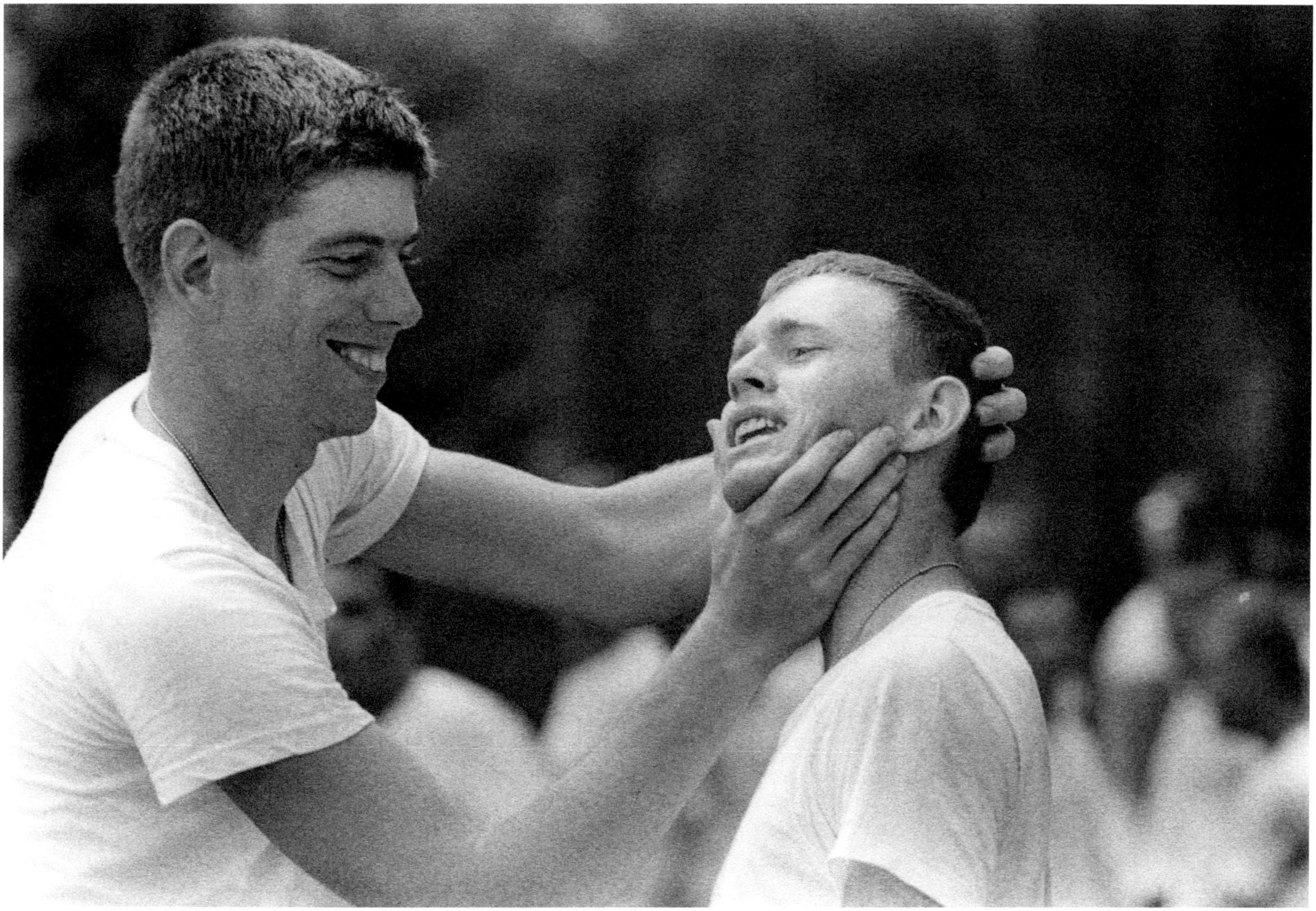

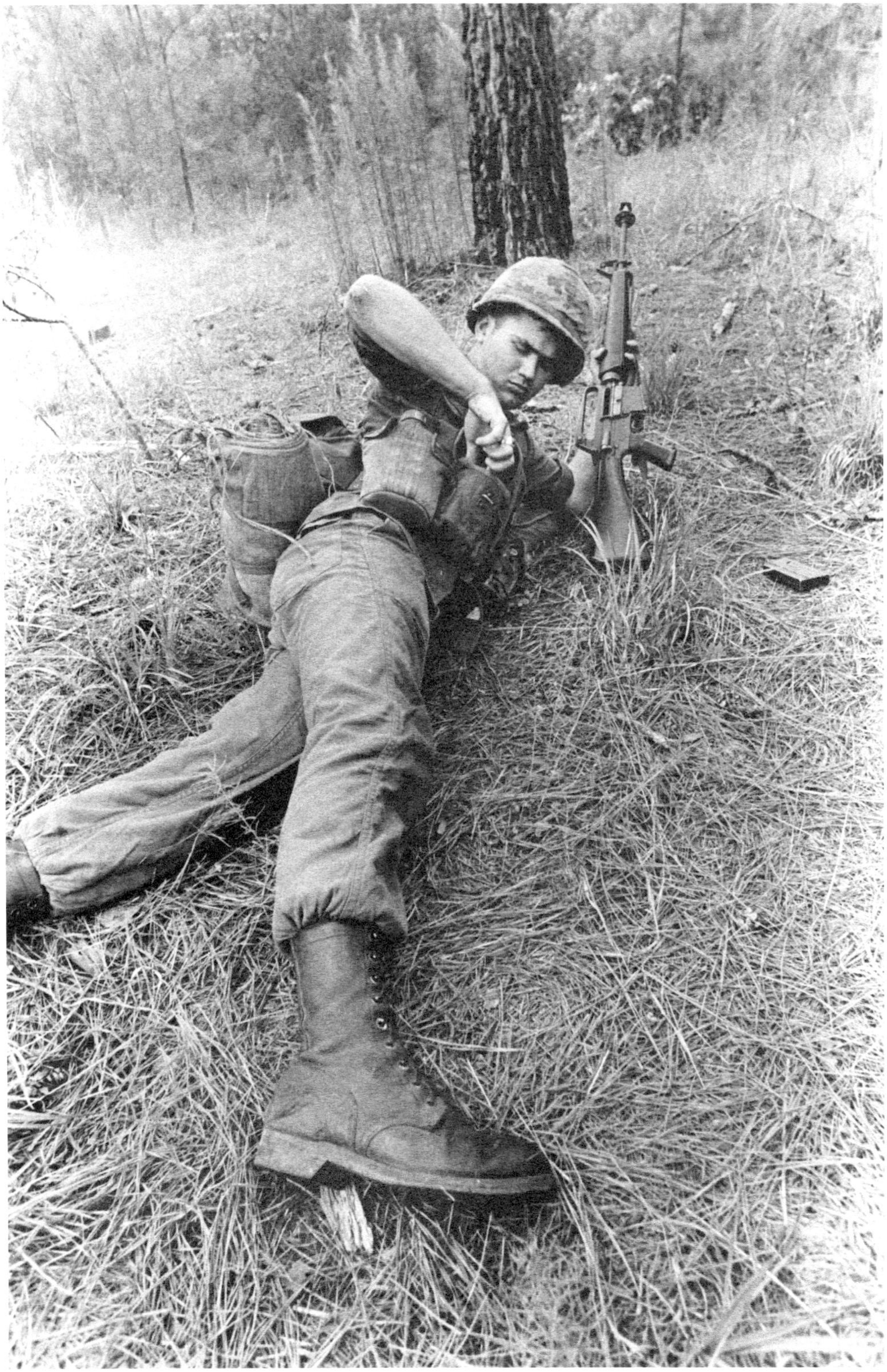

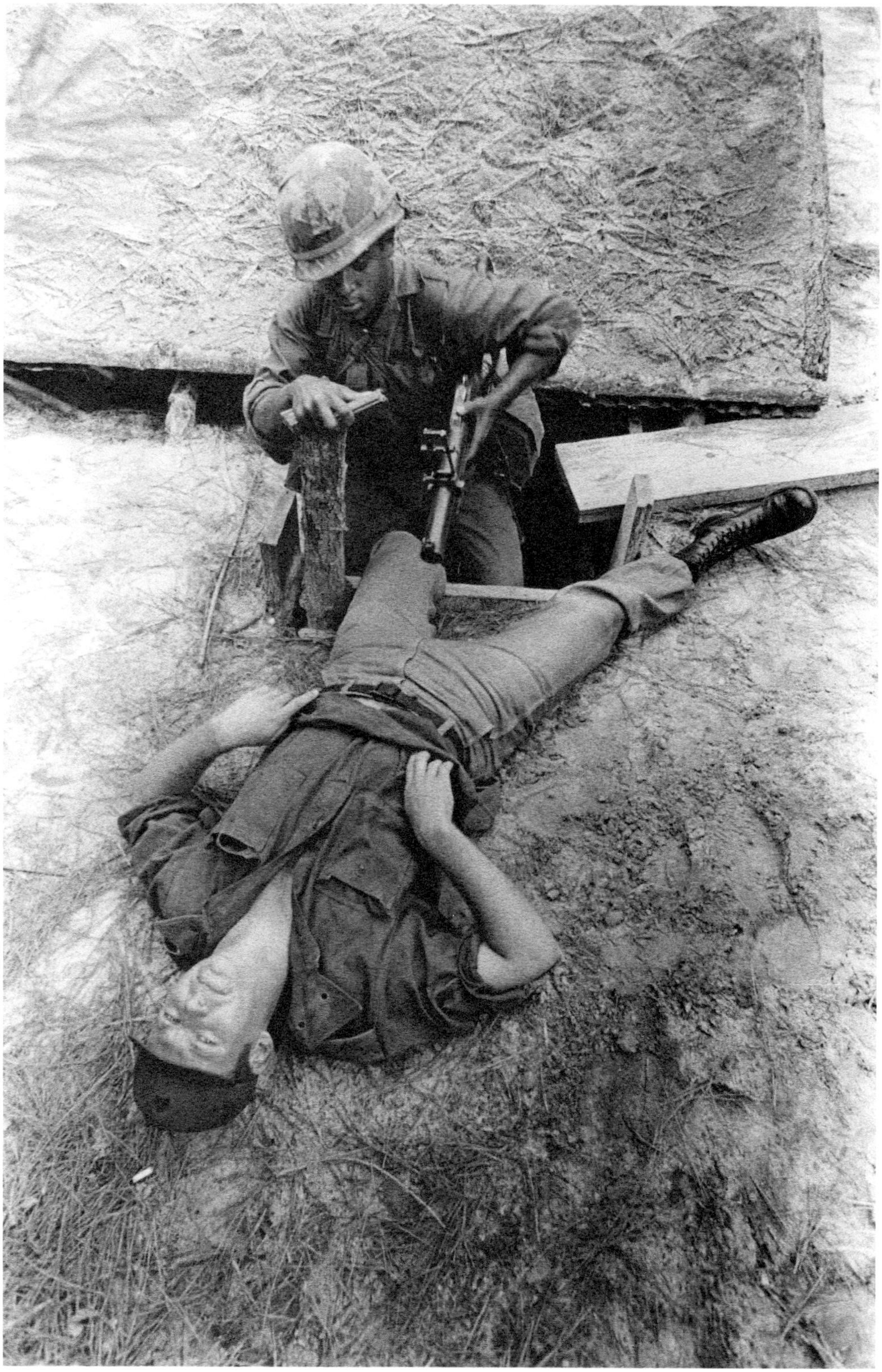

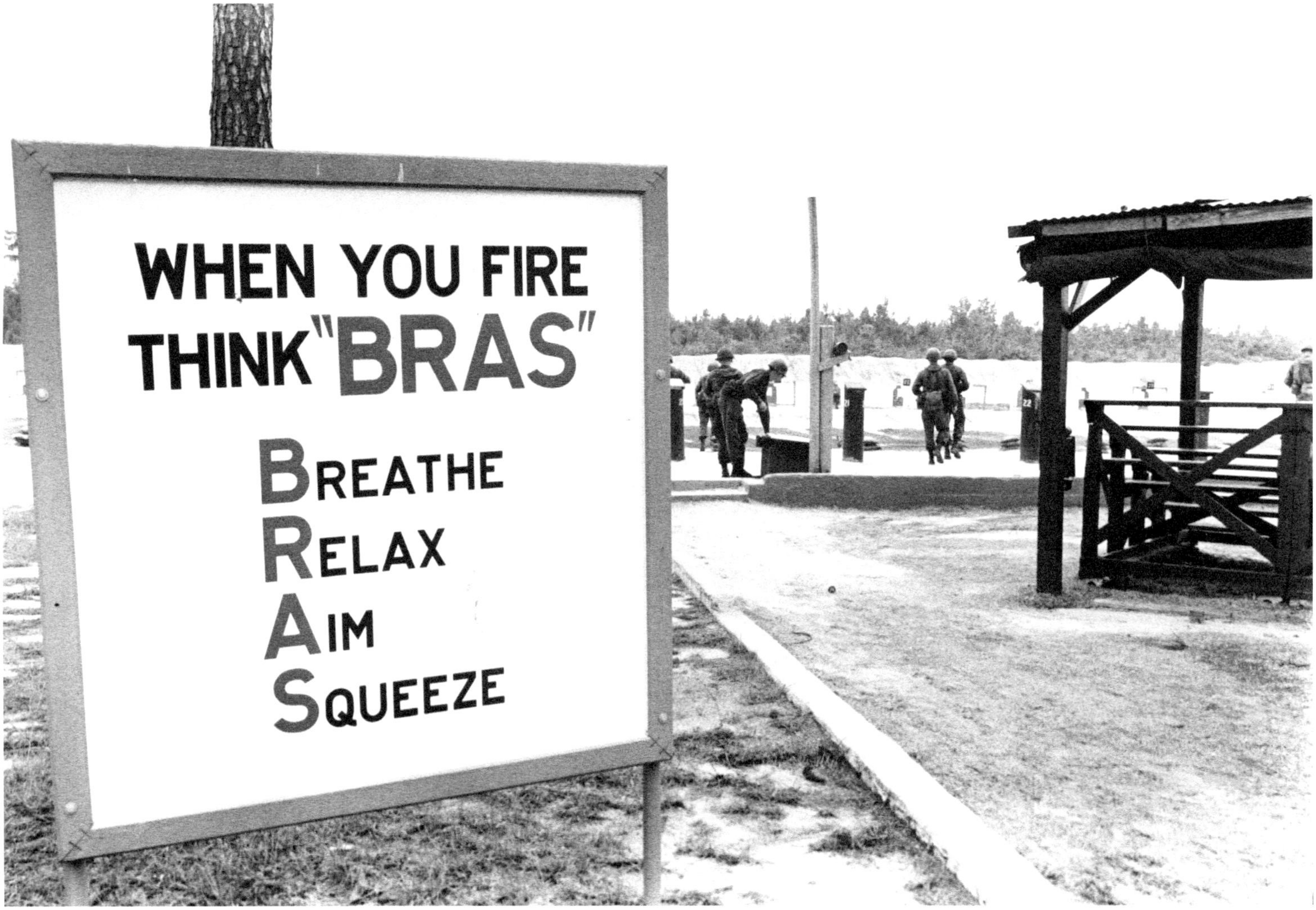
WHEN YOU FIRE
THINK "BRAS"
BREATHE
RELAX
AIM
SQUEEZE

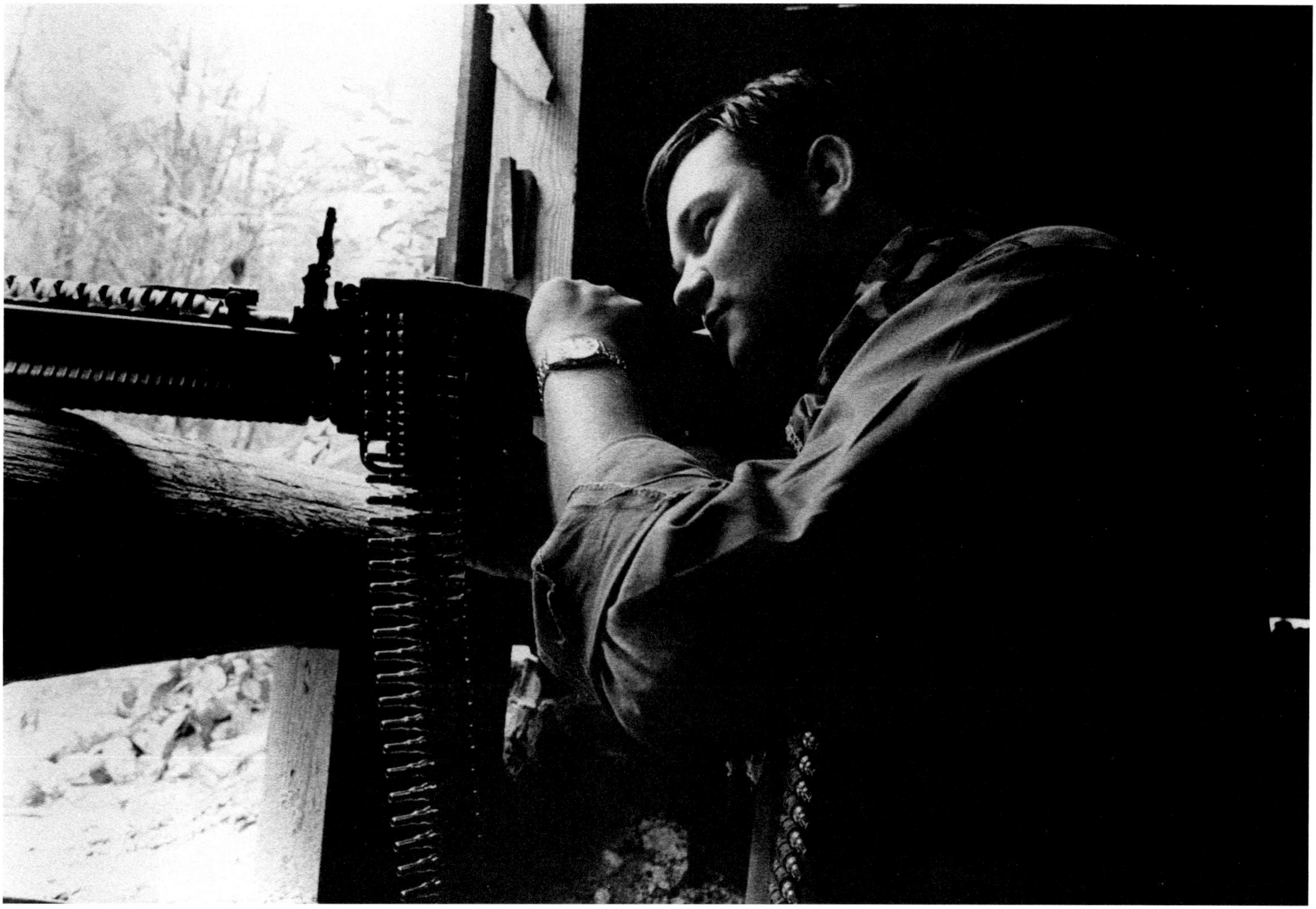

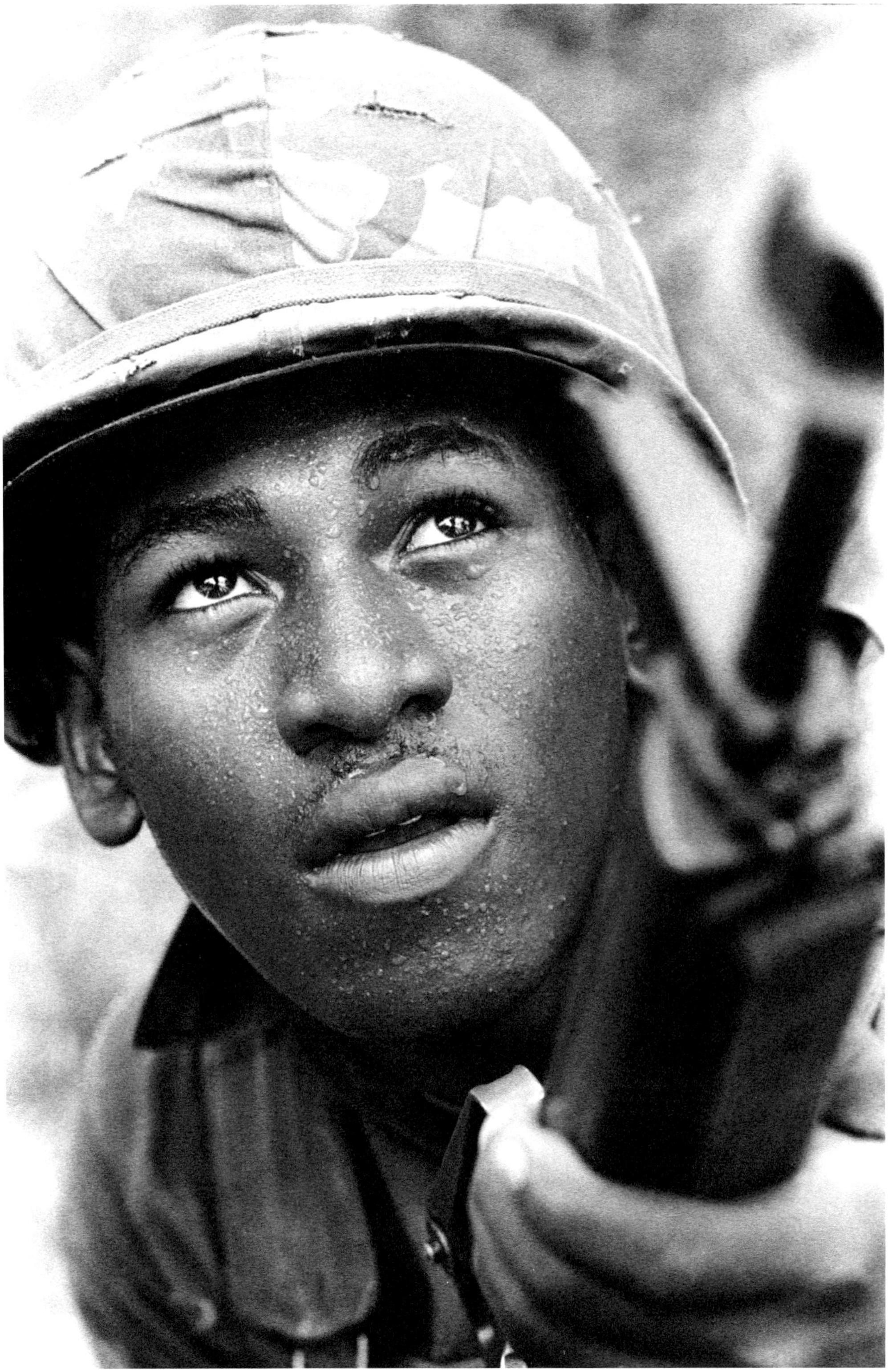

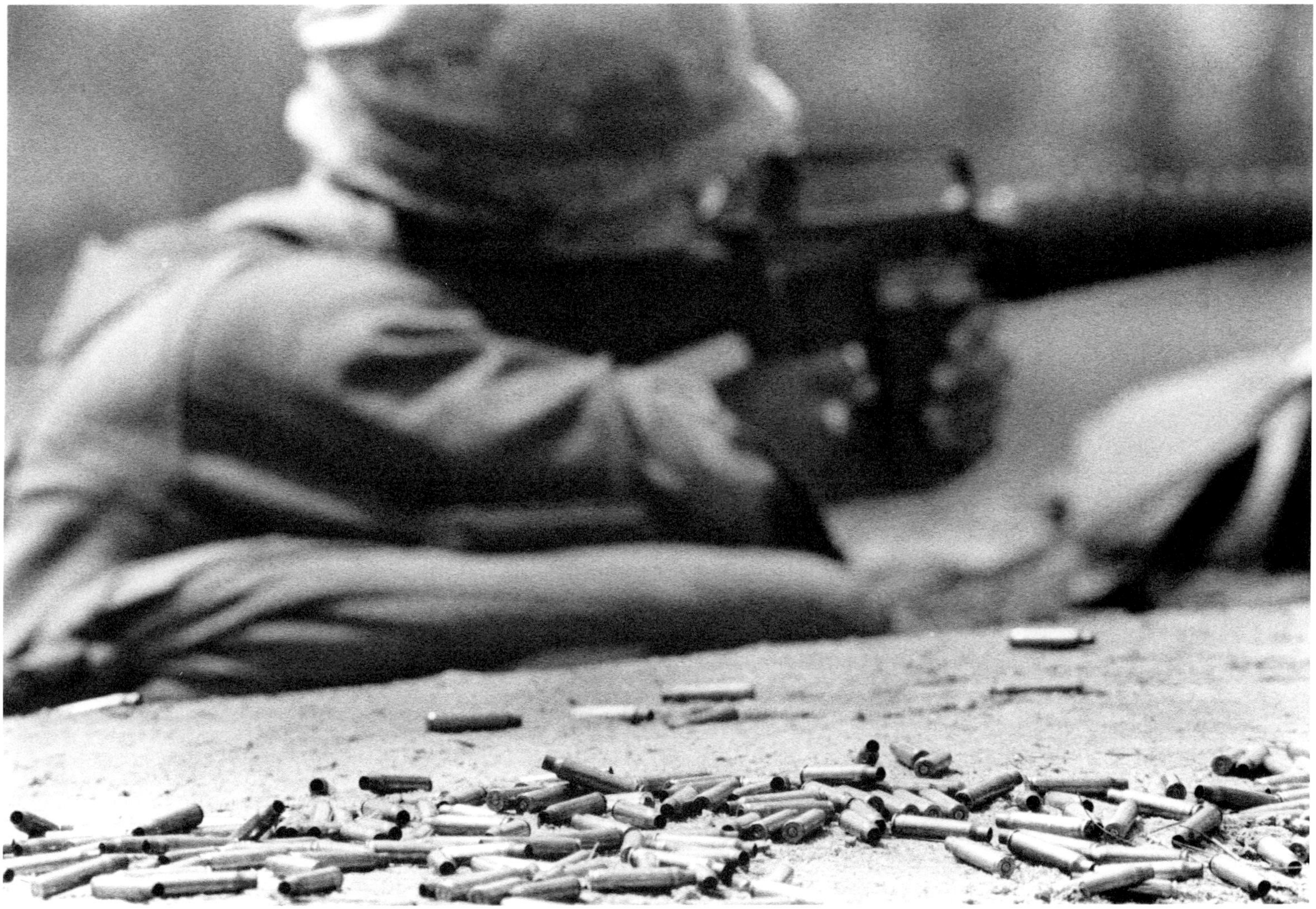

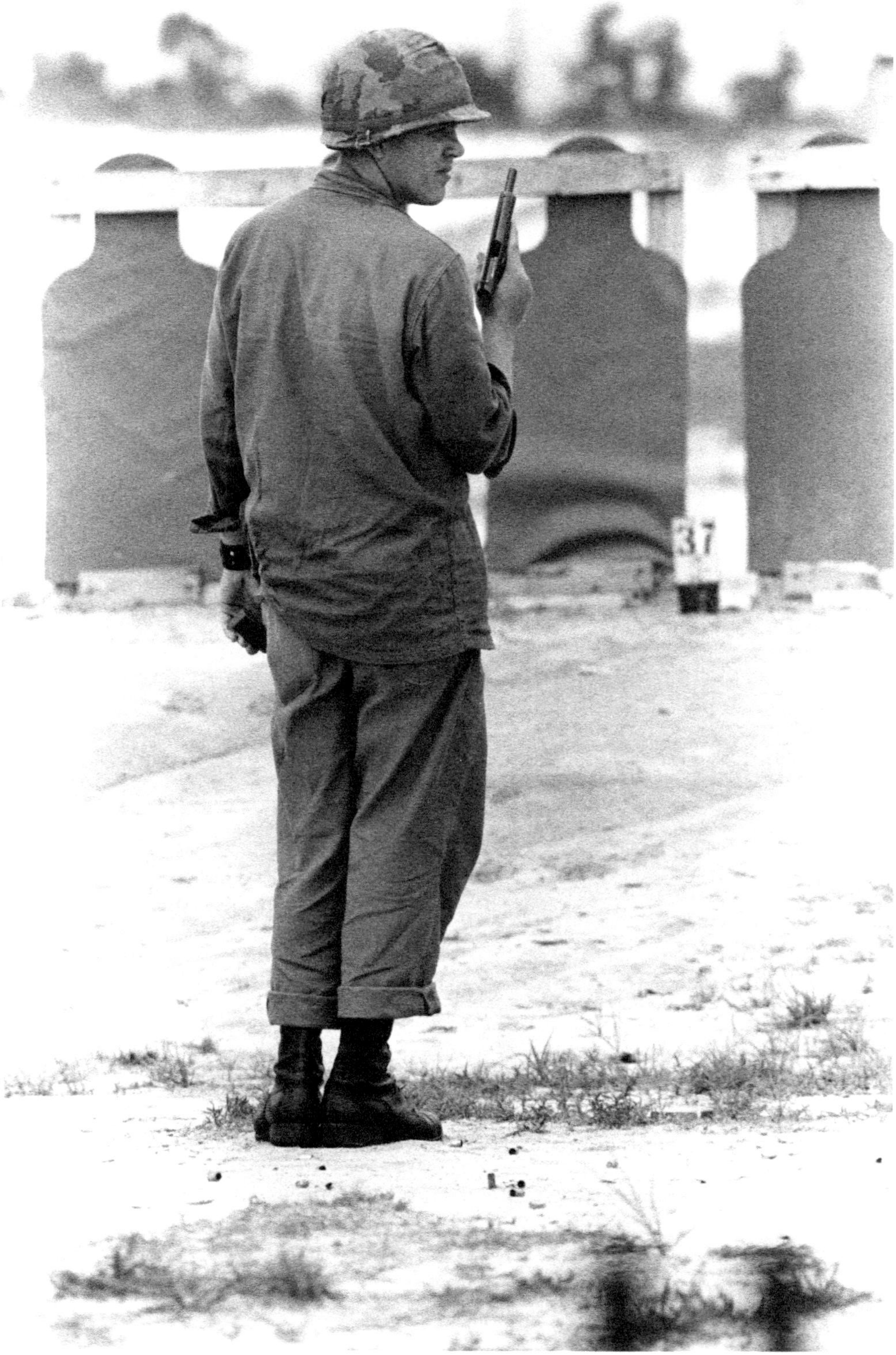
37

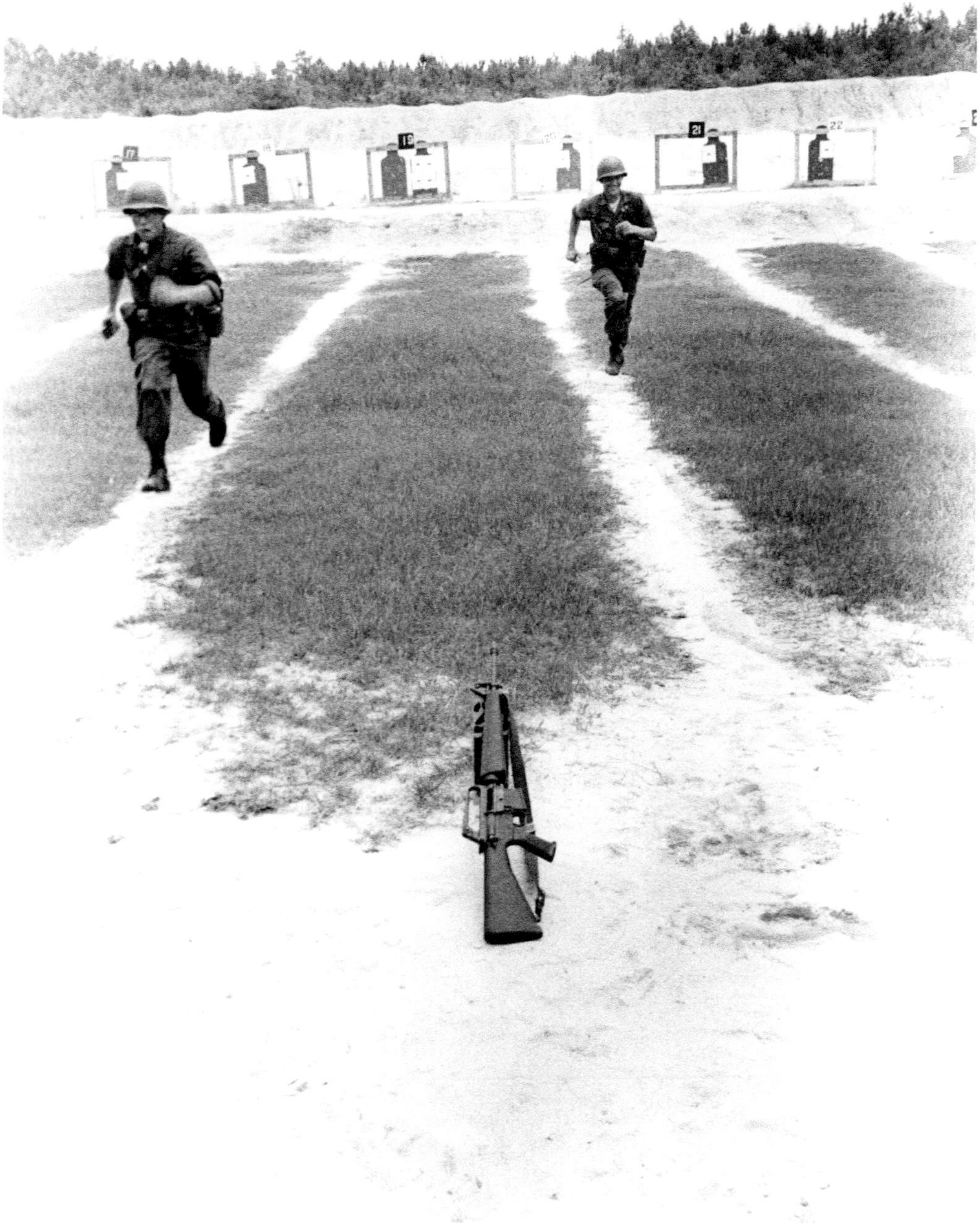

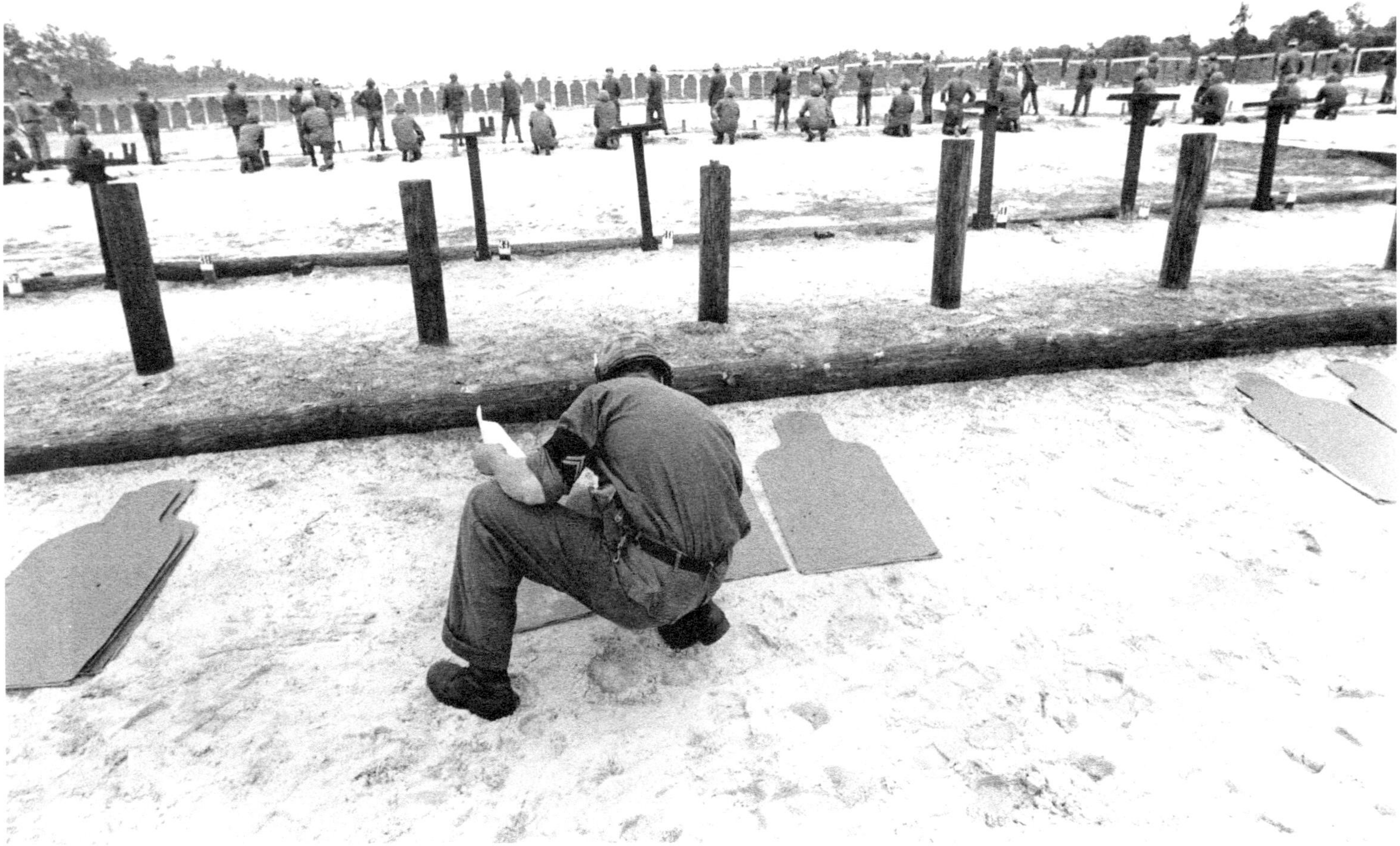

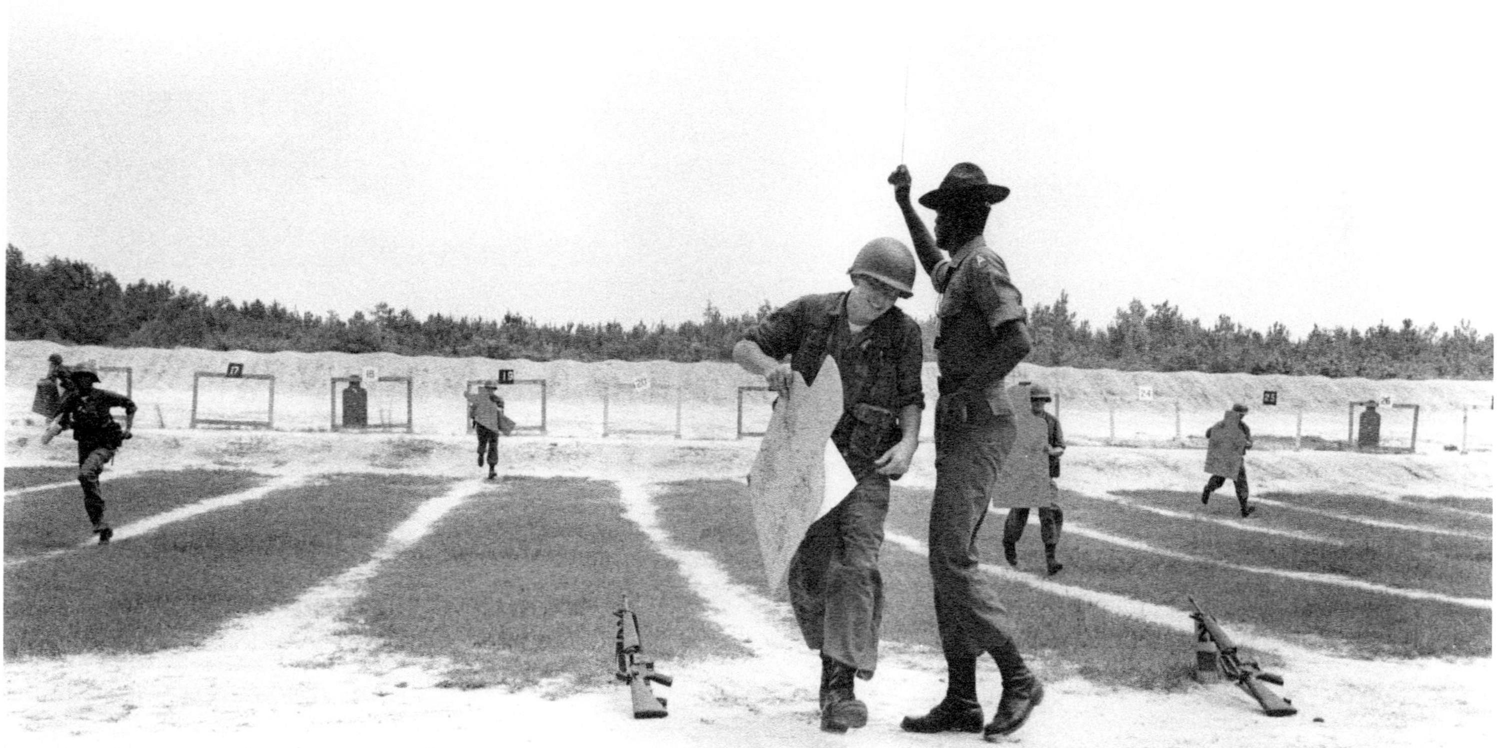

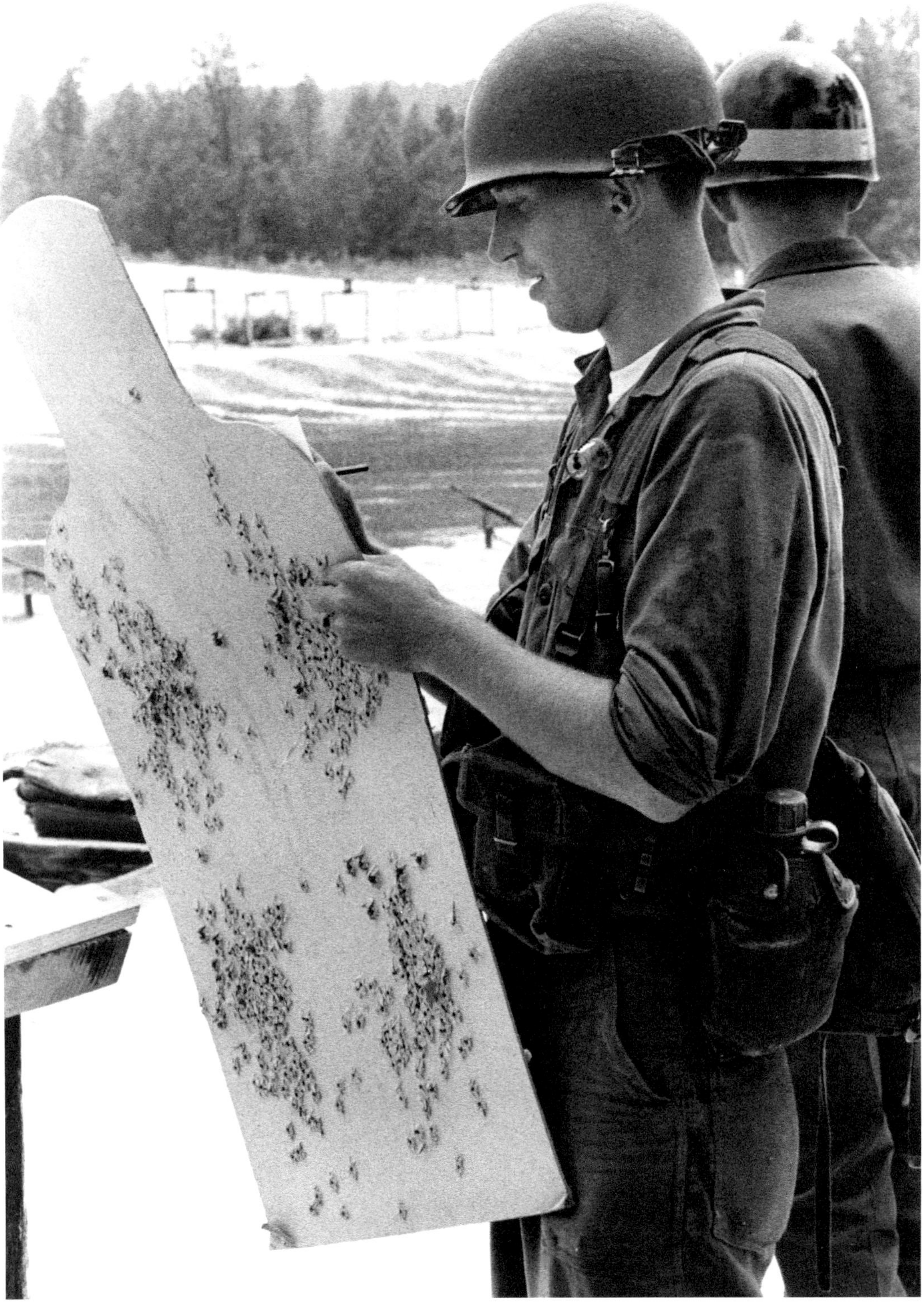

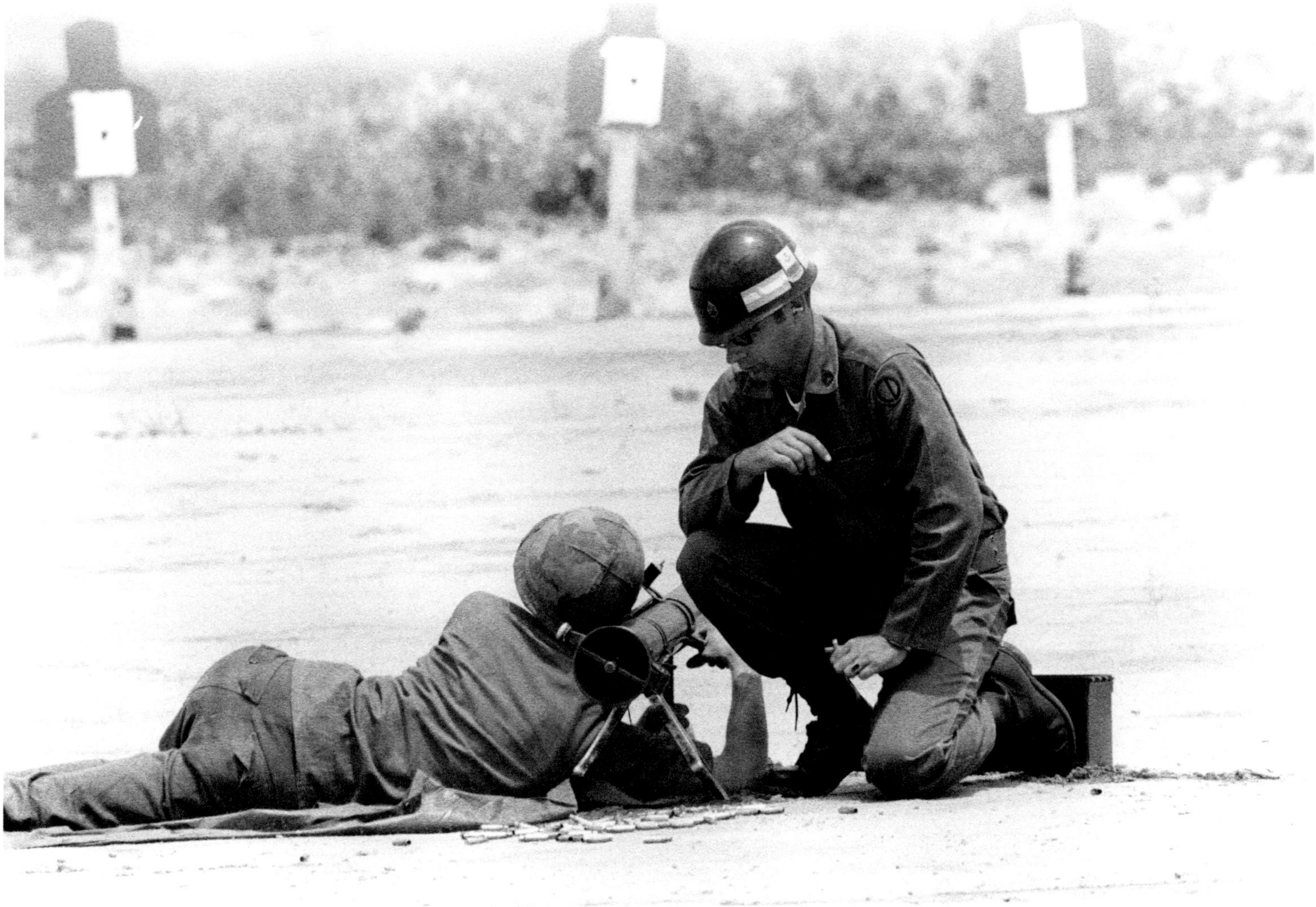

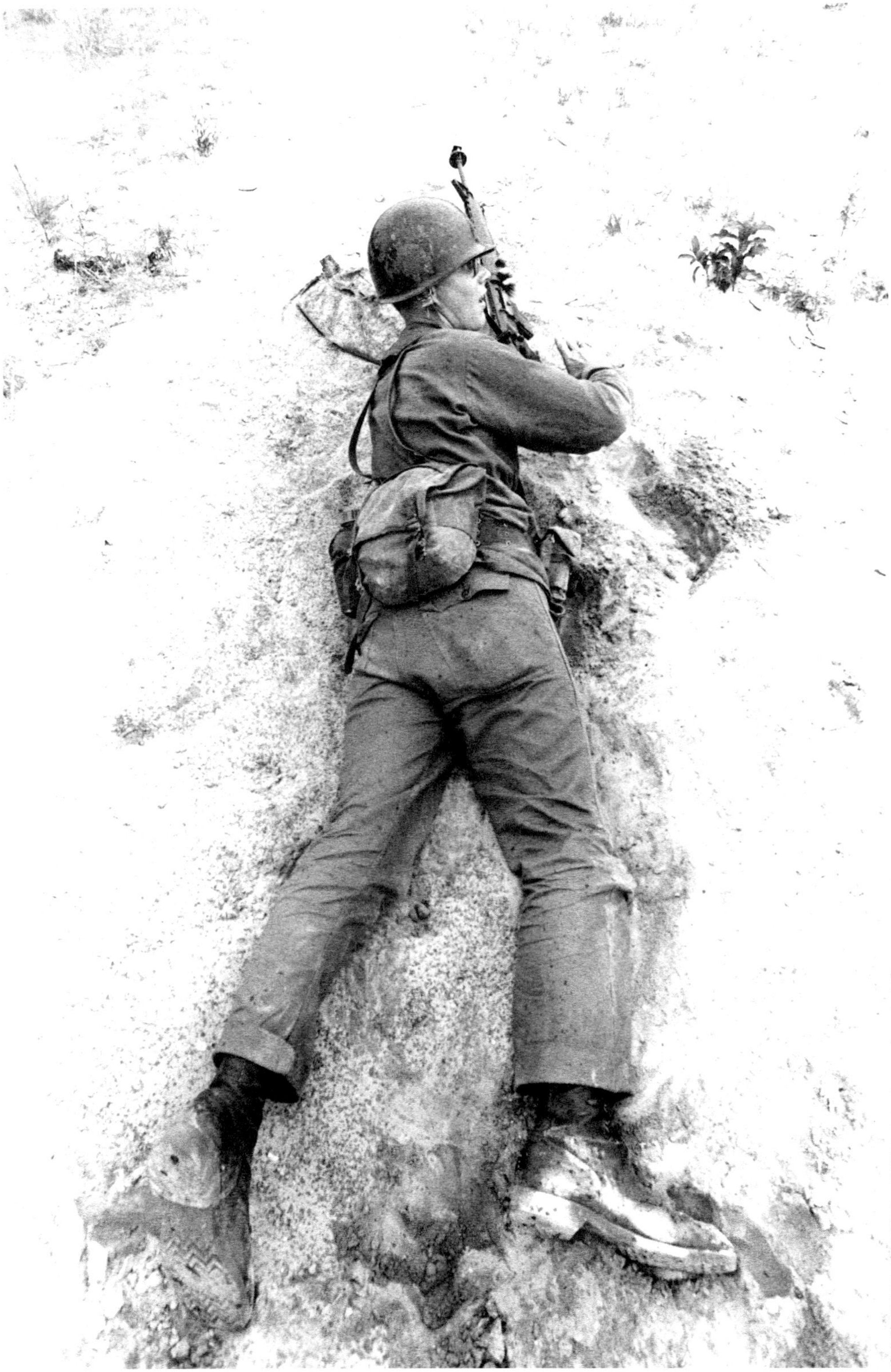

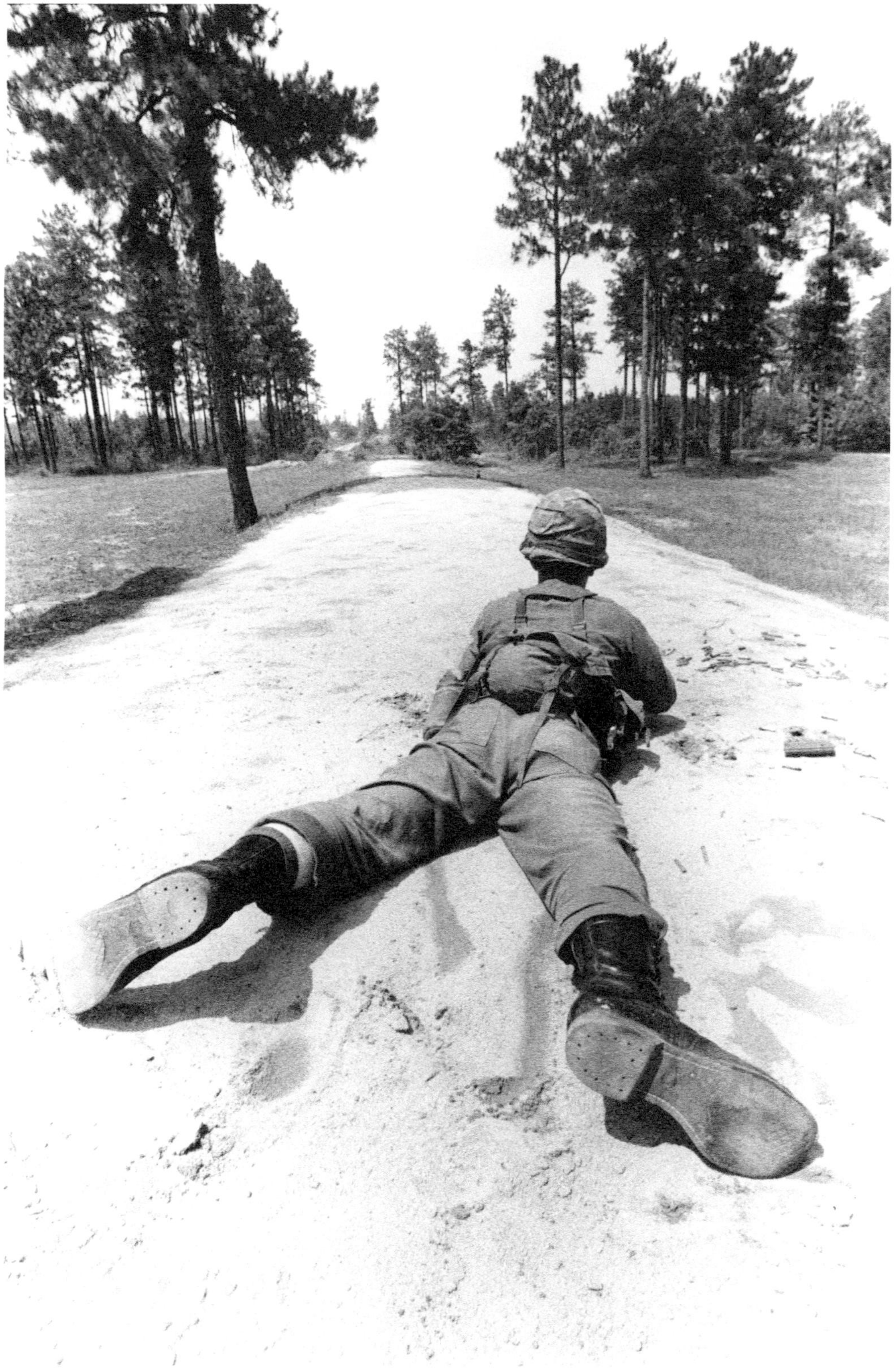

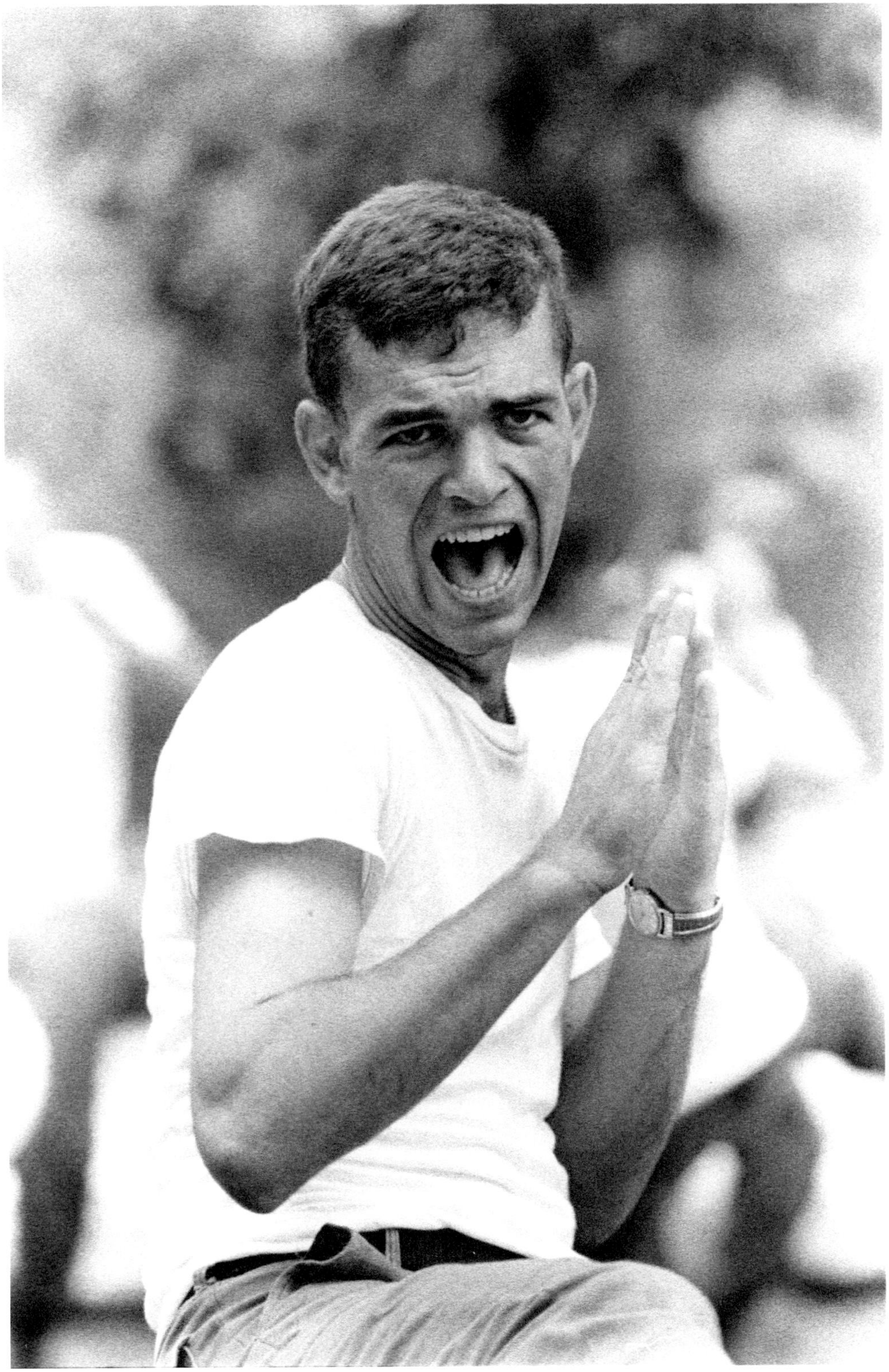

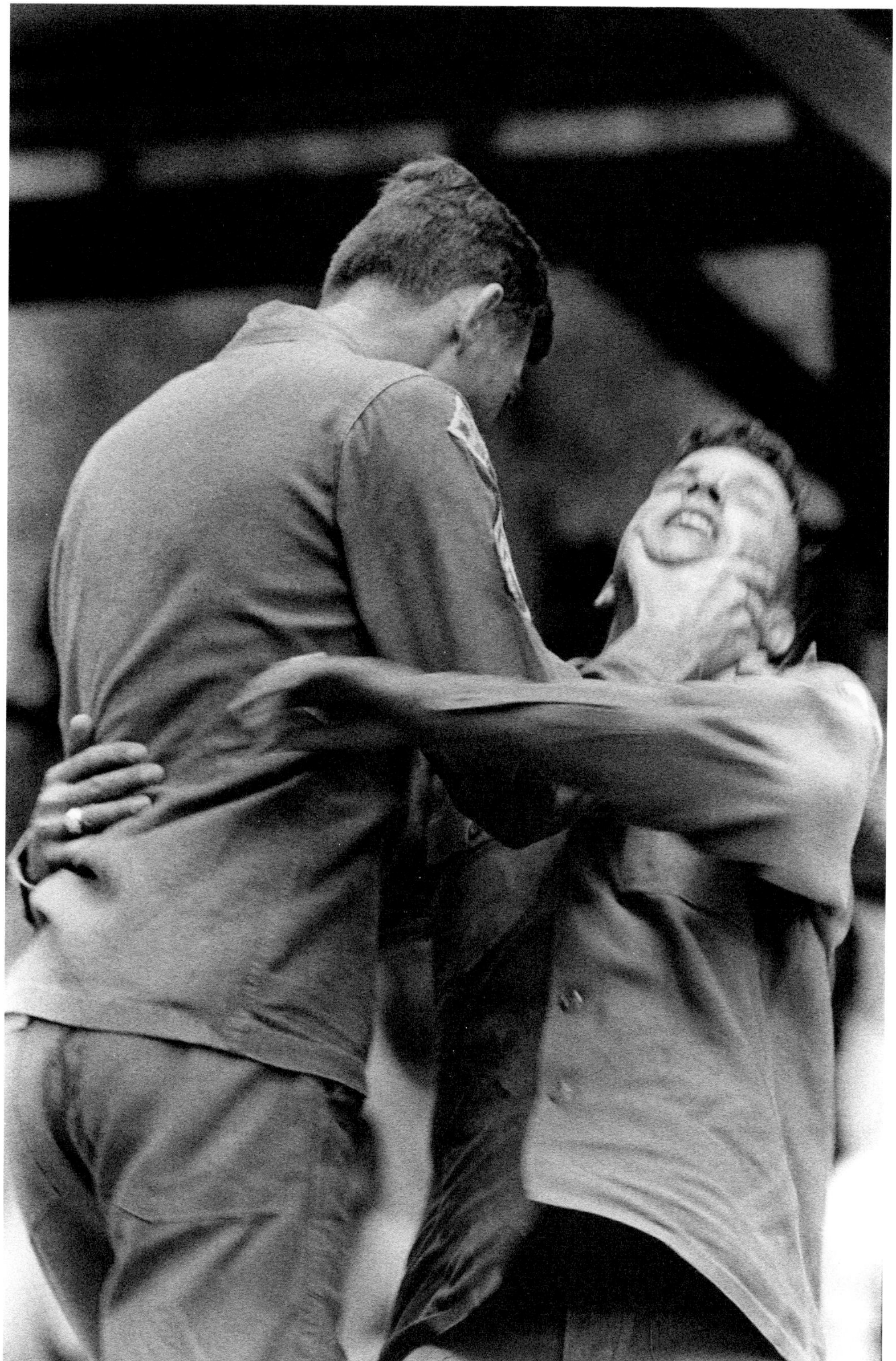

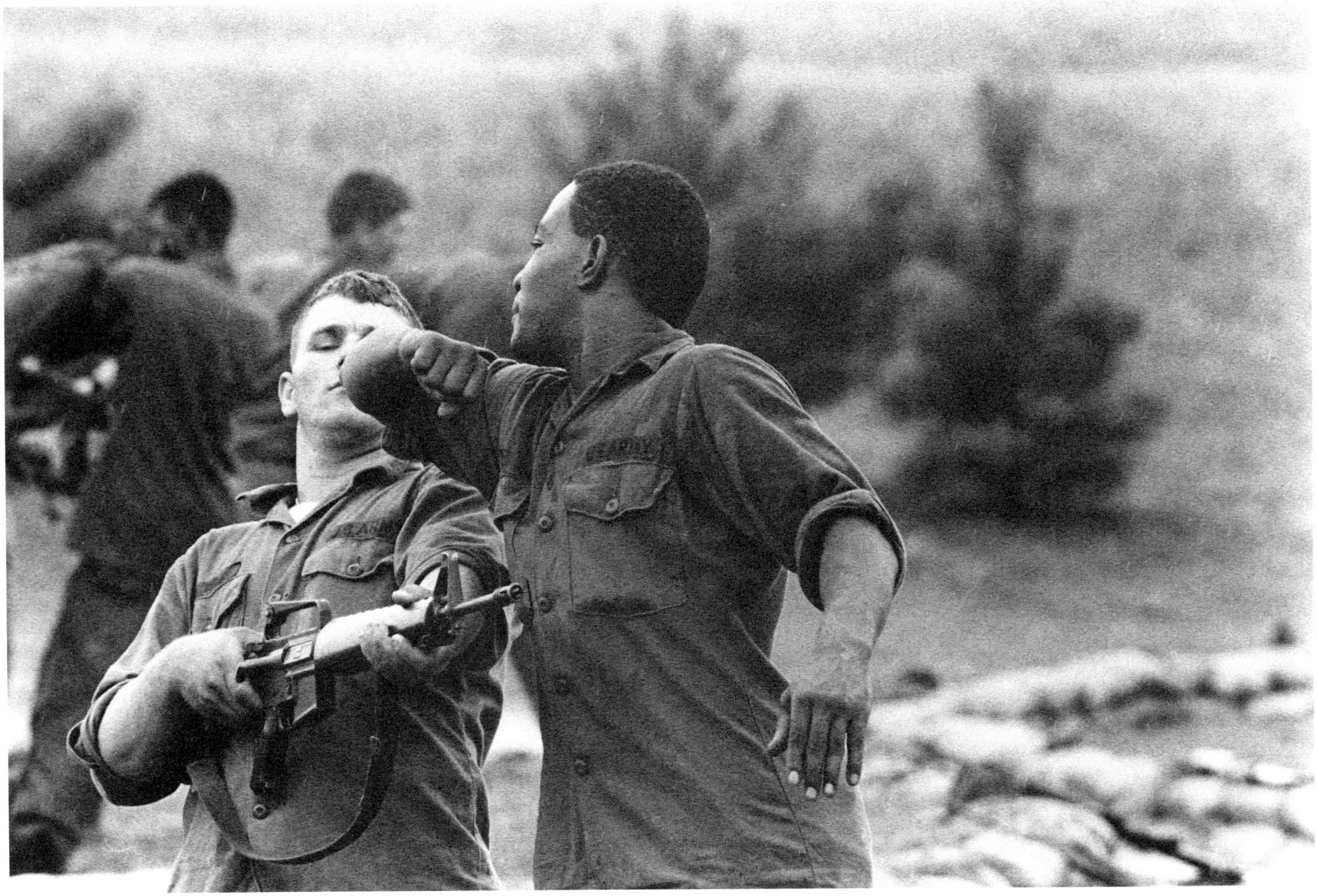

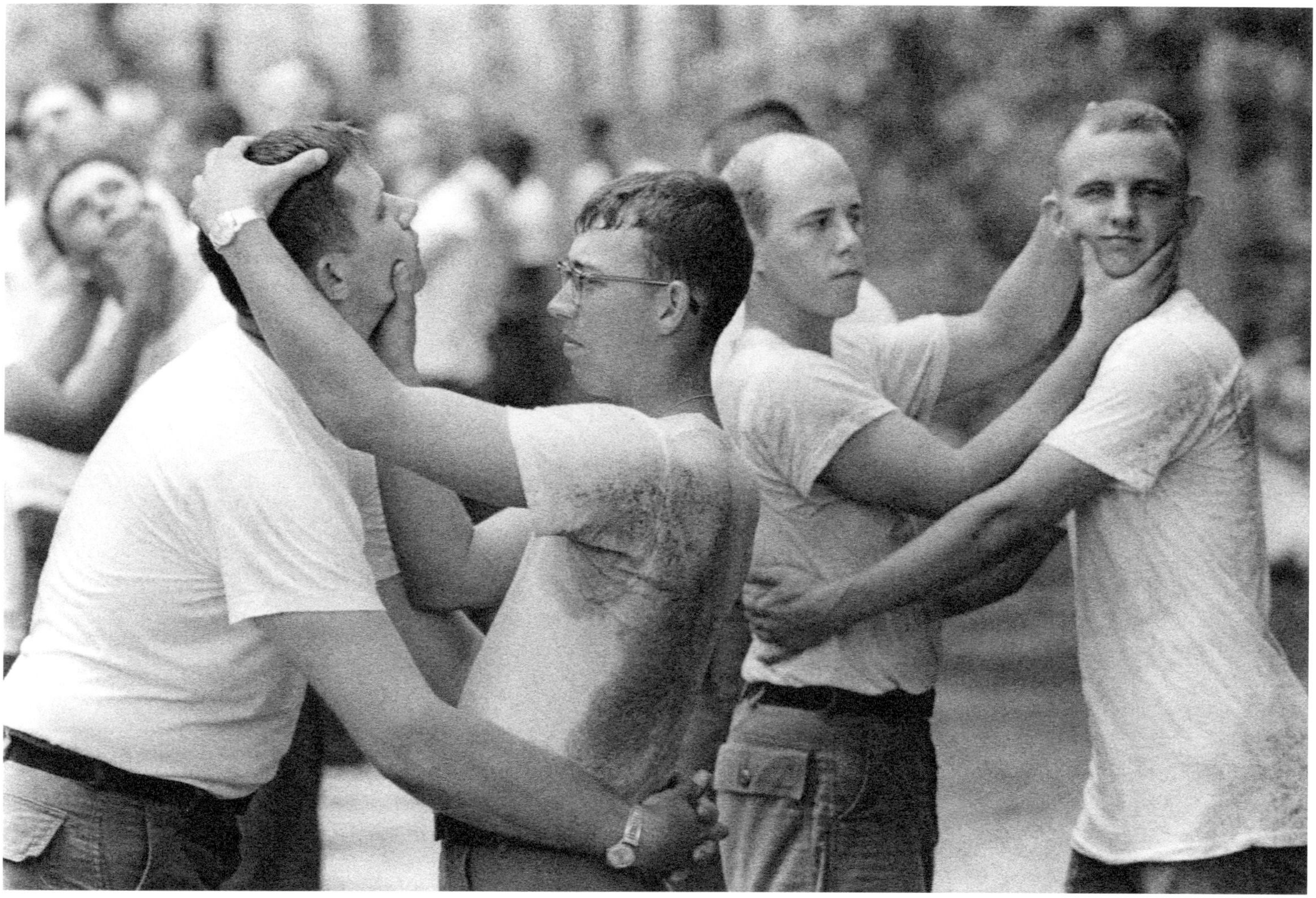

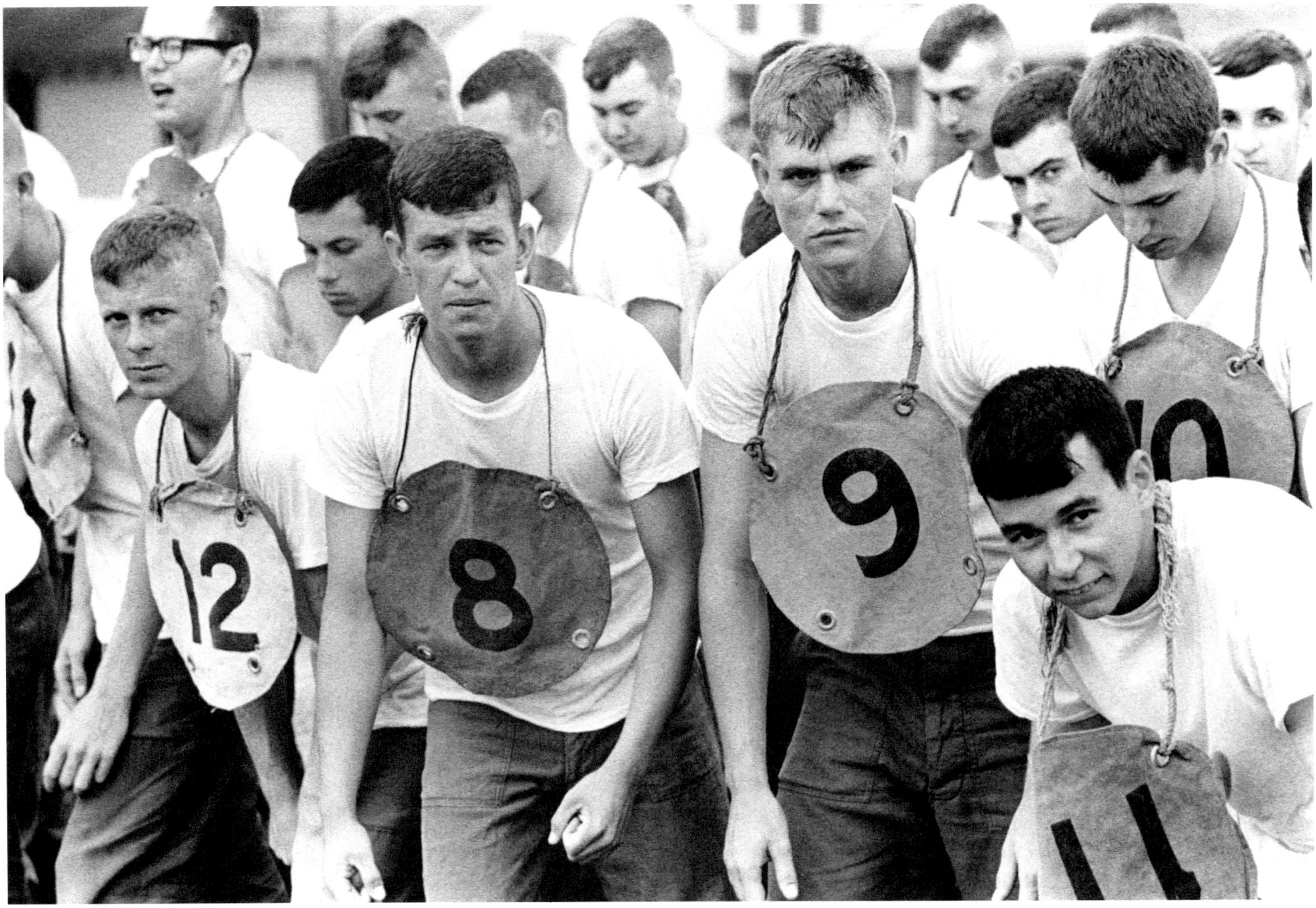
12
8
9
10
11

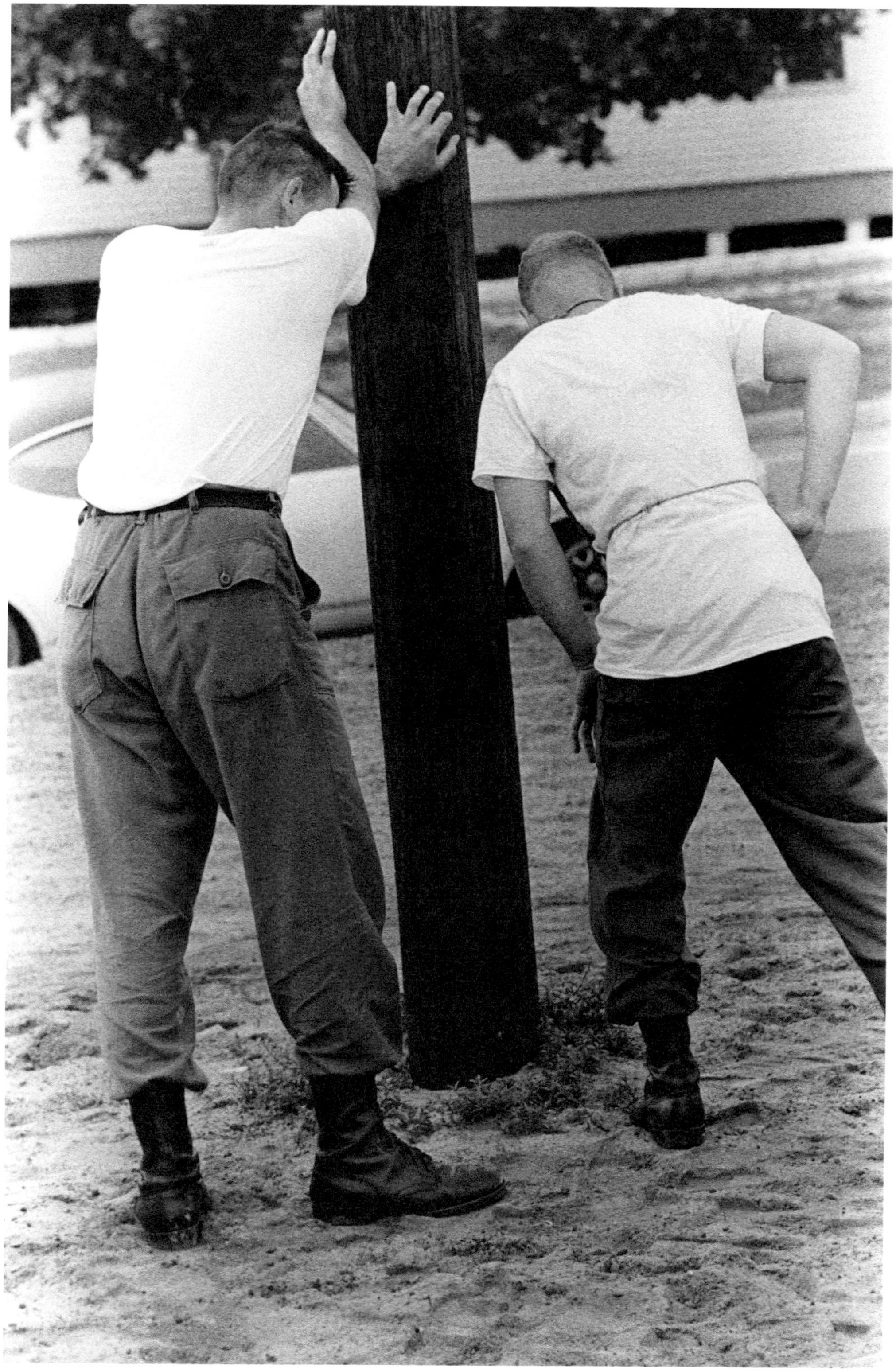

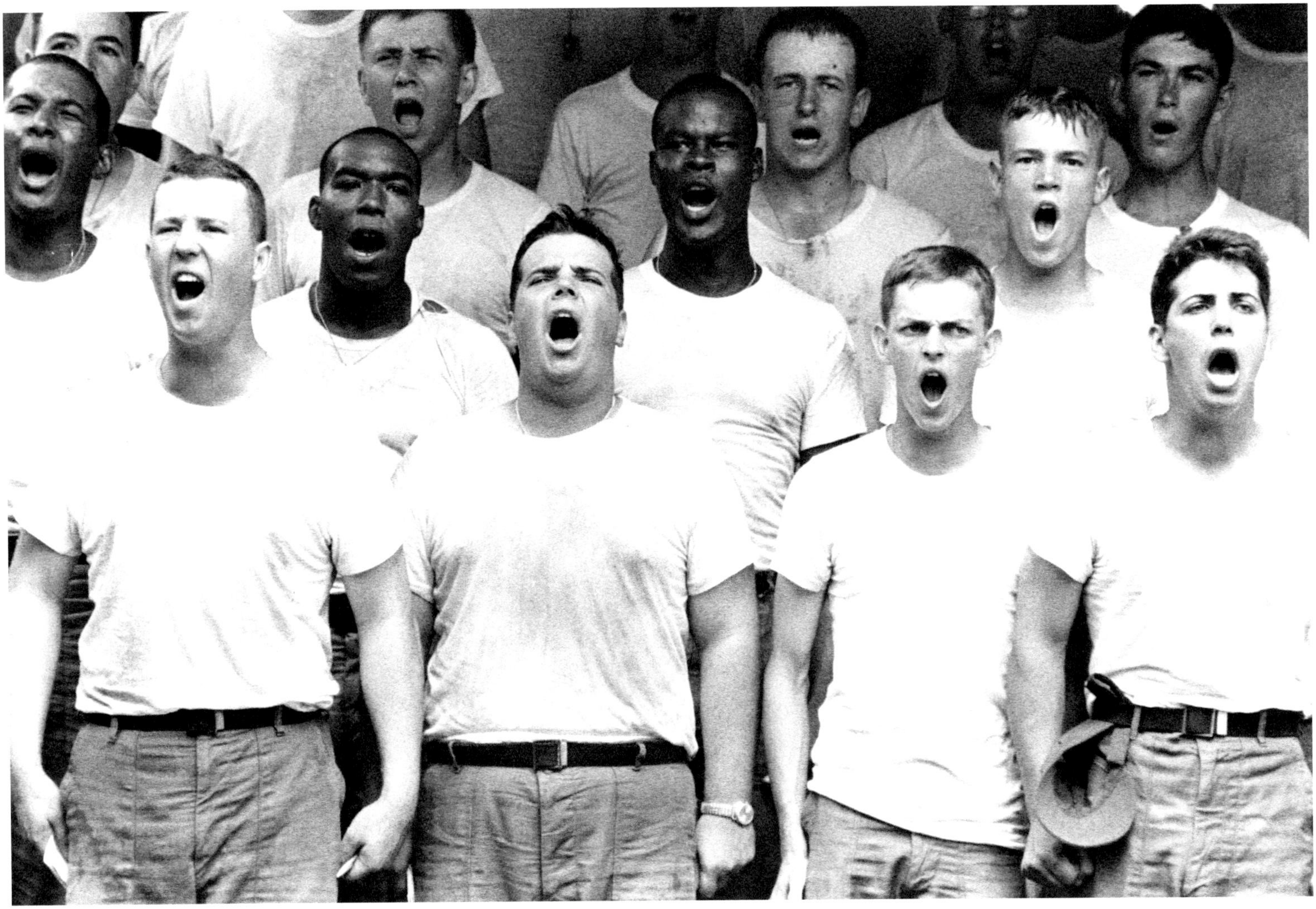

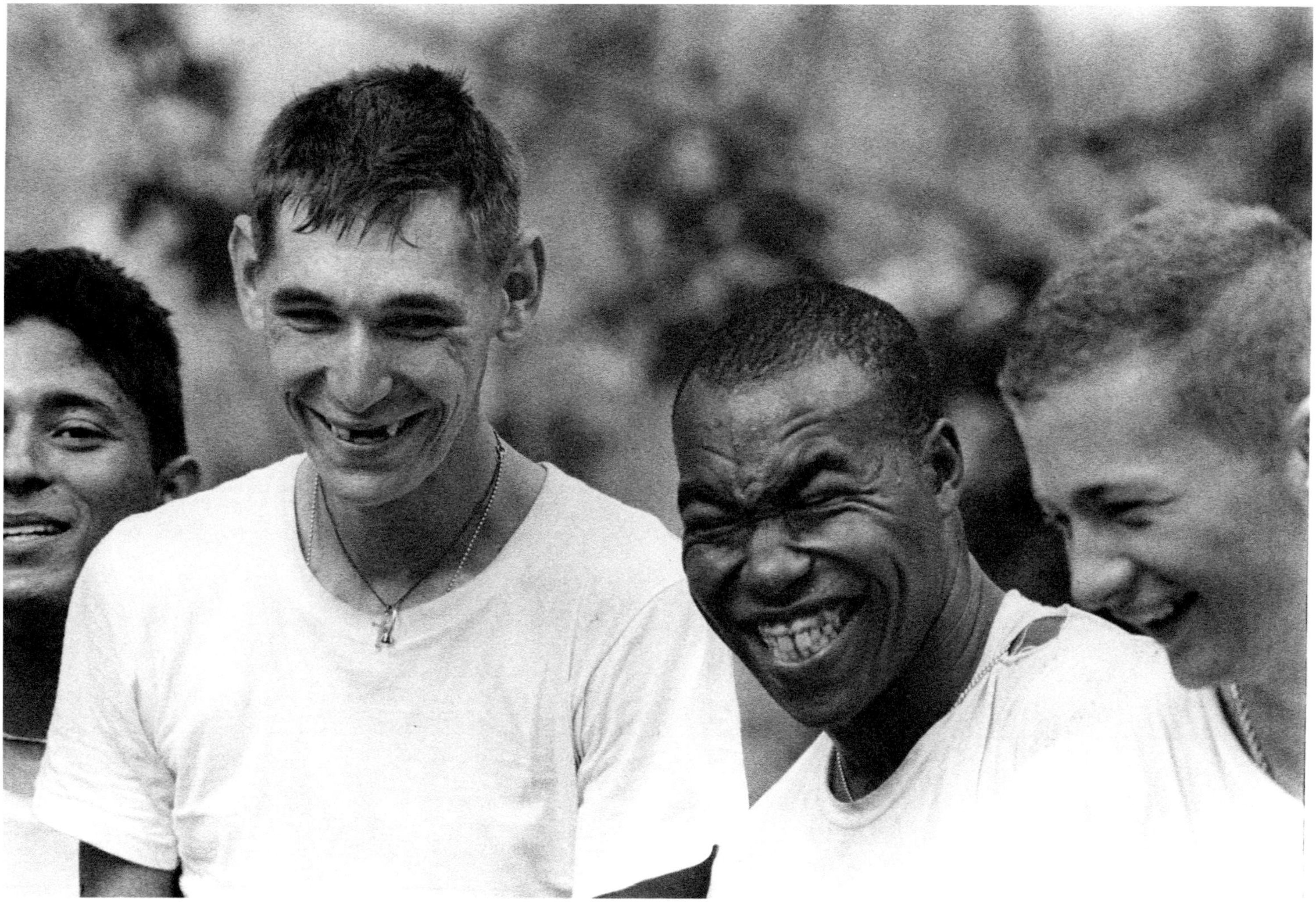

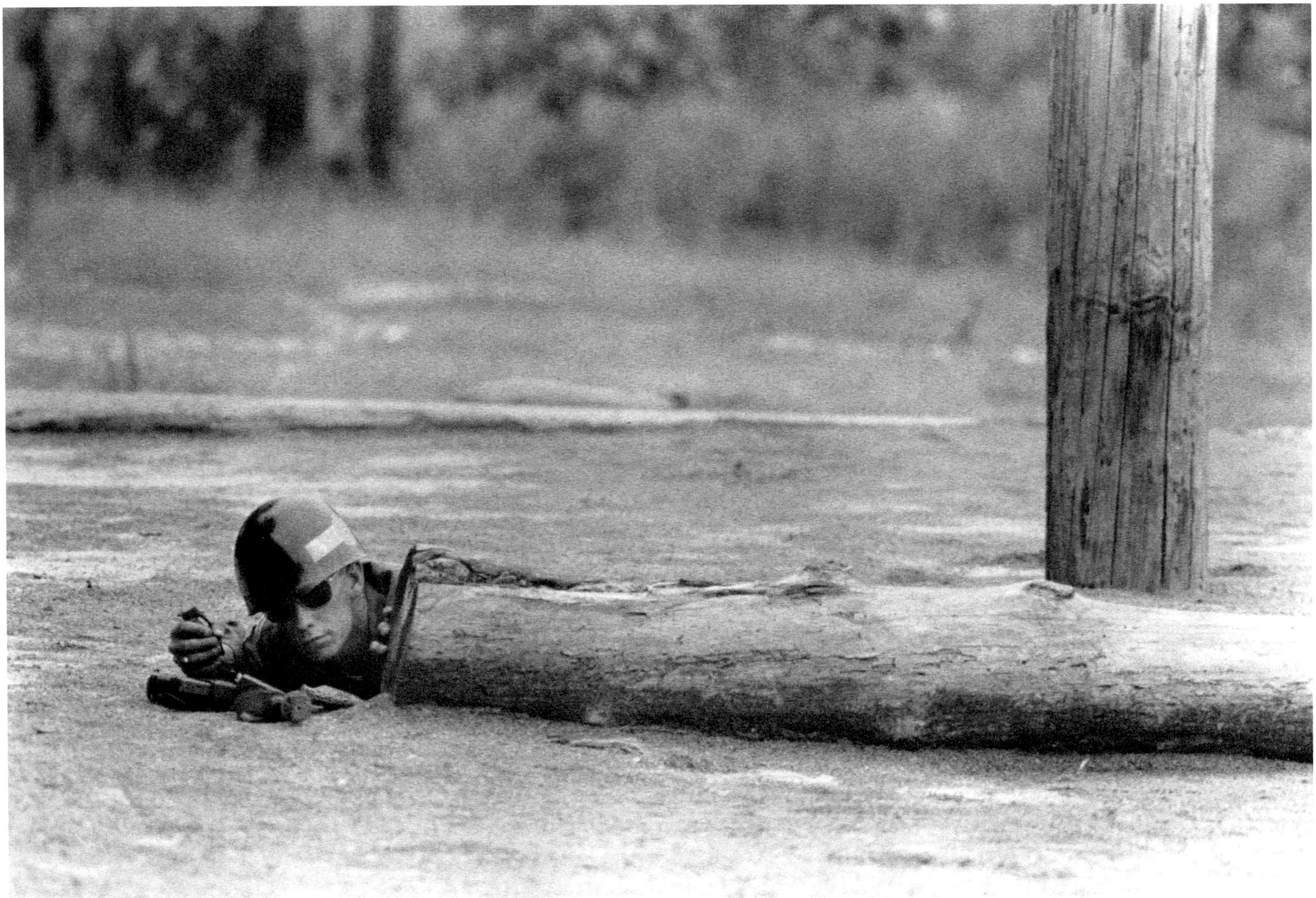

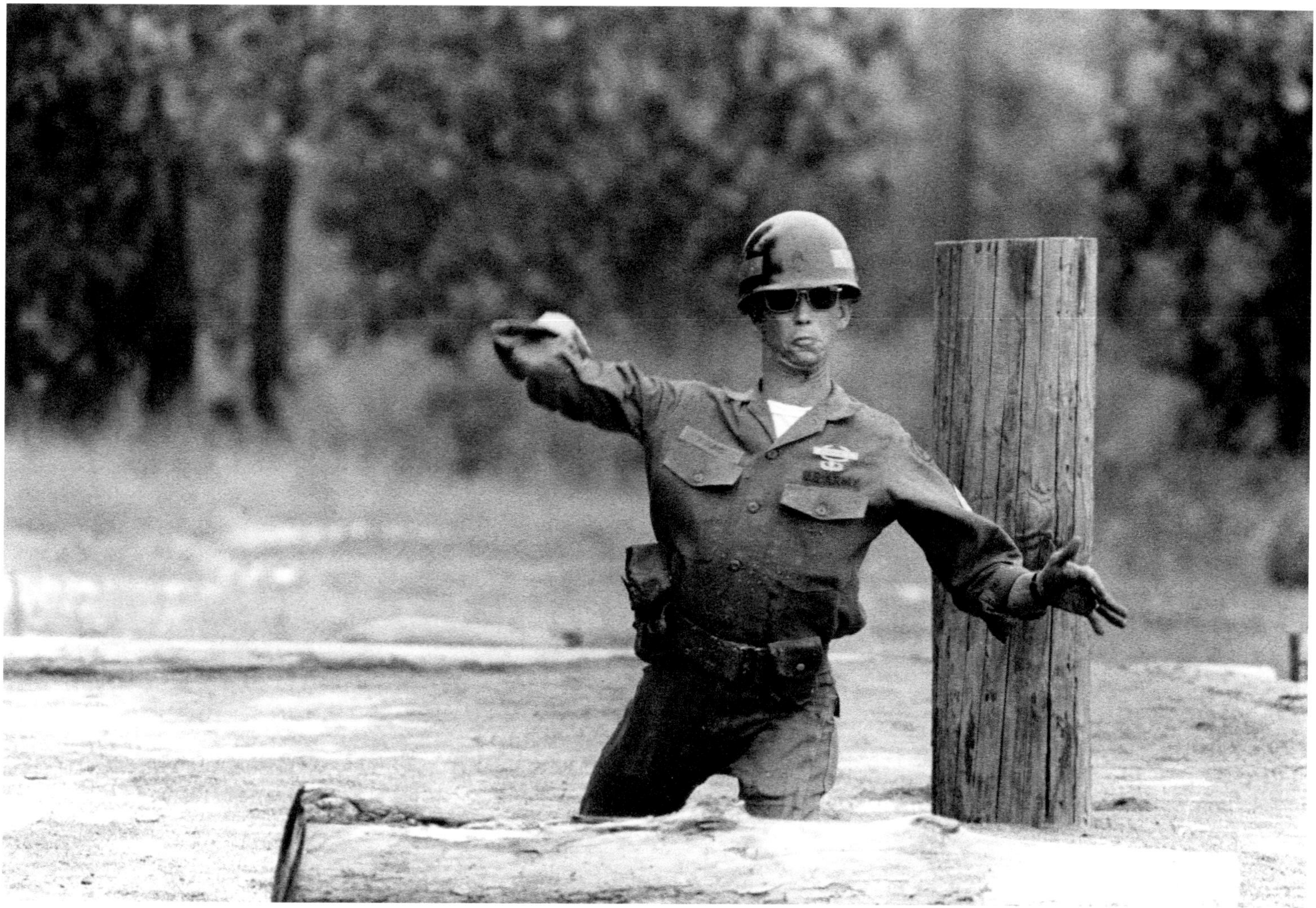

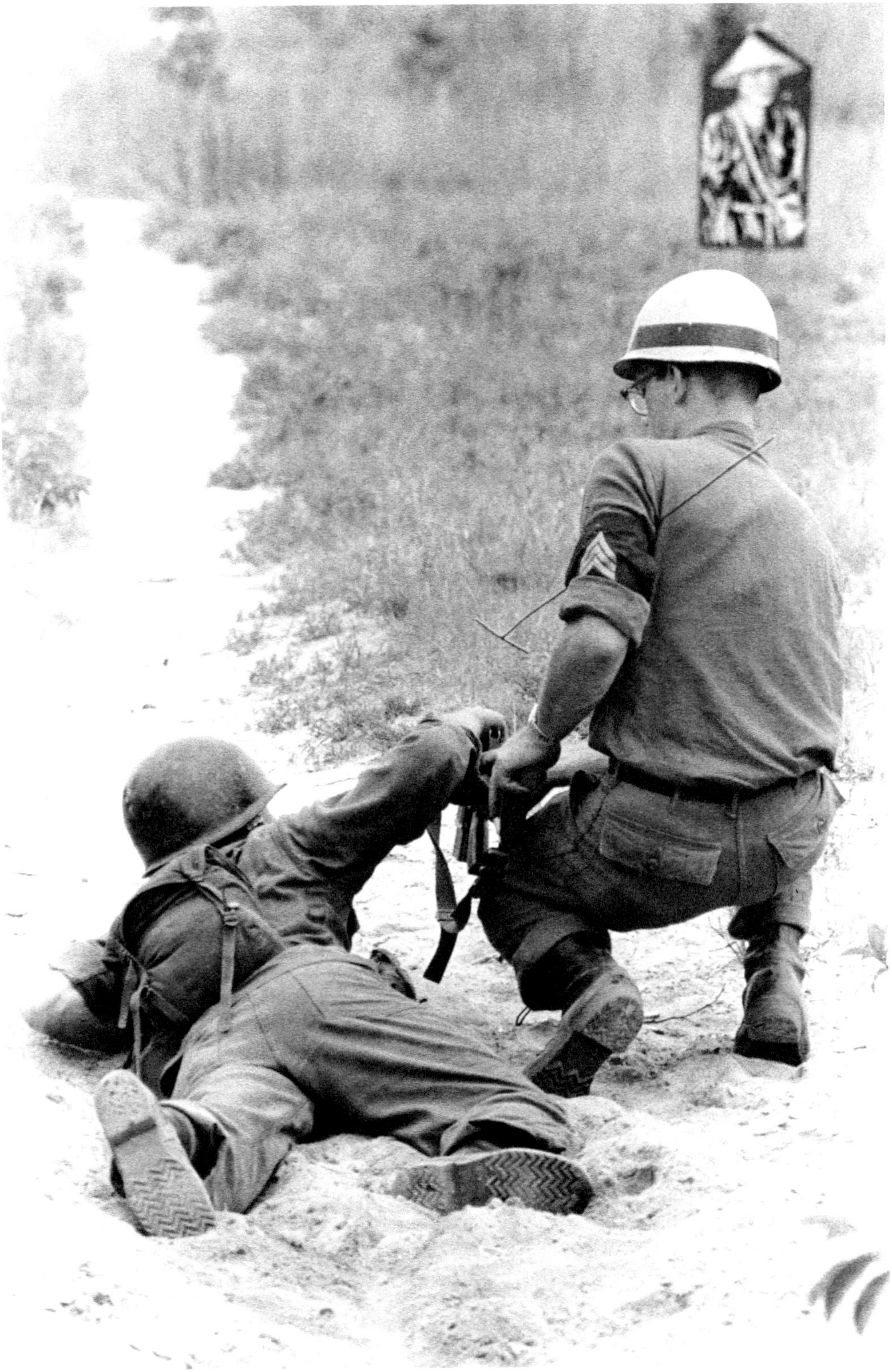

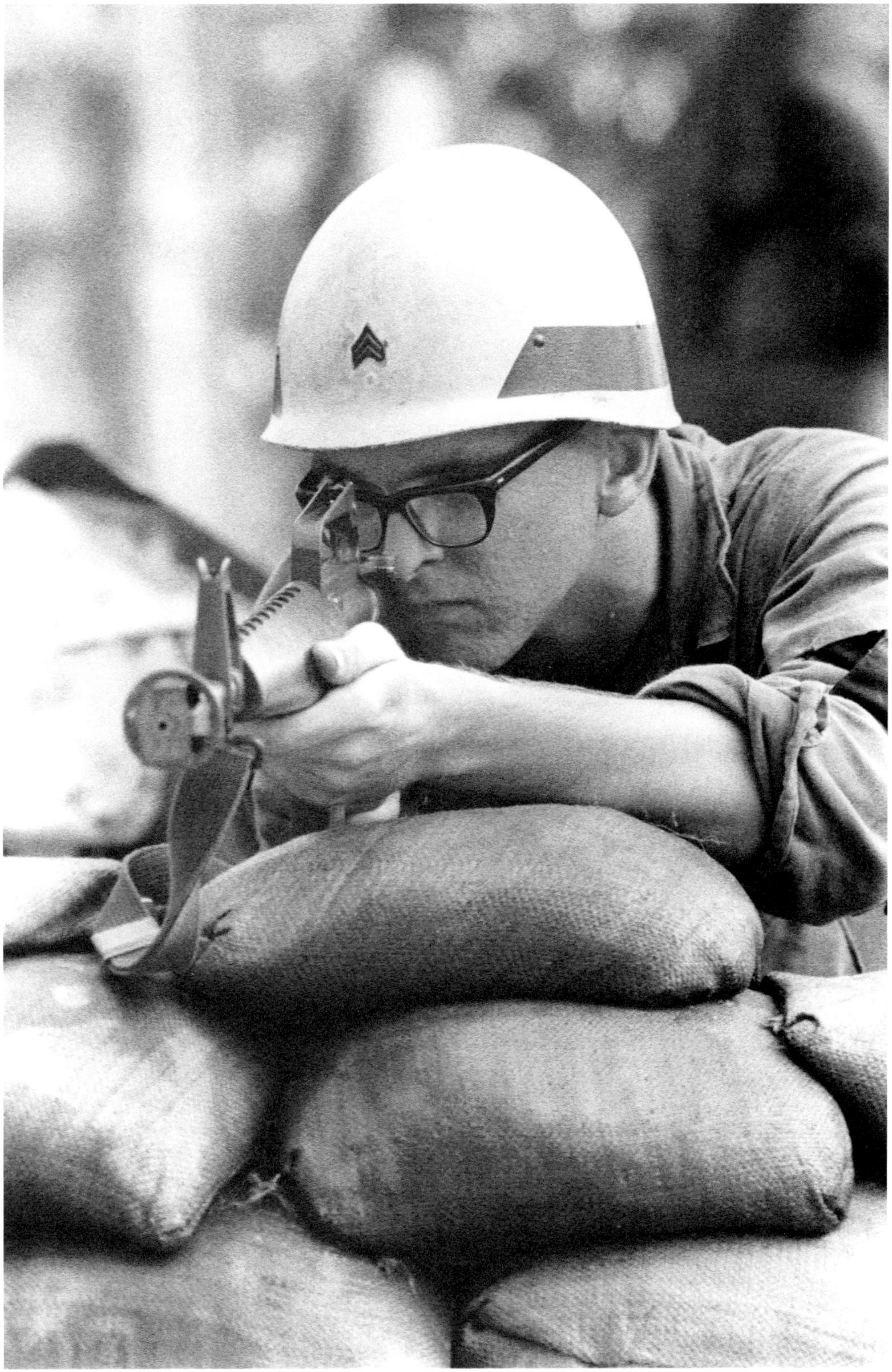

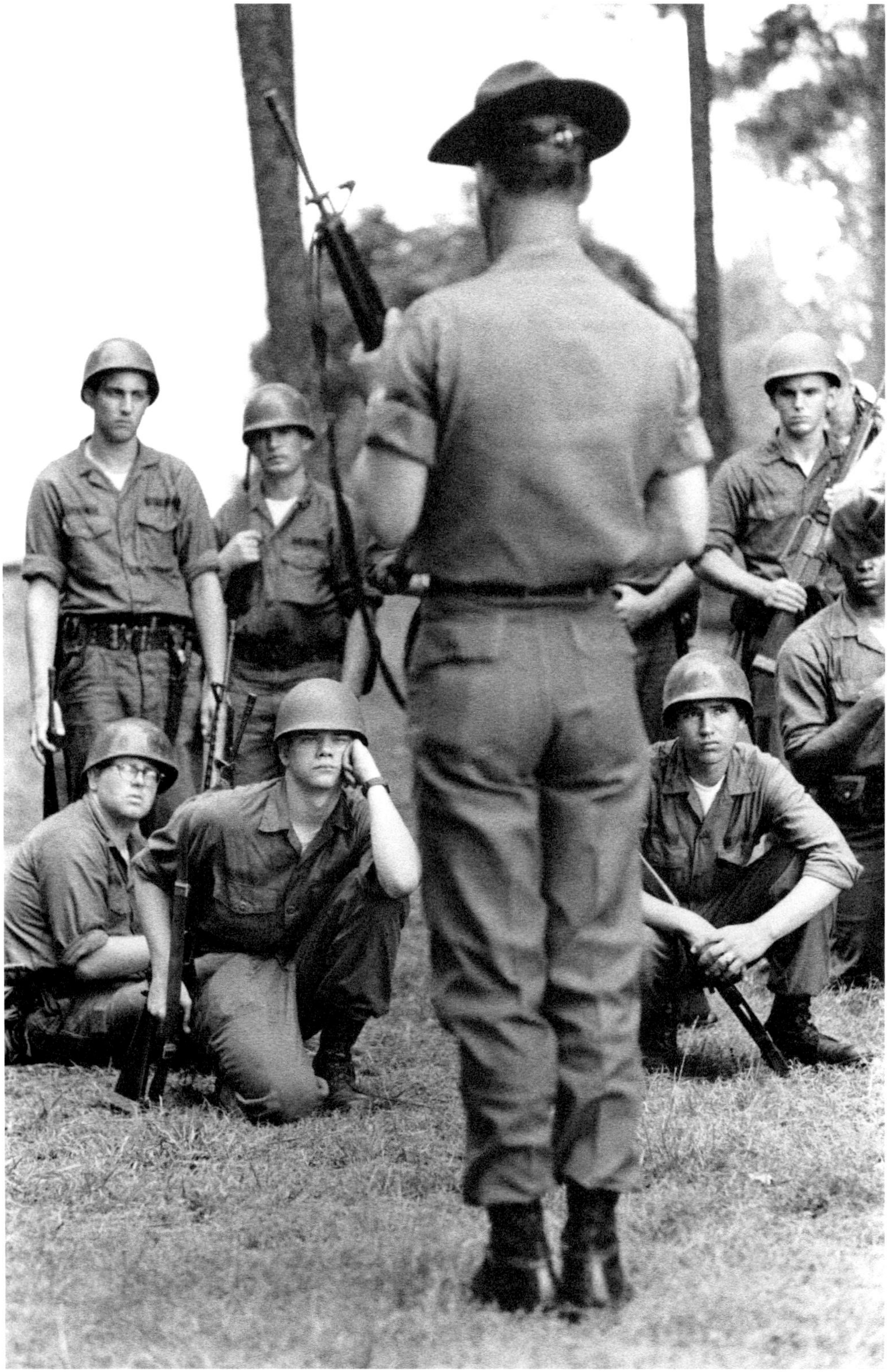

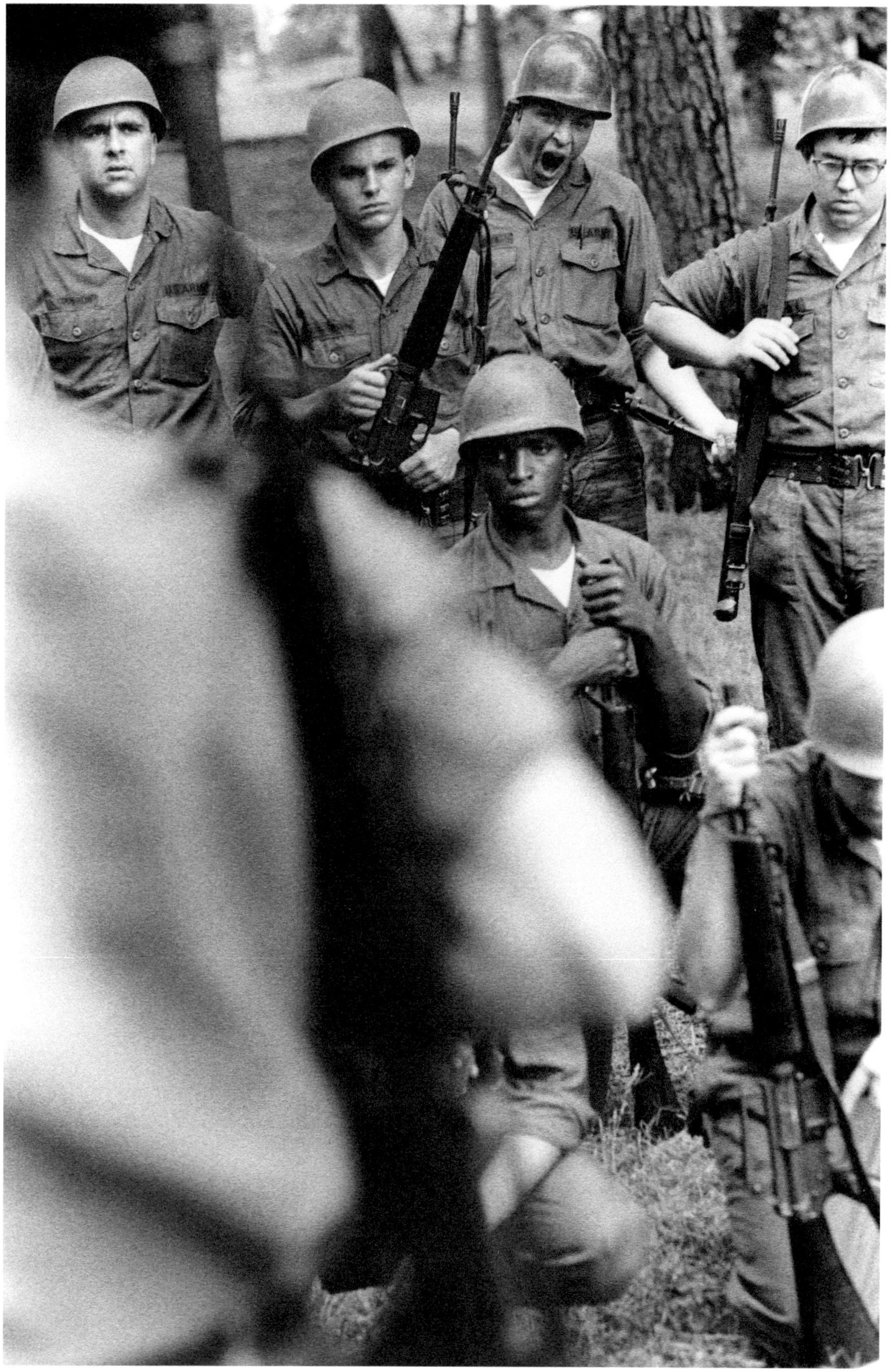

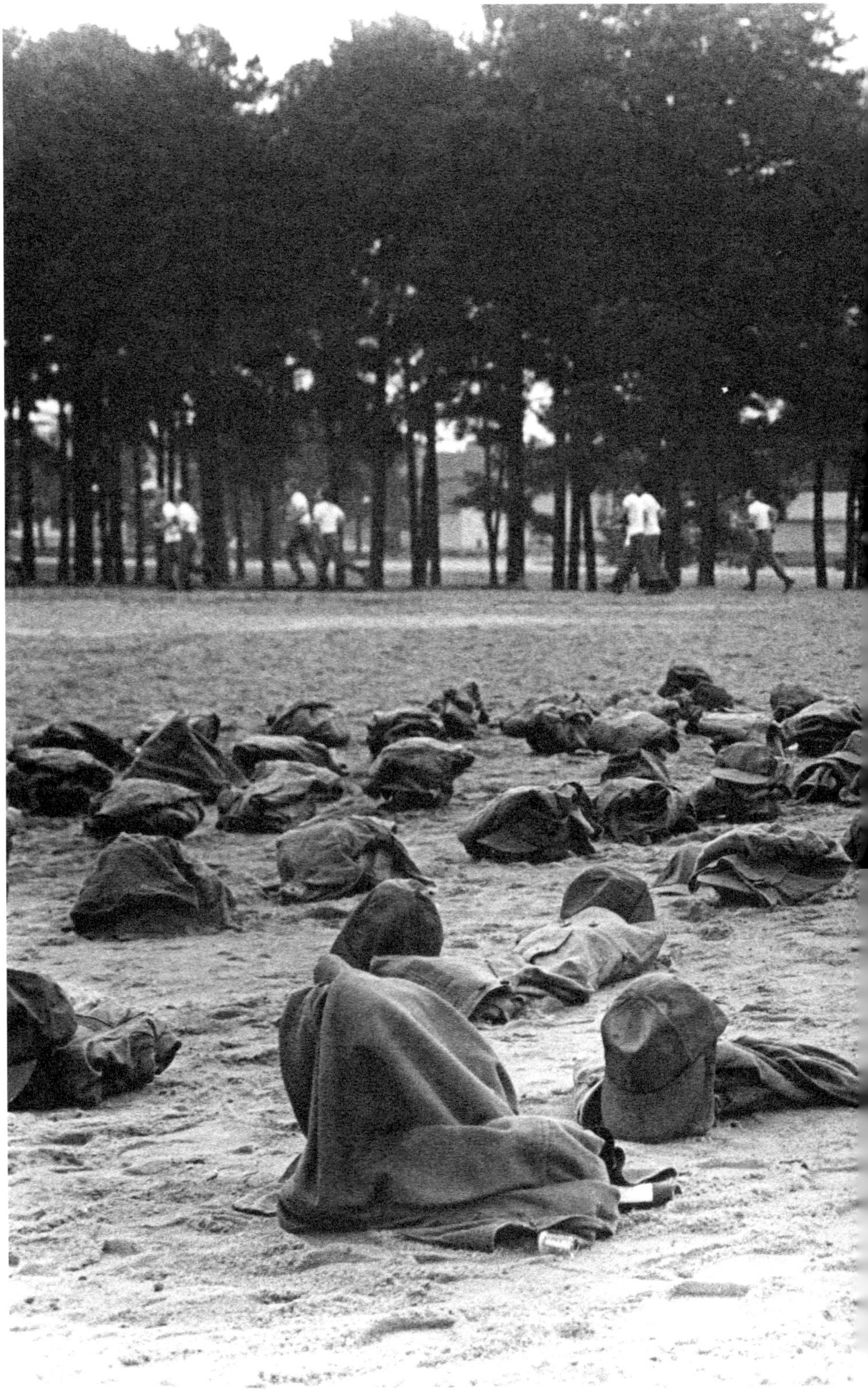

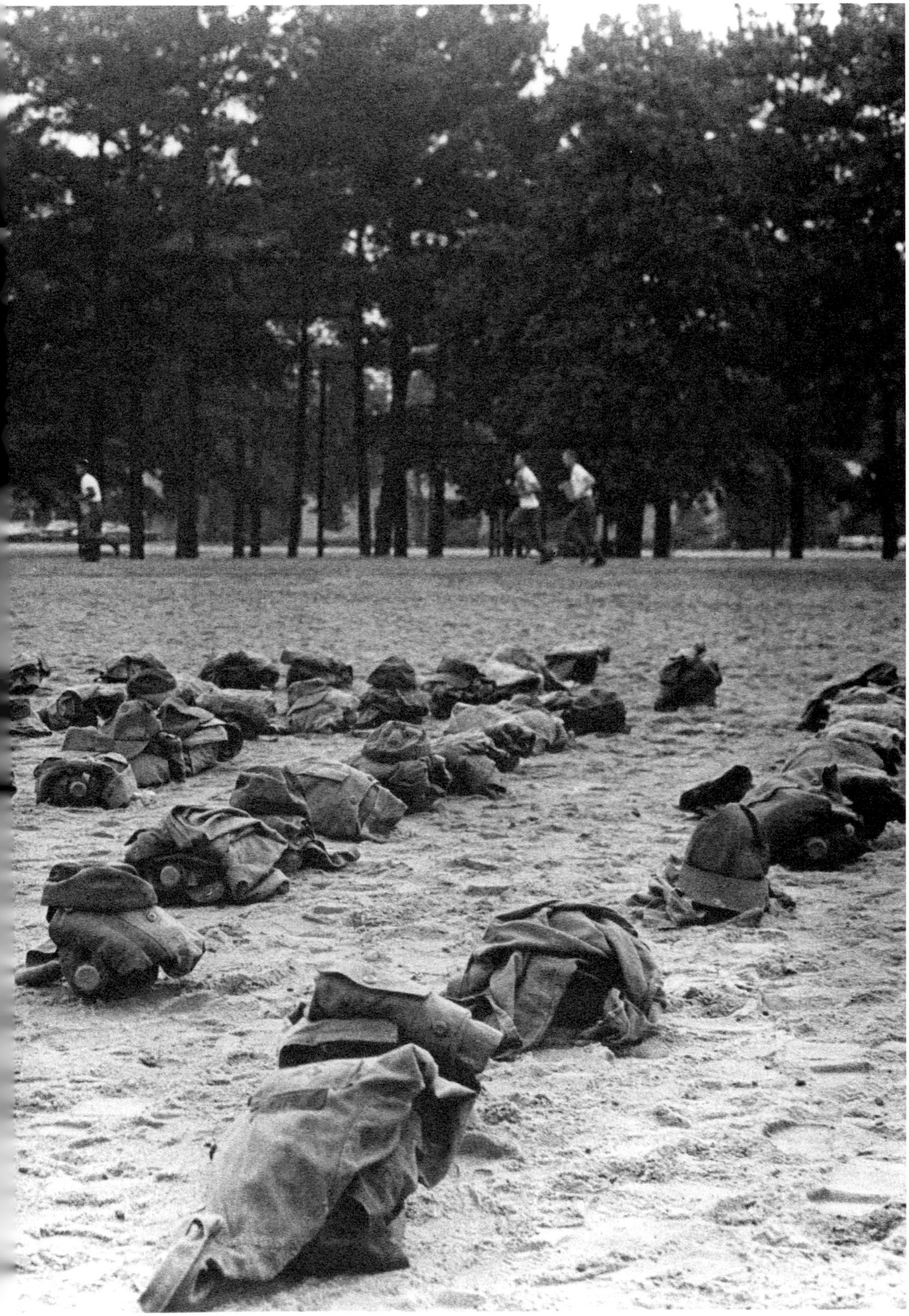

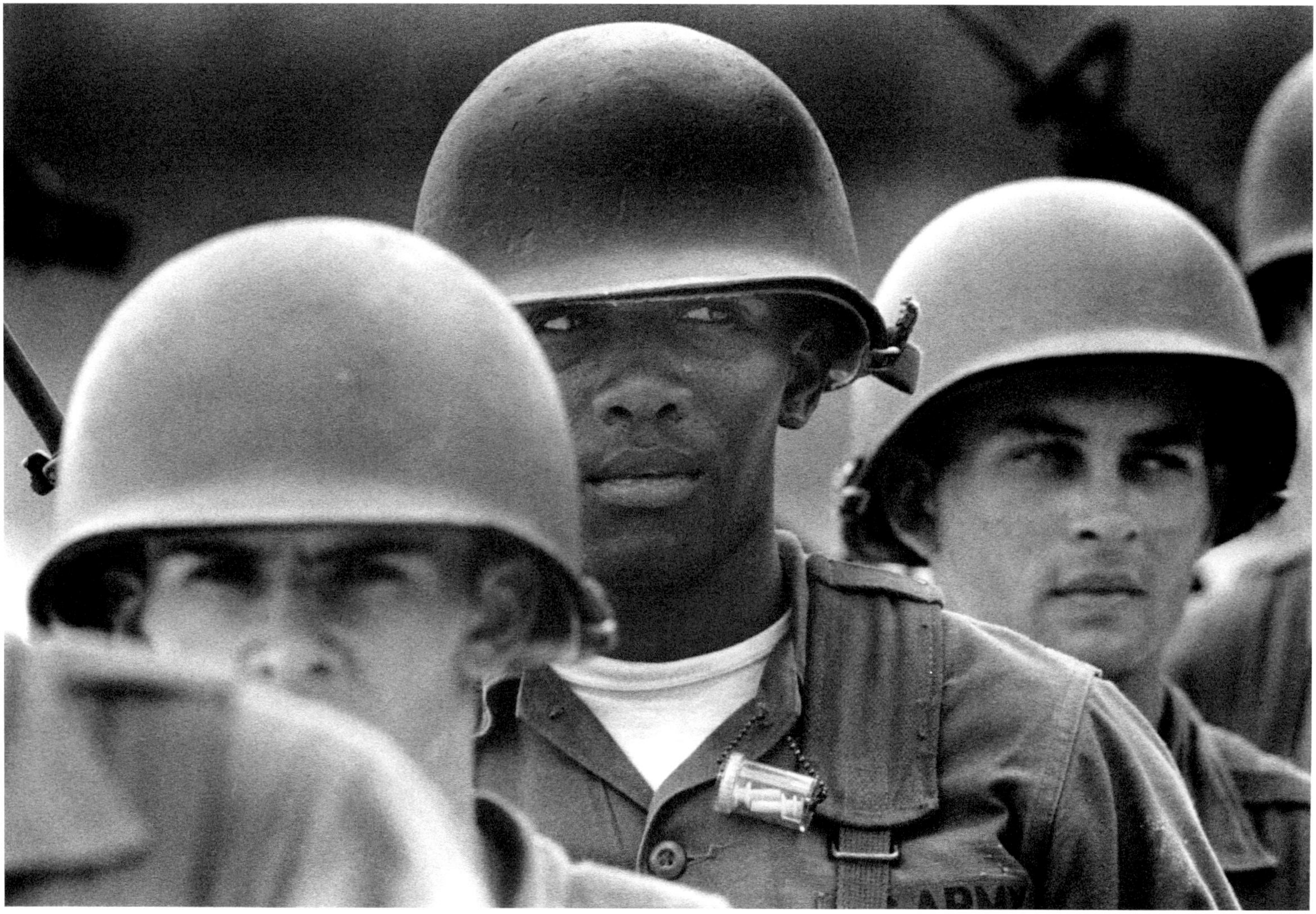
ARMY

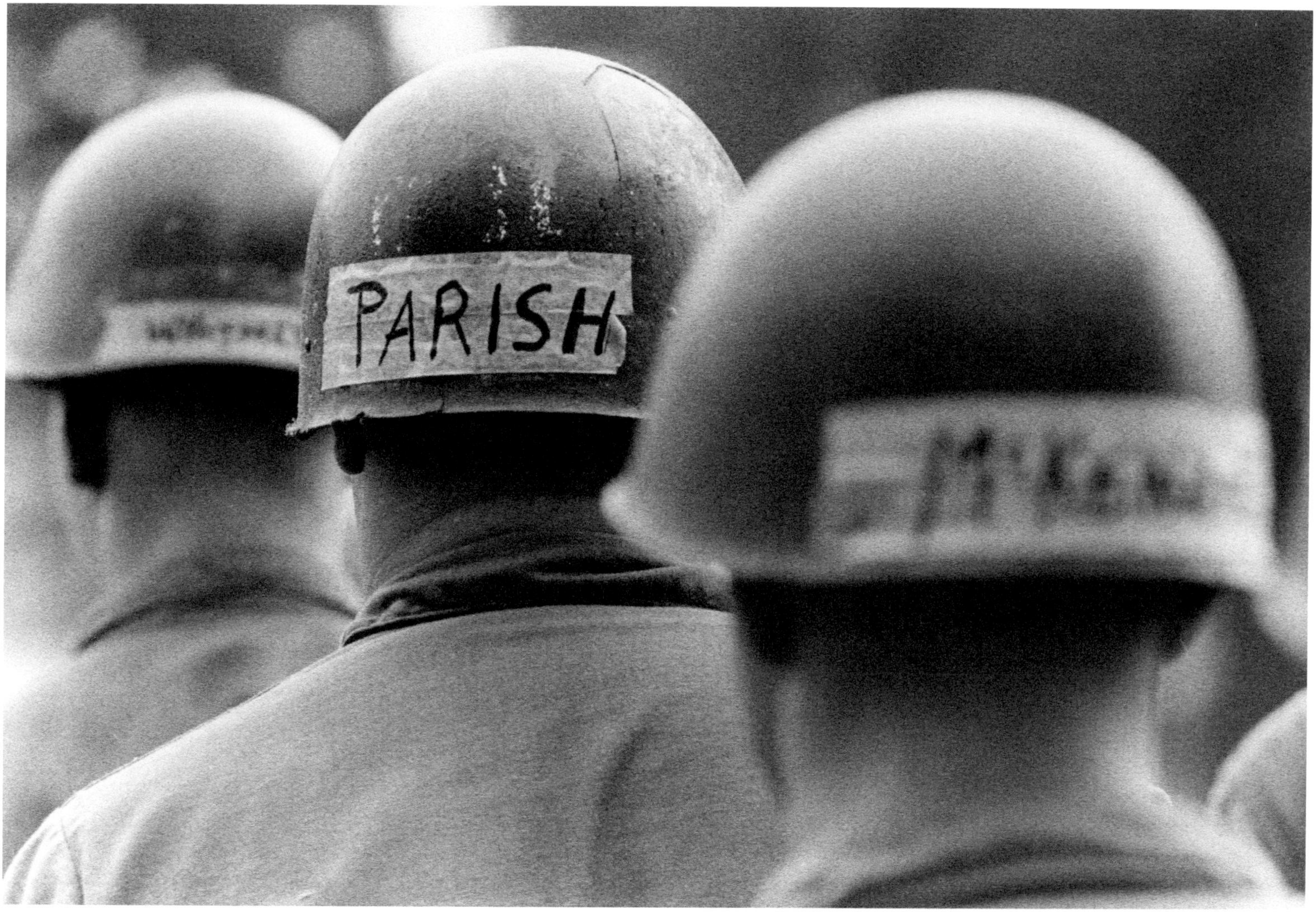
PARISH

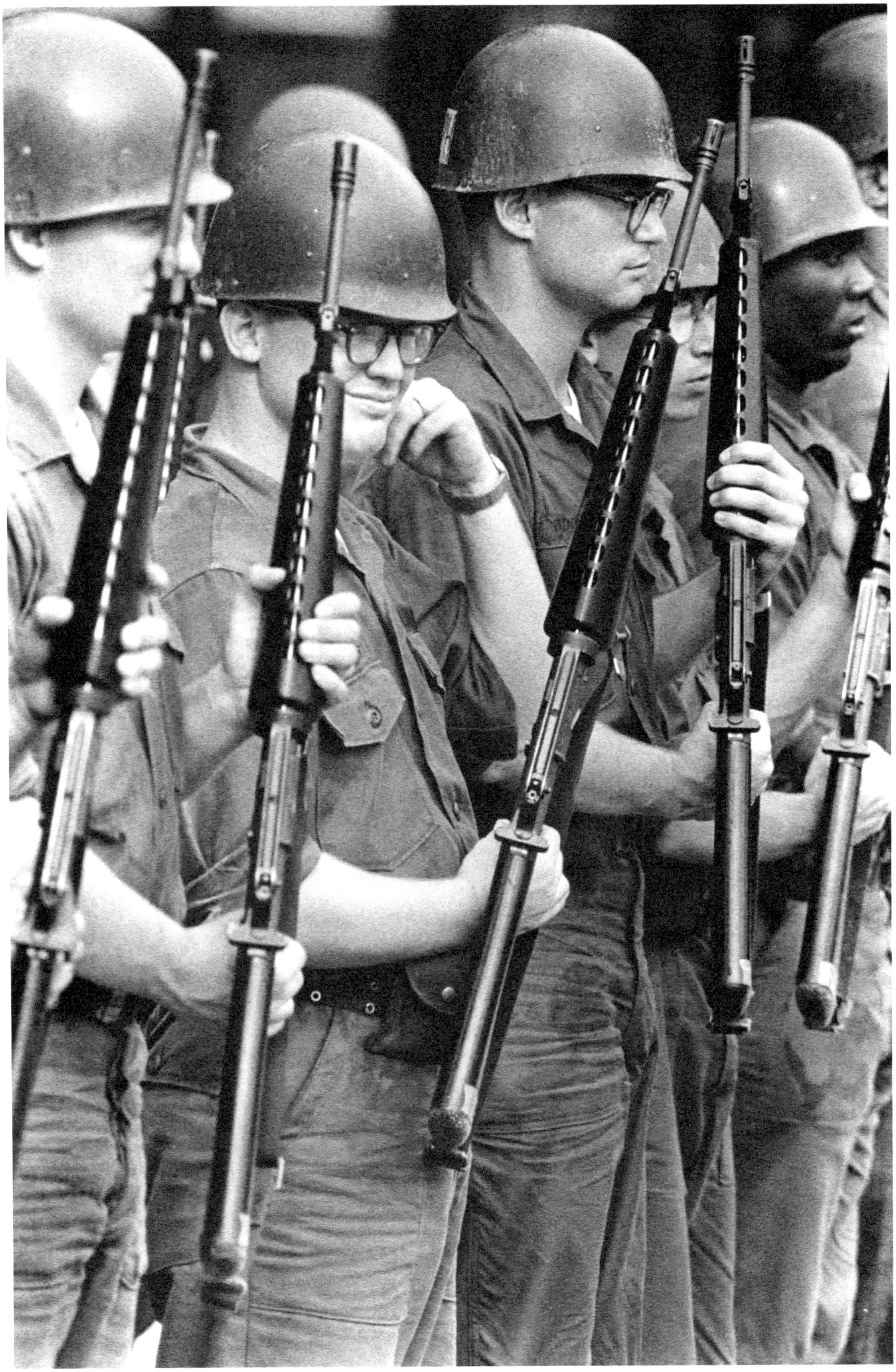

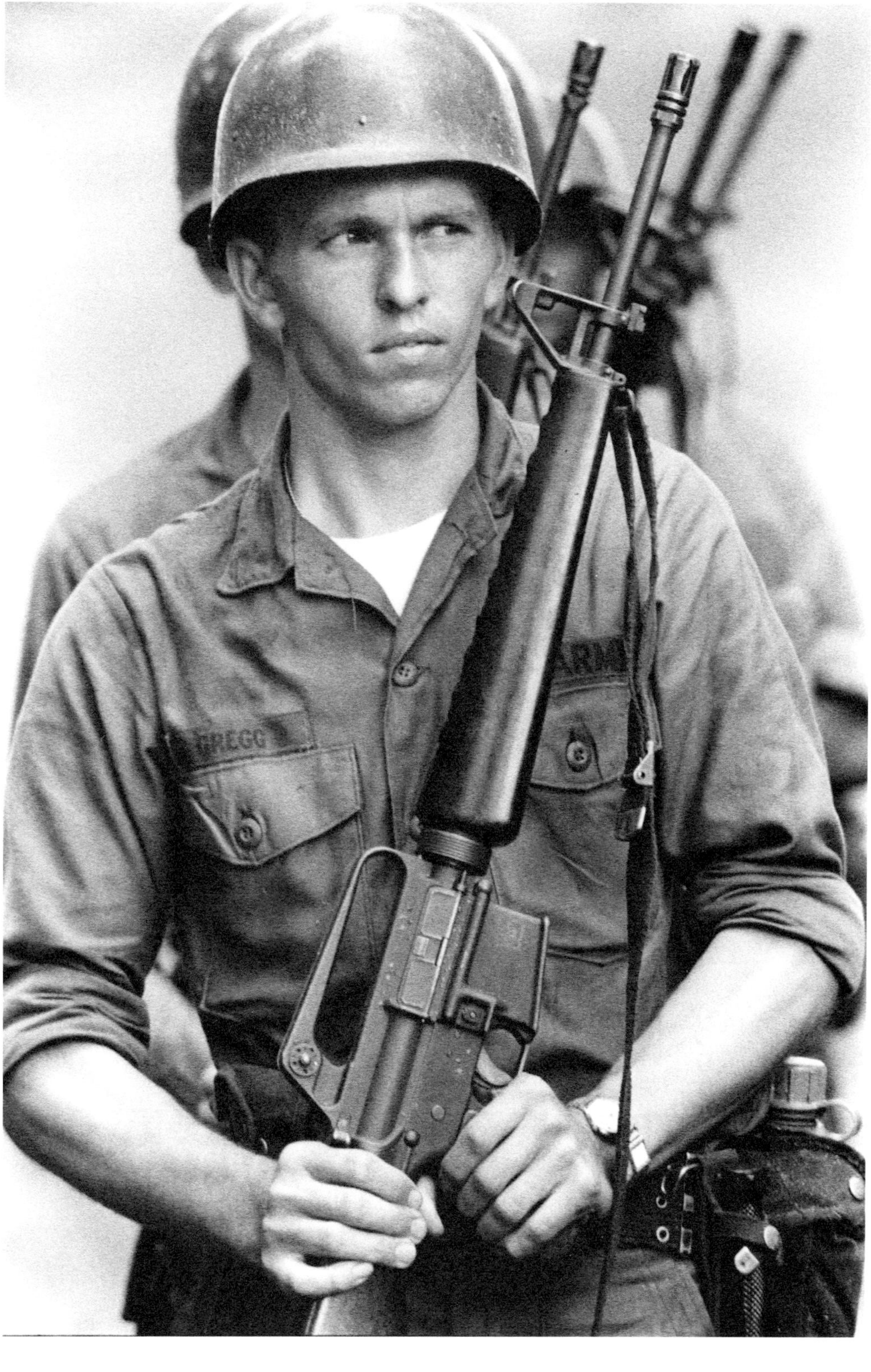
GREGG

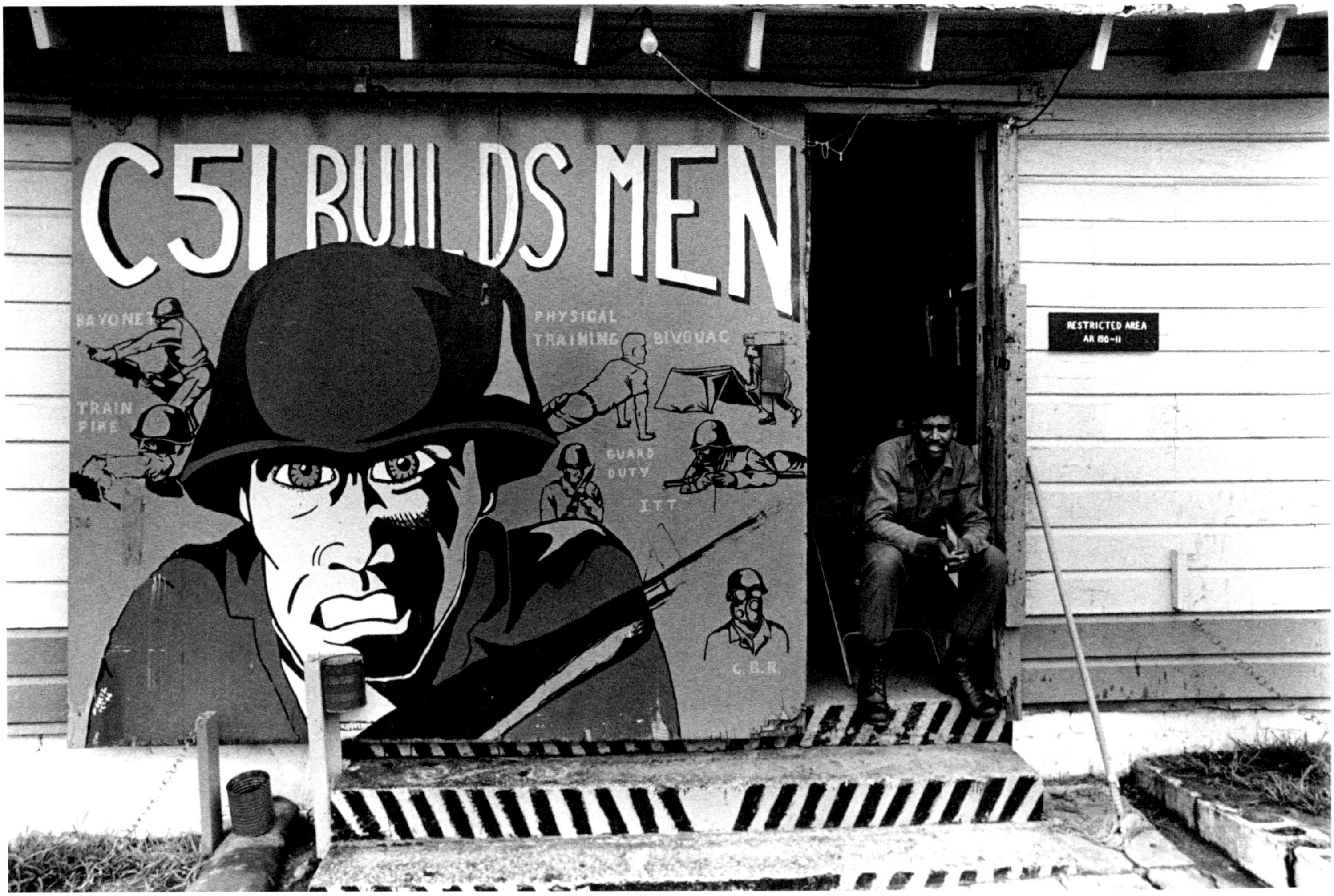
C51 BUILDS MEN
BAYONET
PHYSICAL TRAINING
BIVOUAC
TRAIN FIRE
GUARD DUTY
ITT
C.B.R.
RESTRICTED AREA
AR 190-11

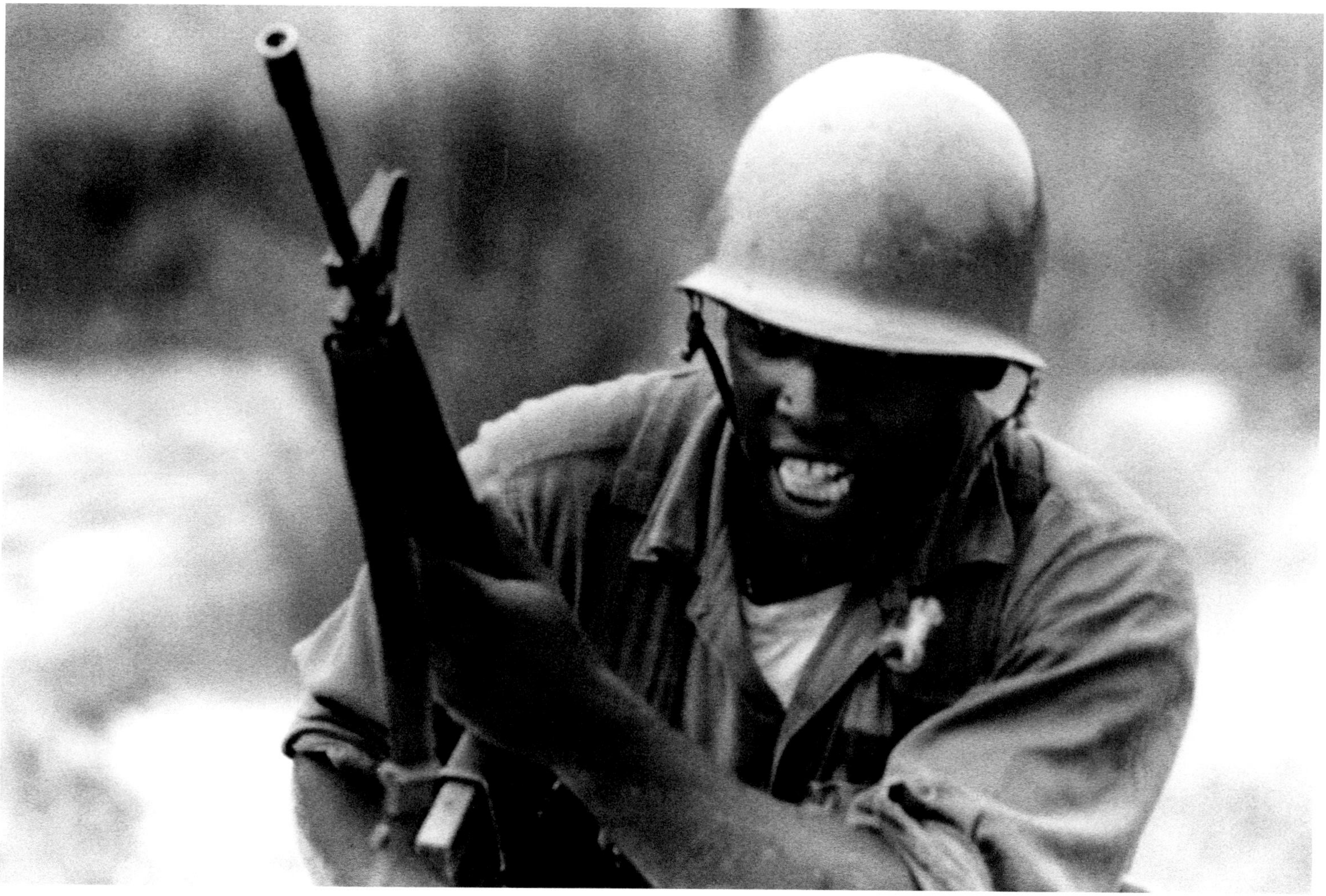

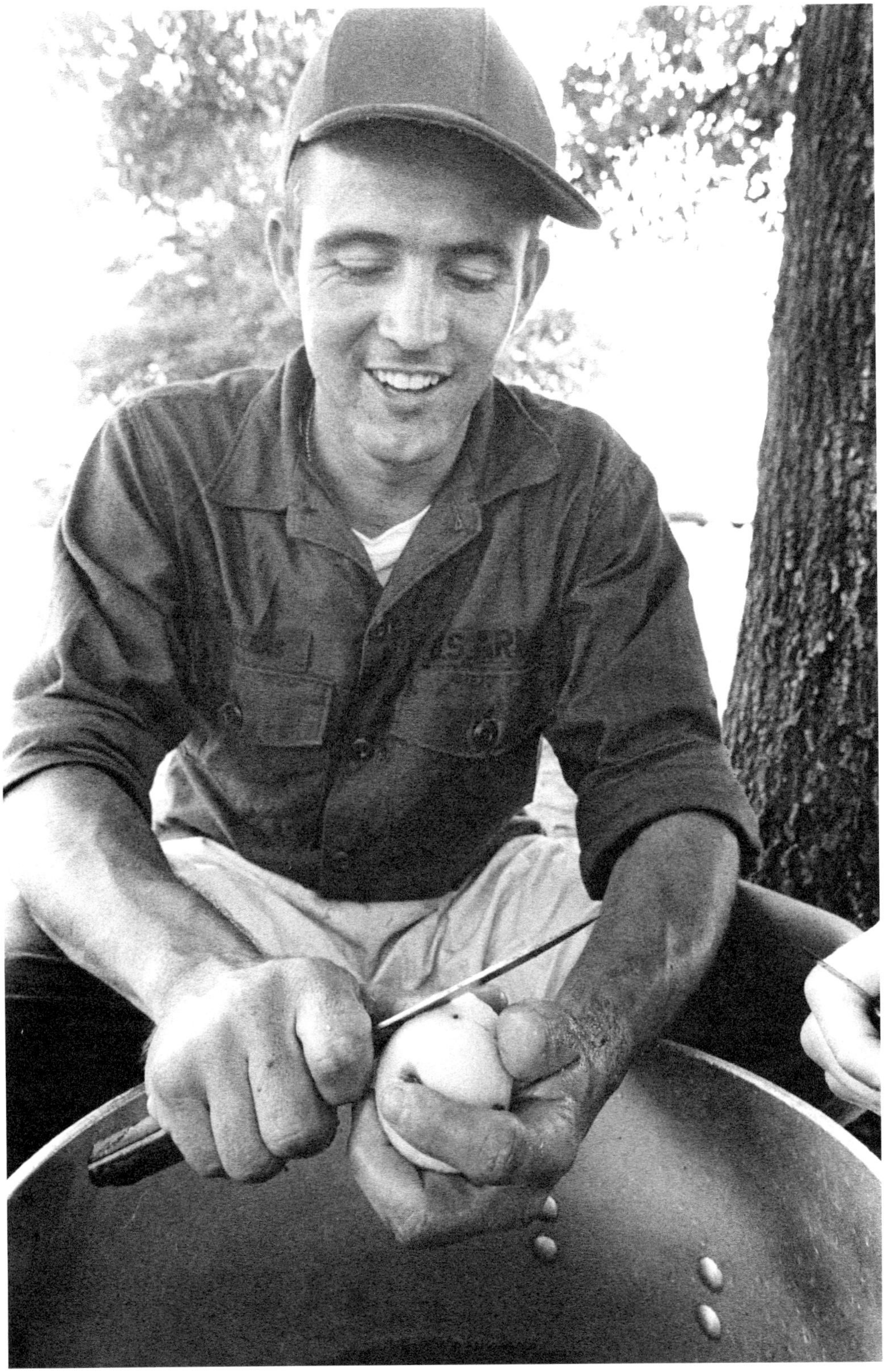

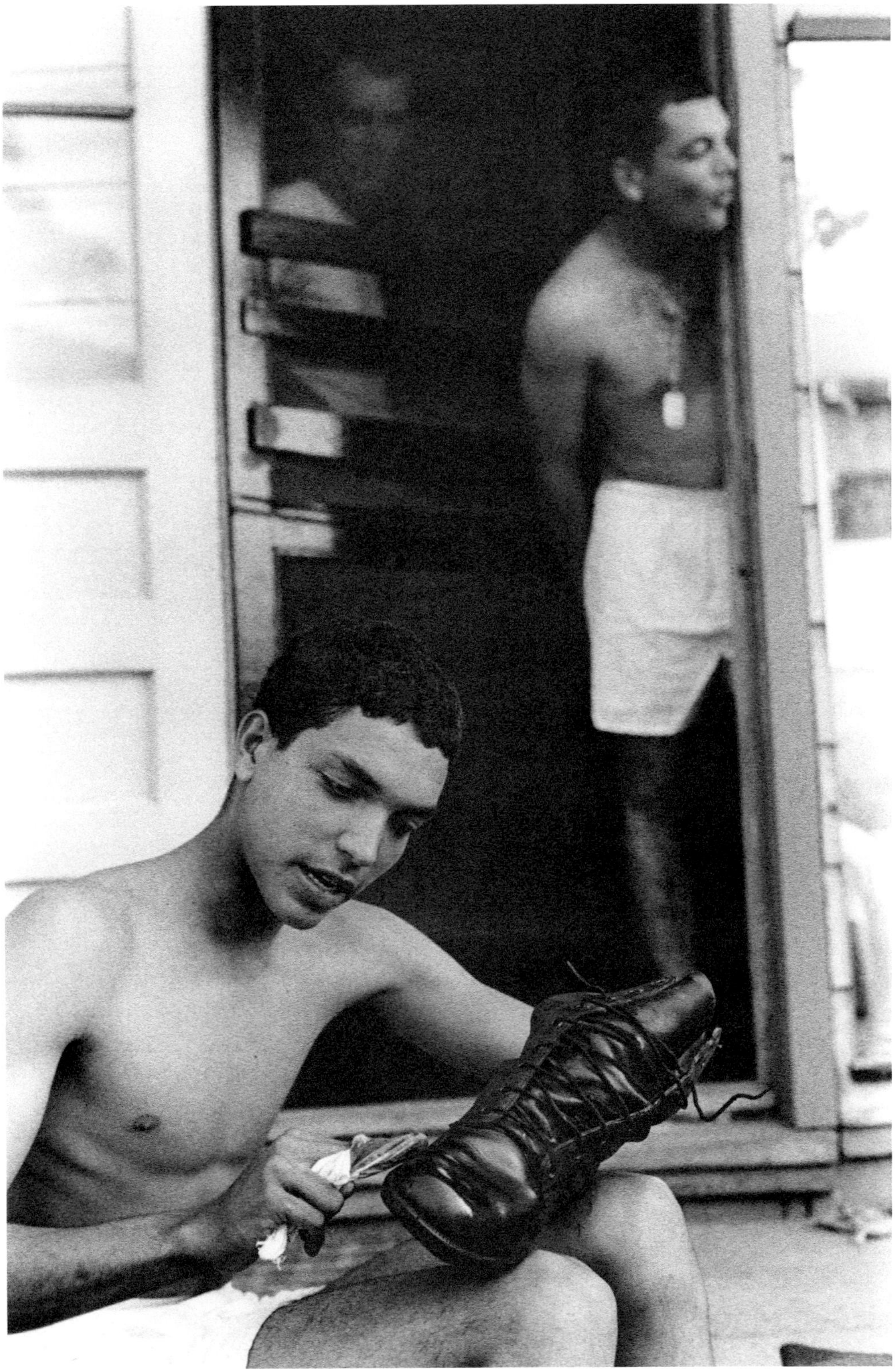

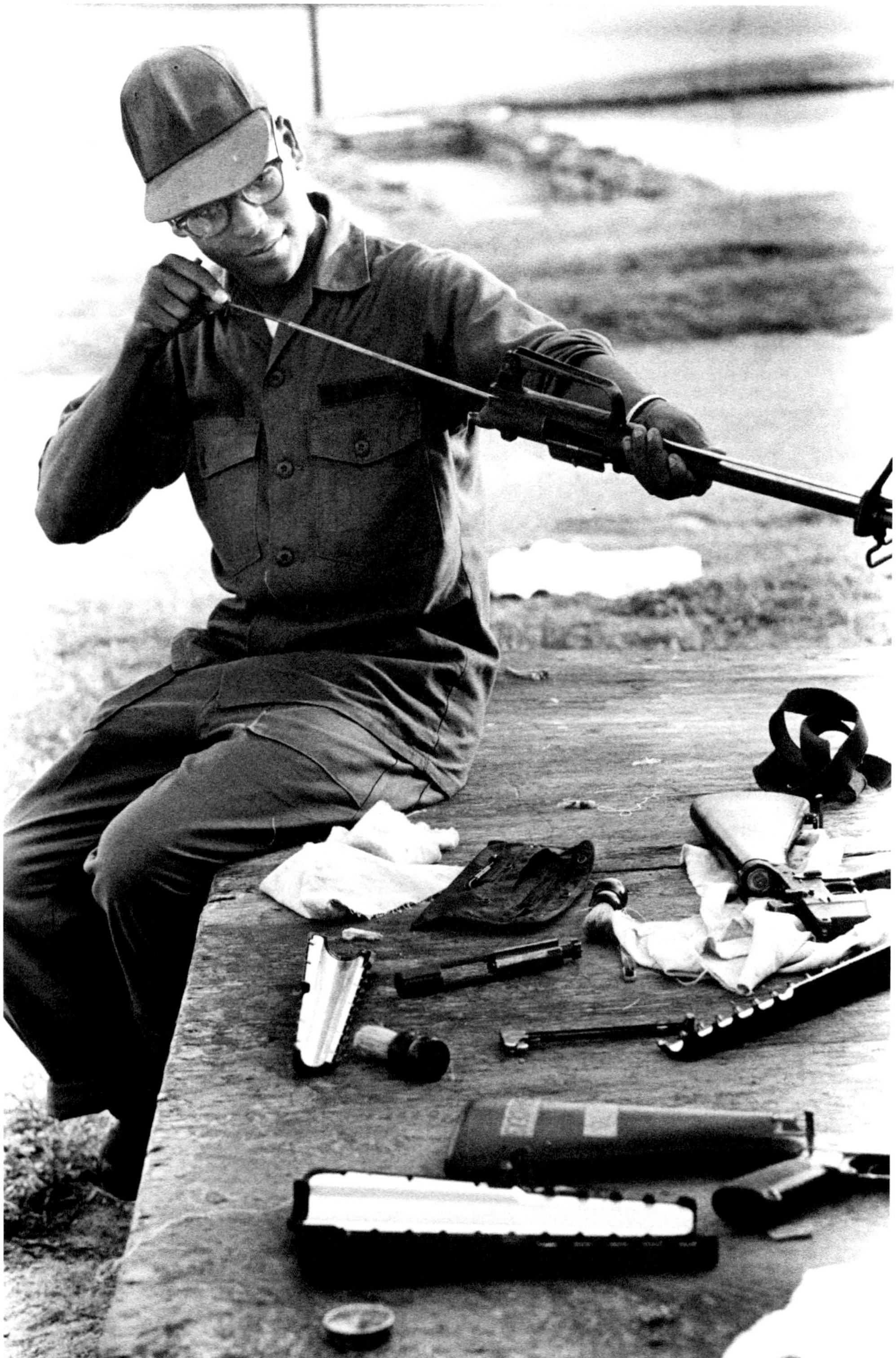

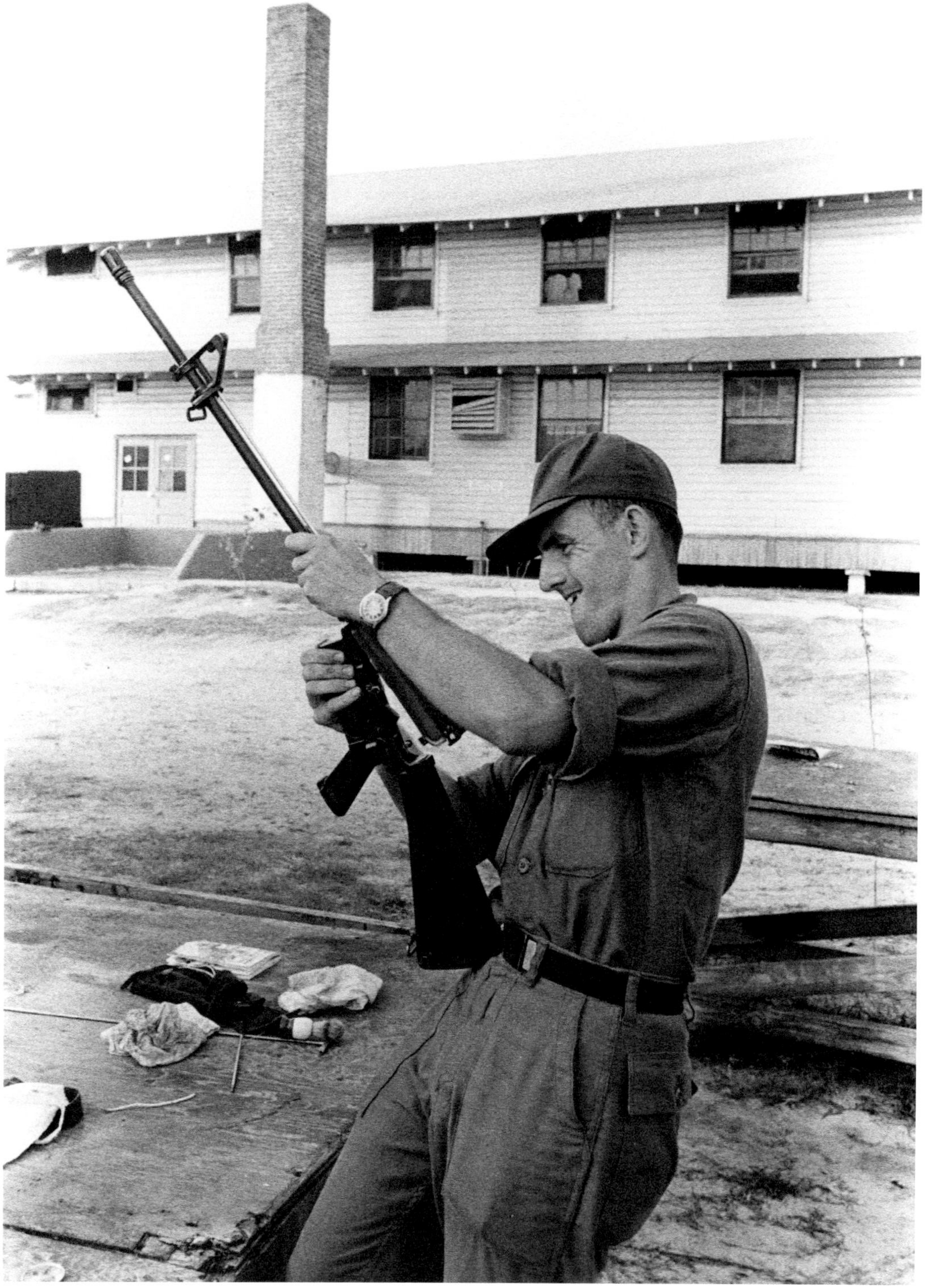

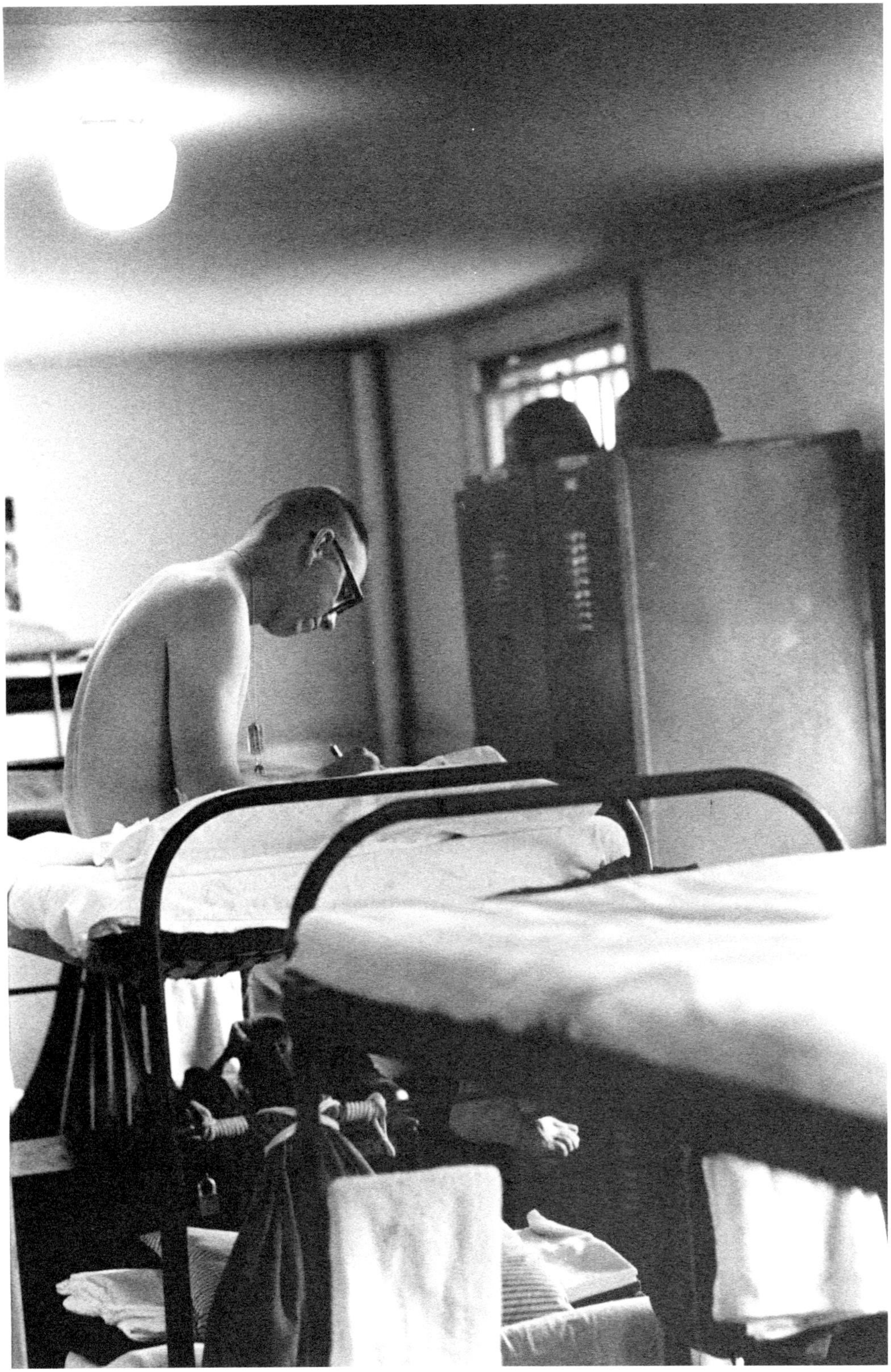

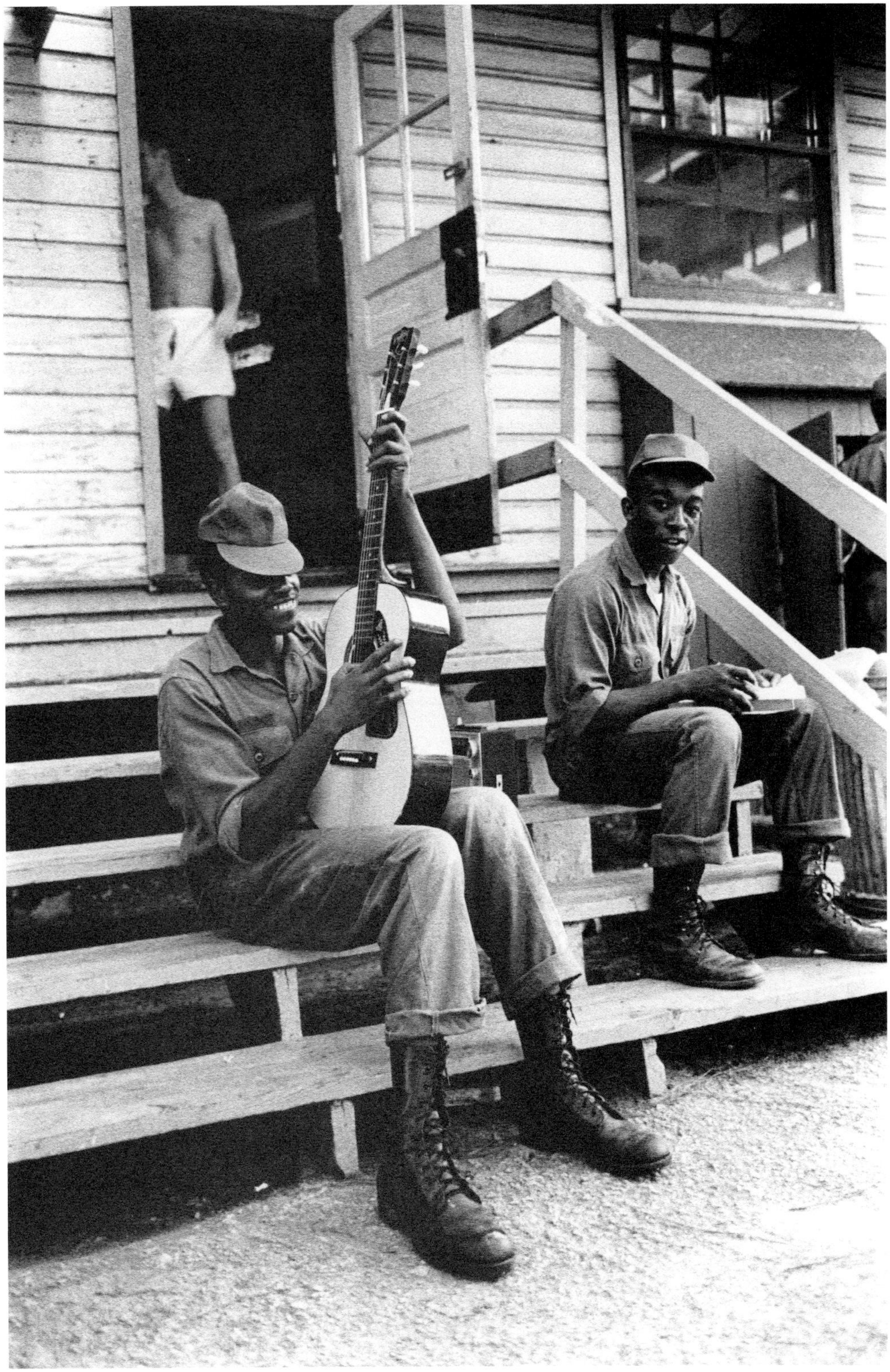

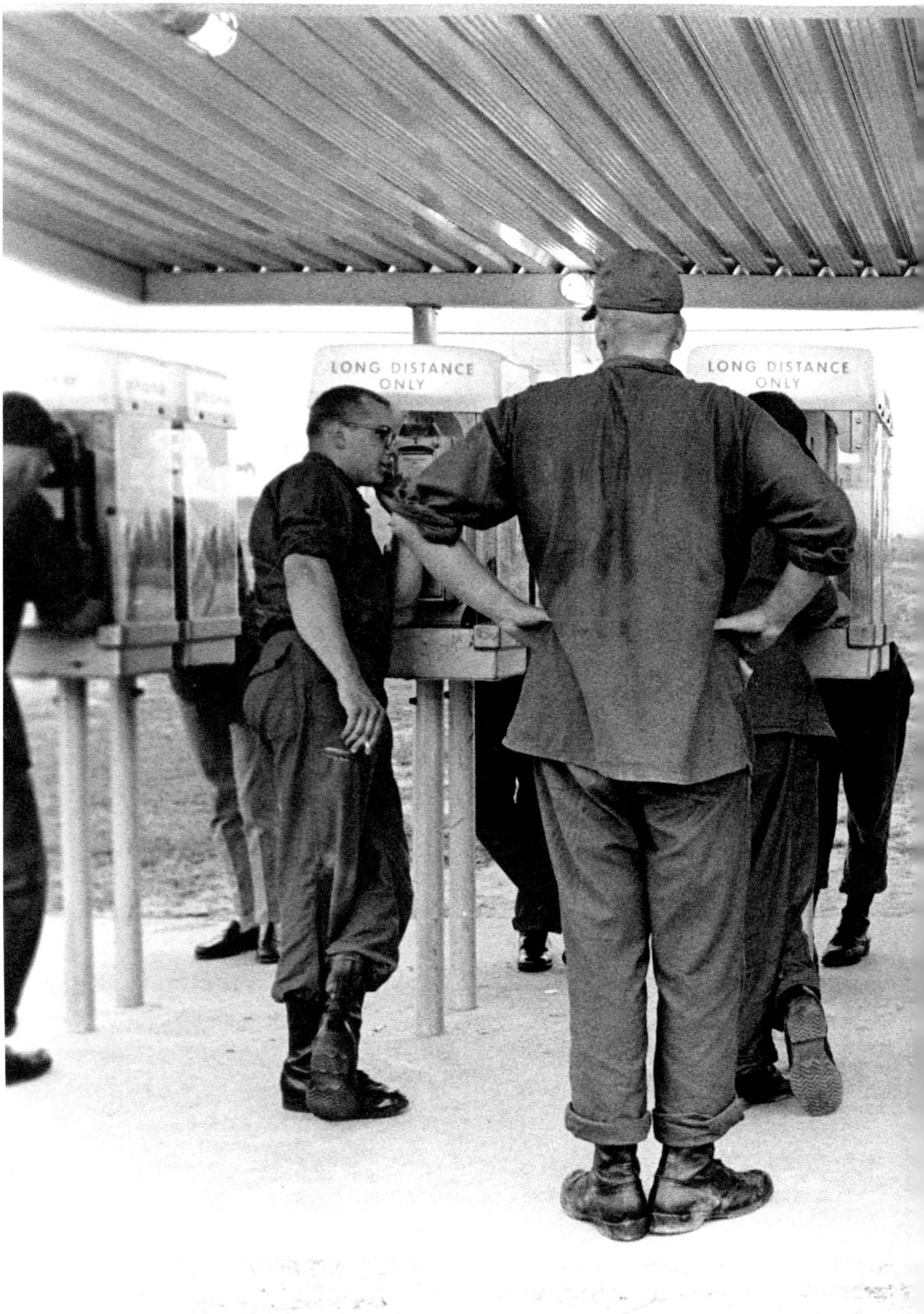
LONG DISTANCE
ONLY
LONG DISTANCE
ONLY

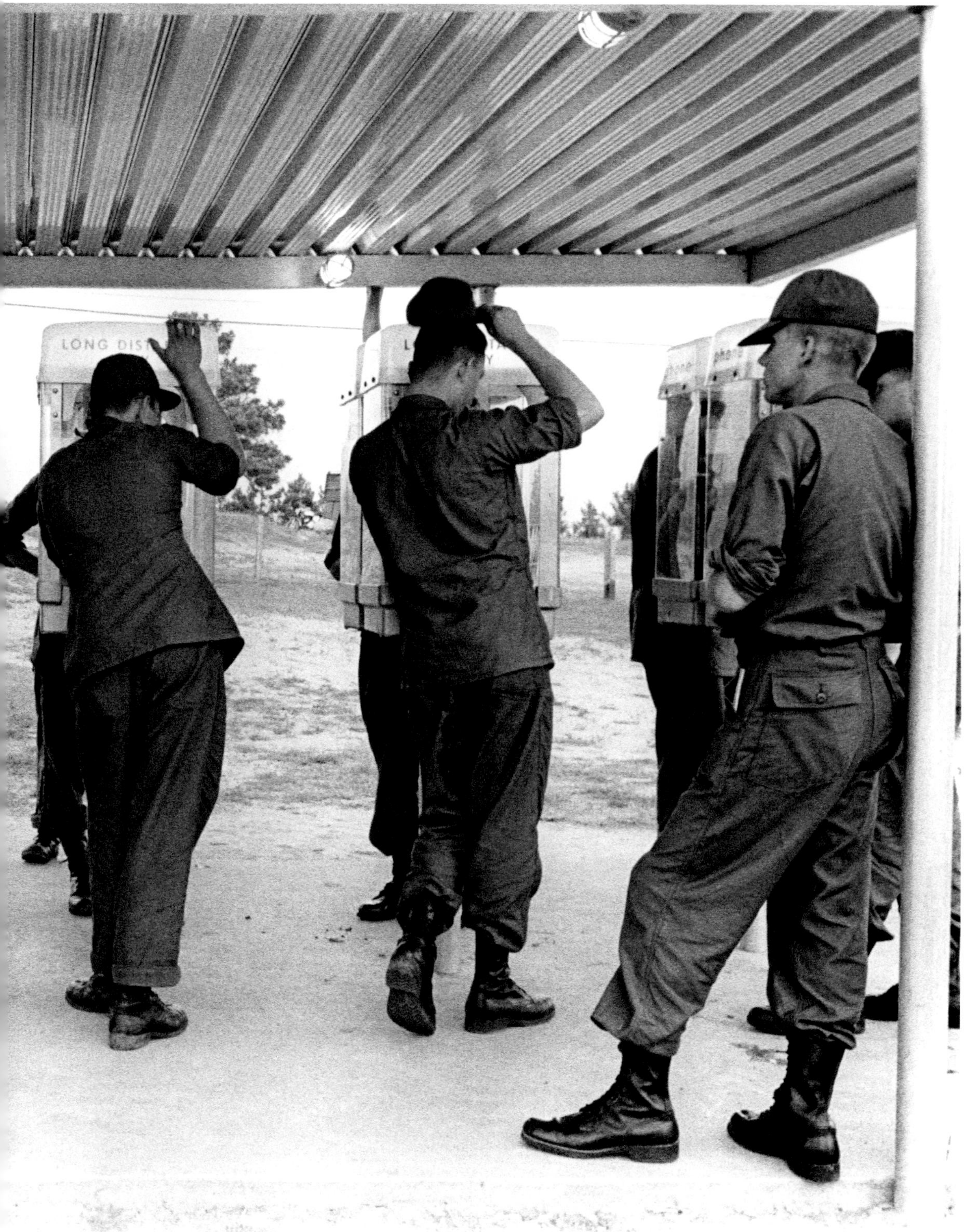

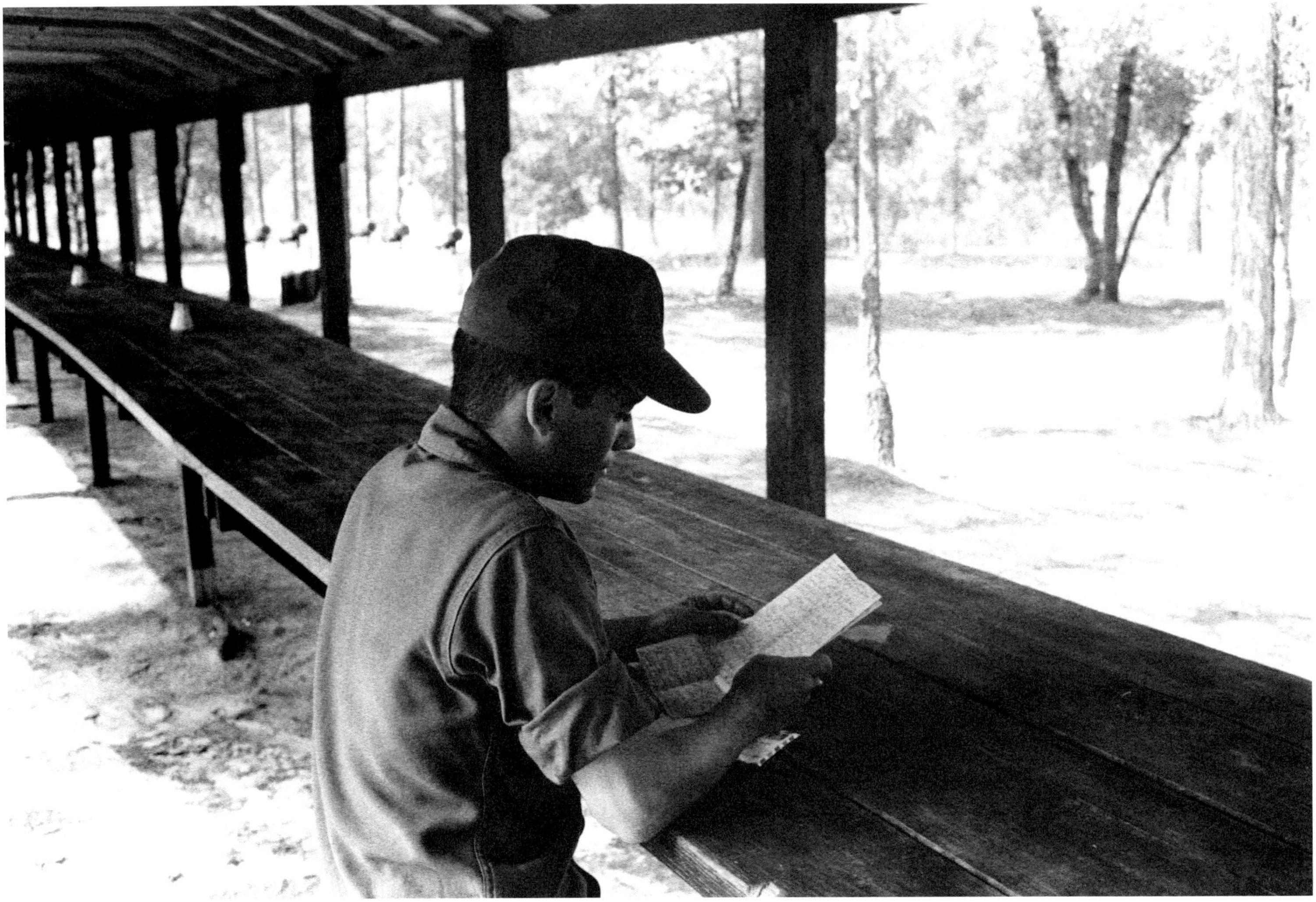

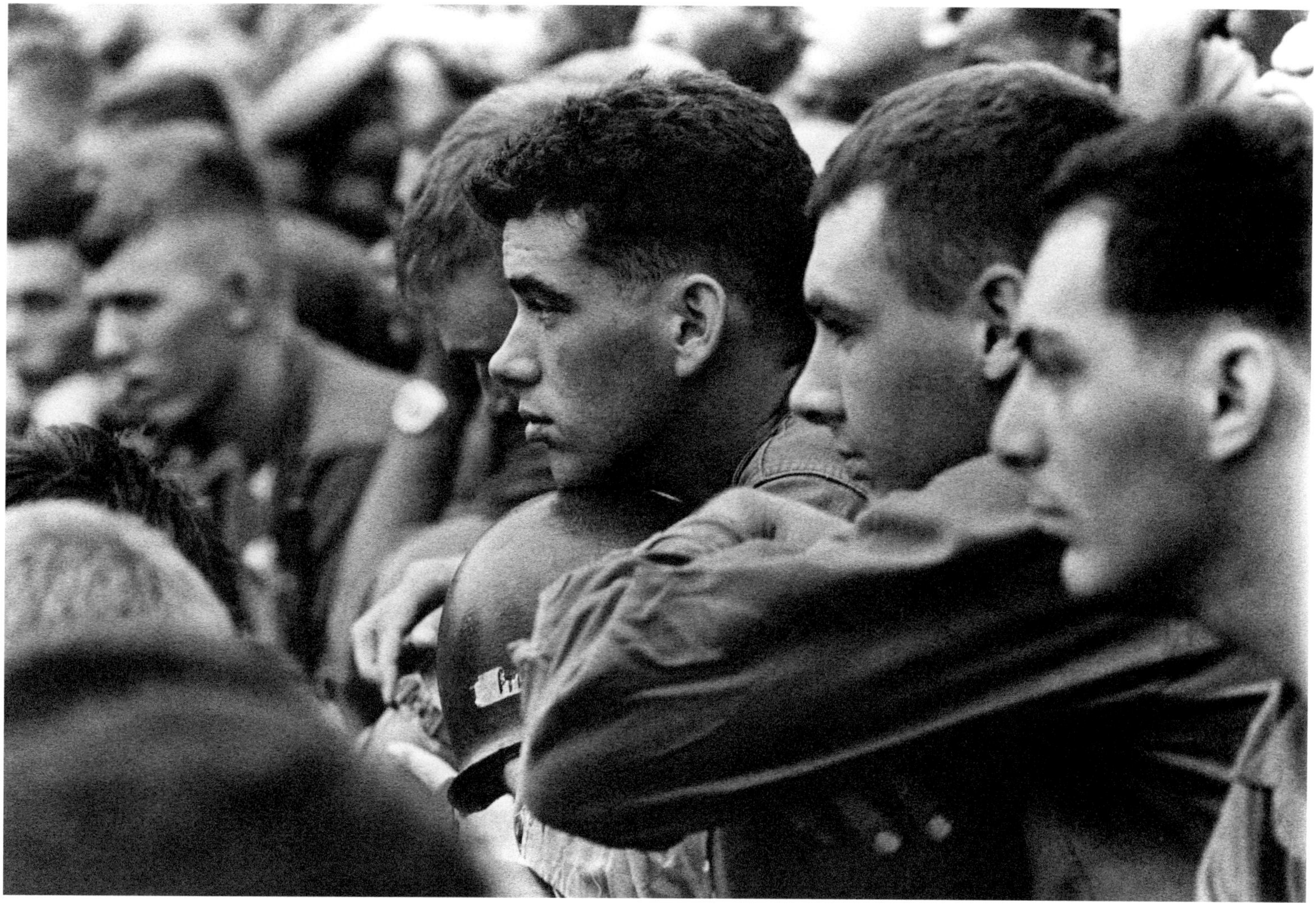

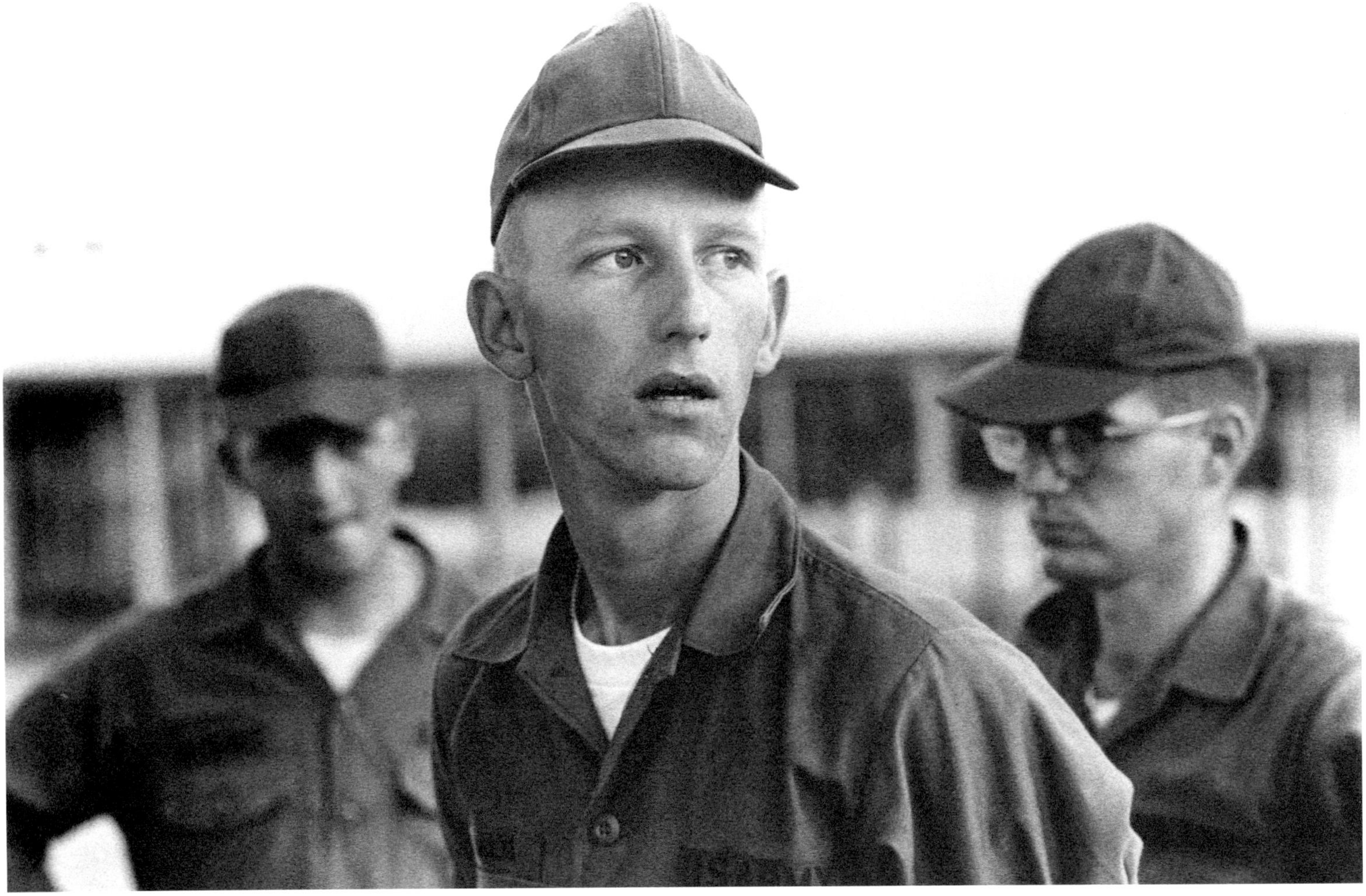

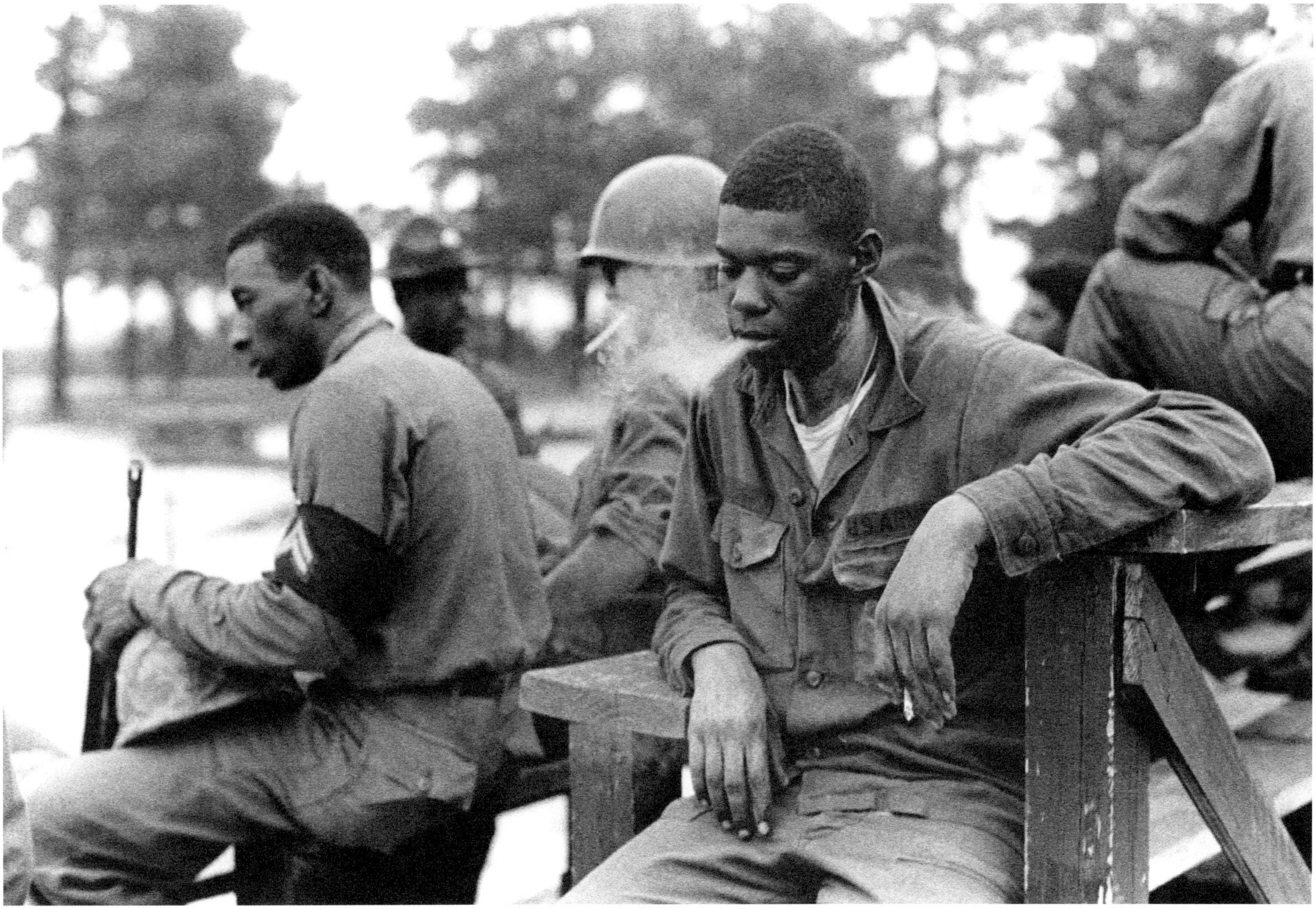

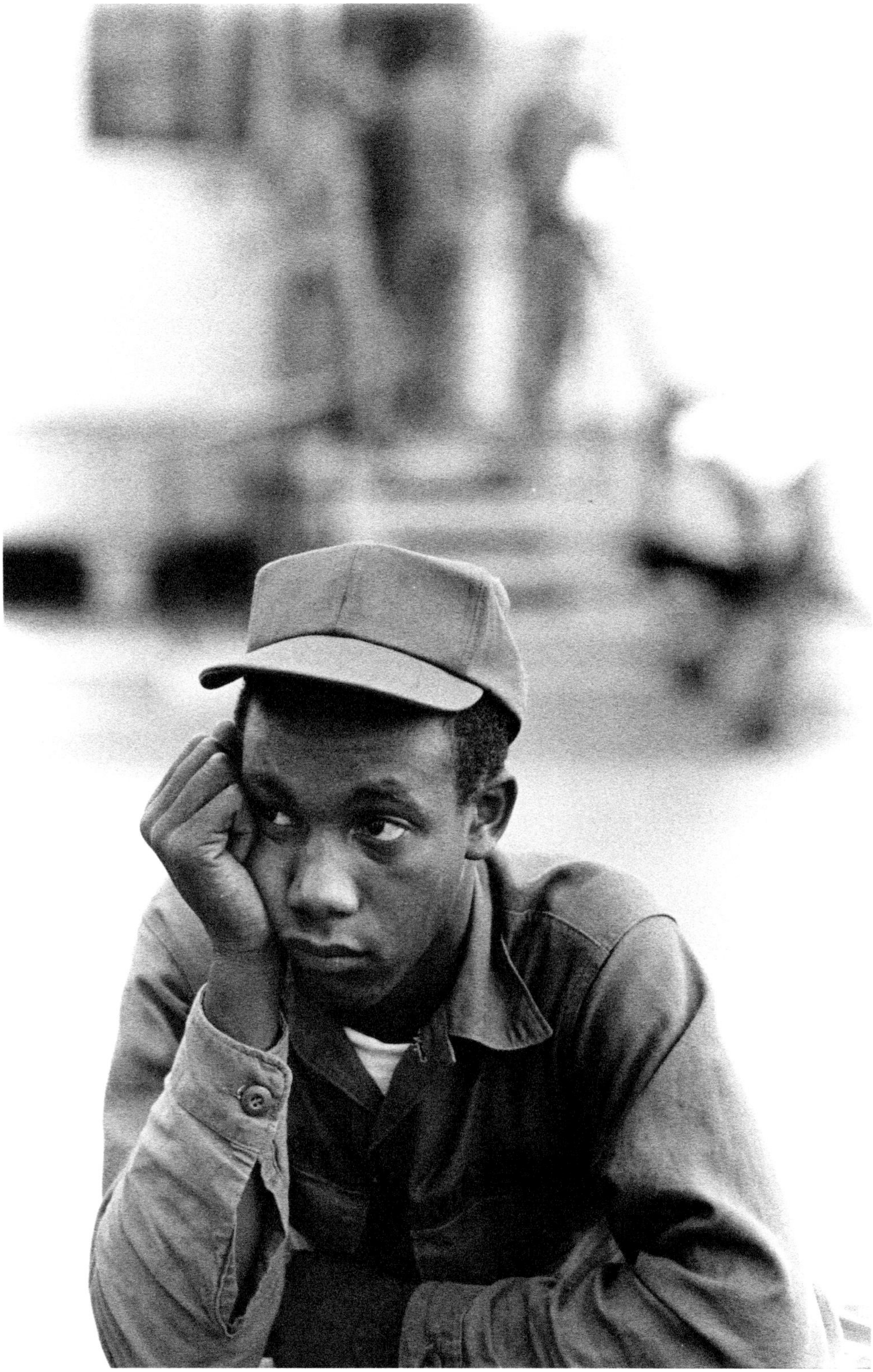

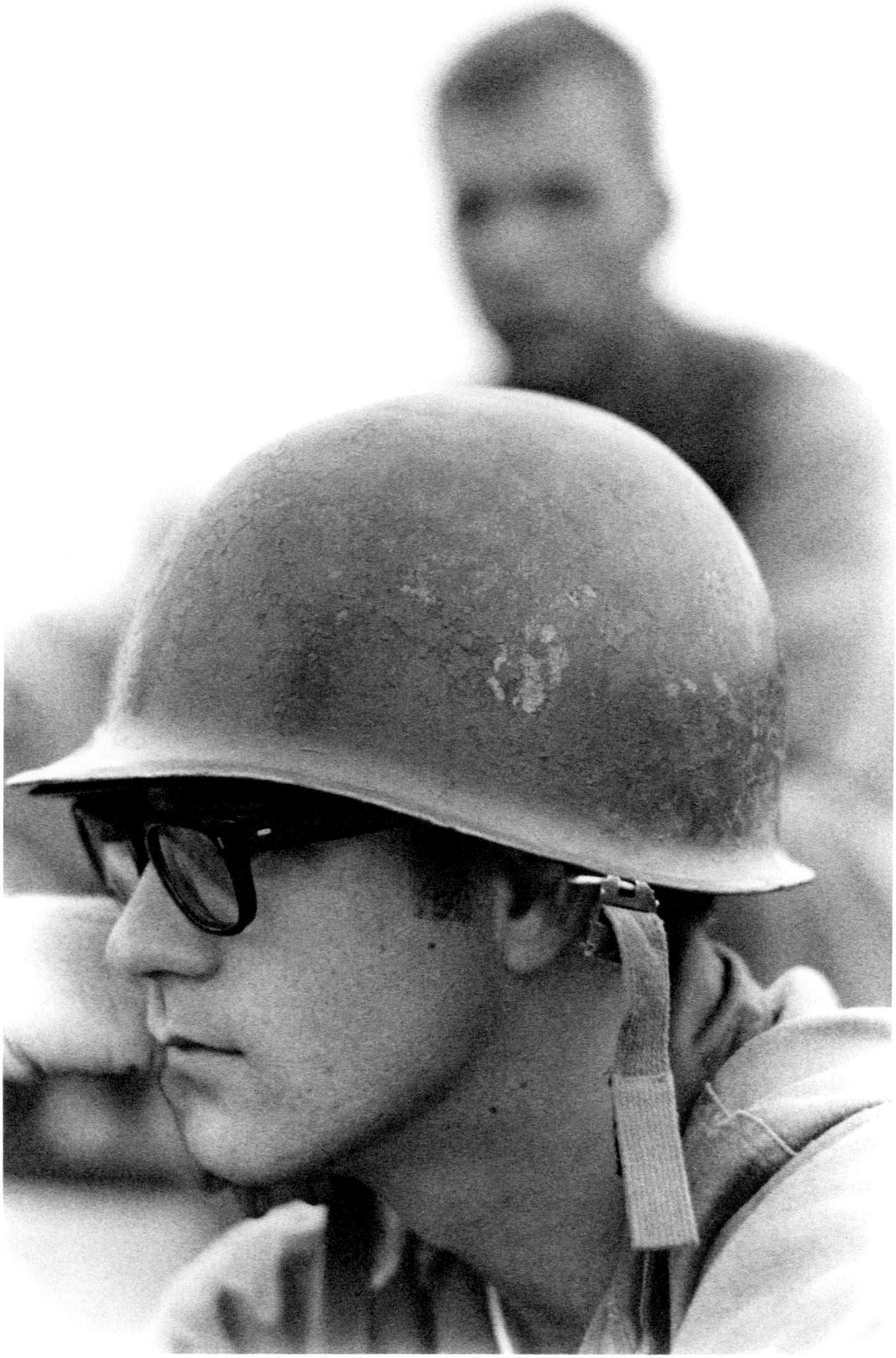

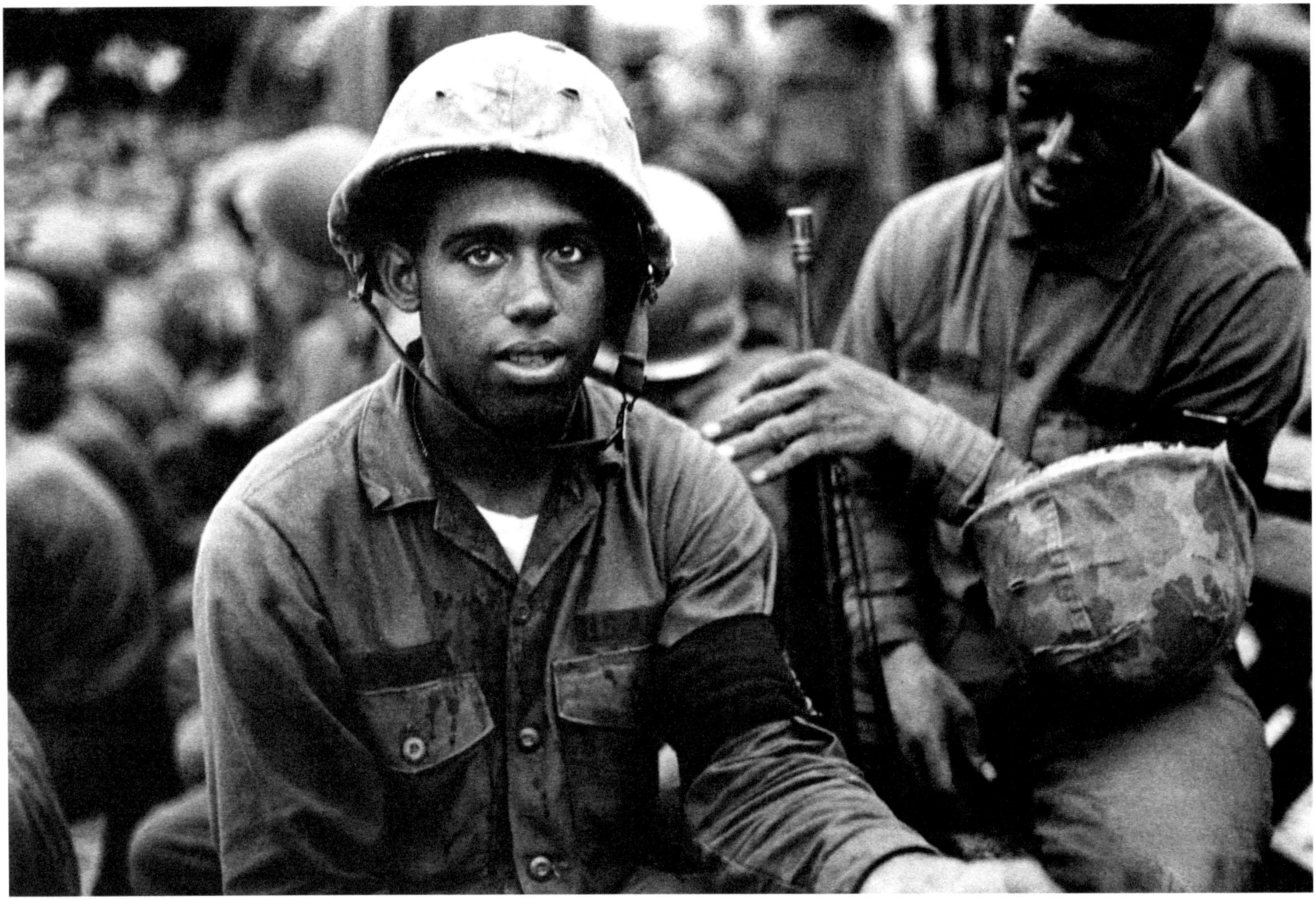

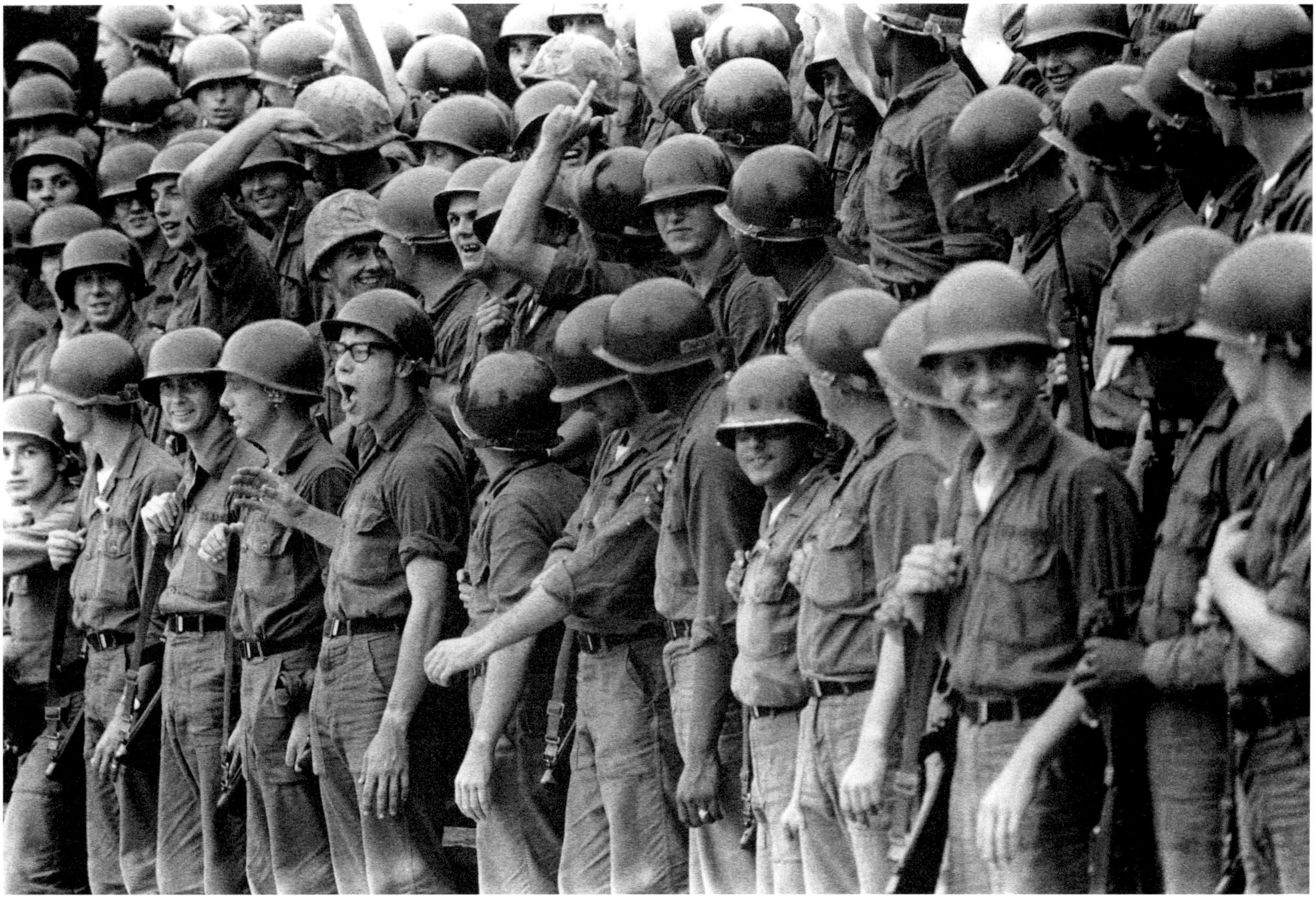

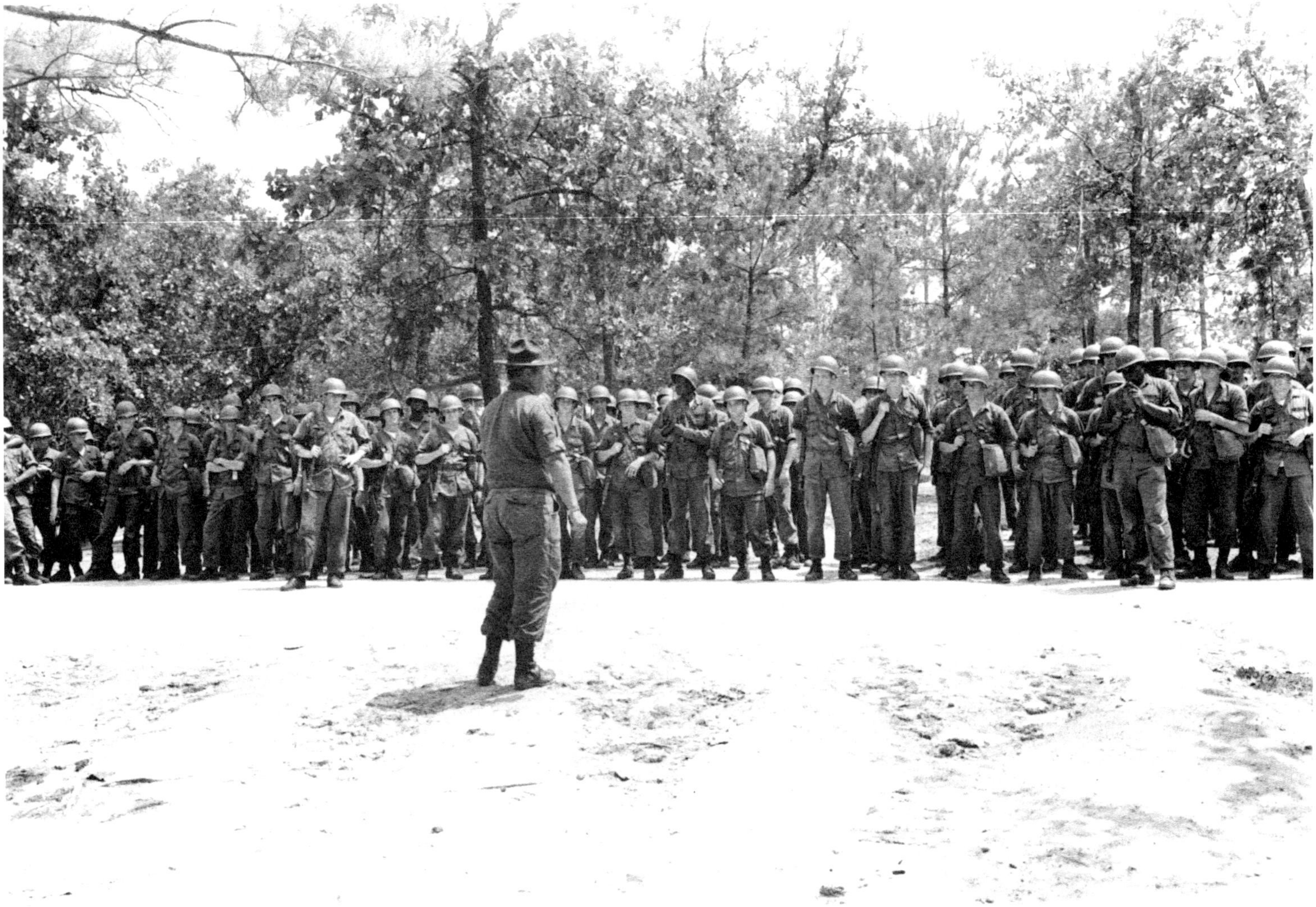

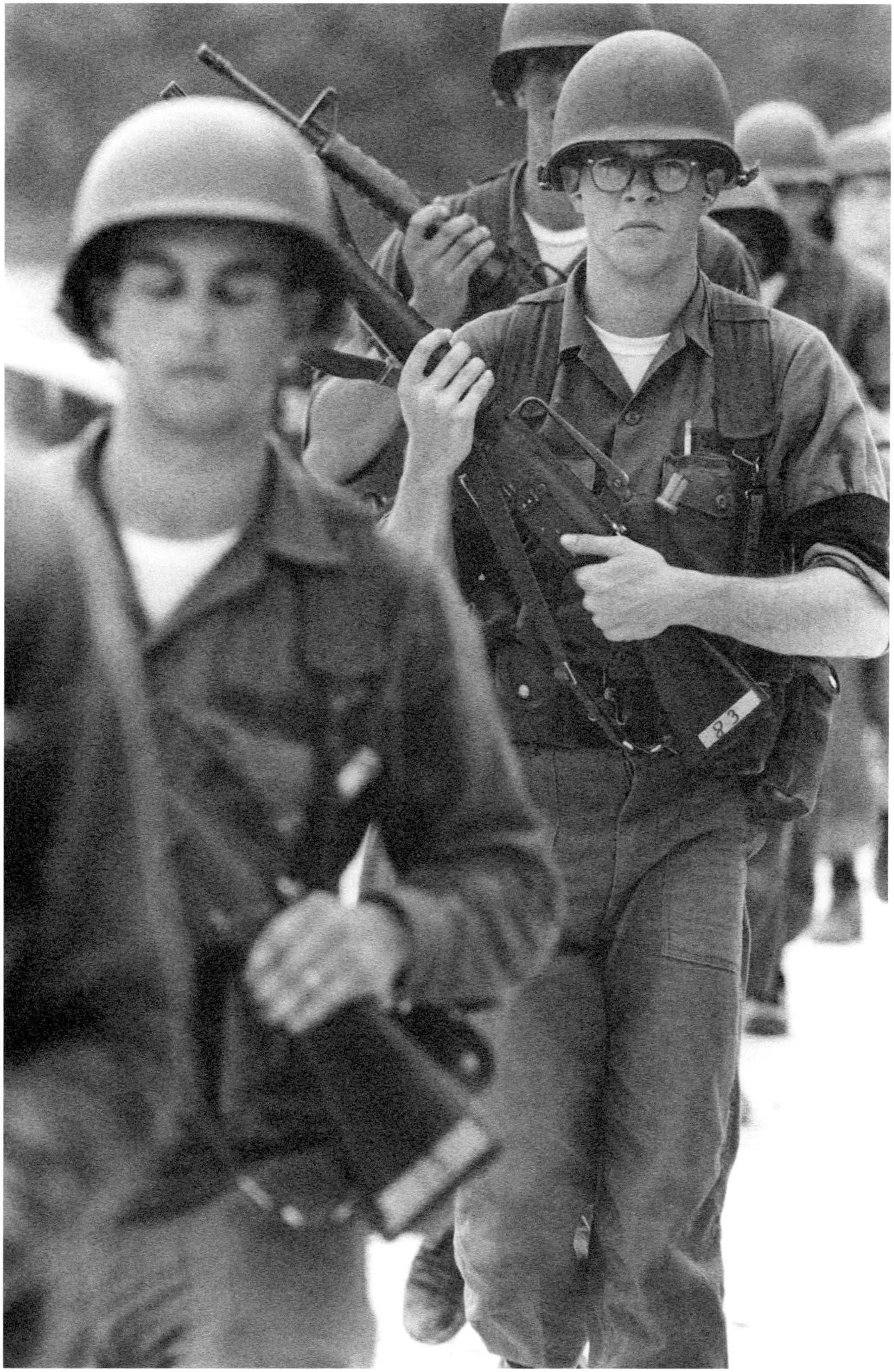
83

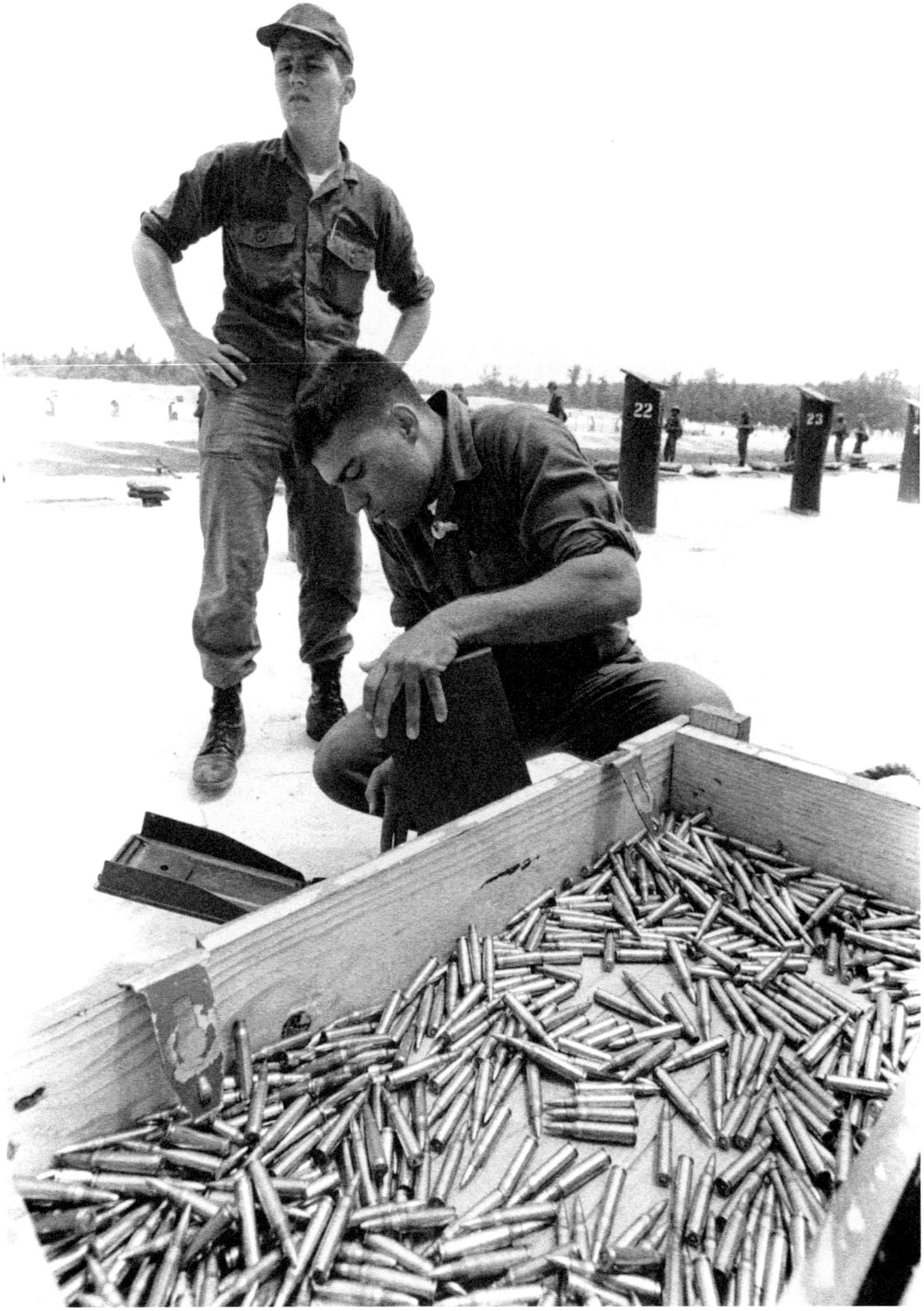
22
23

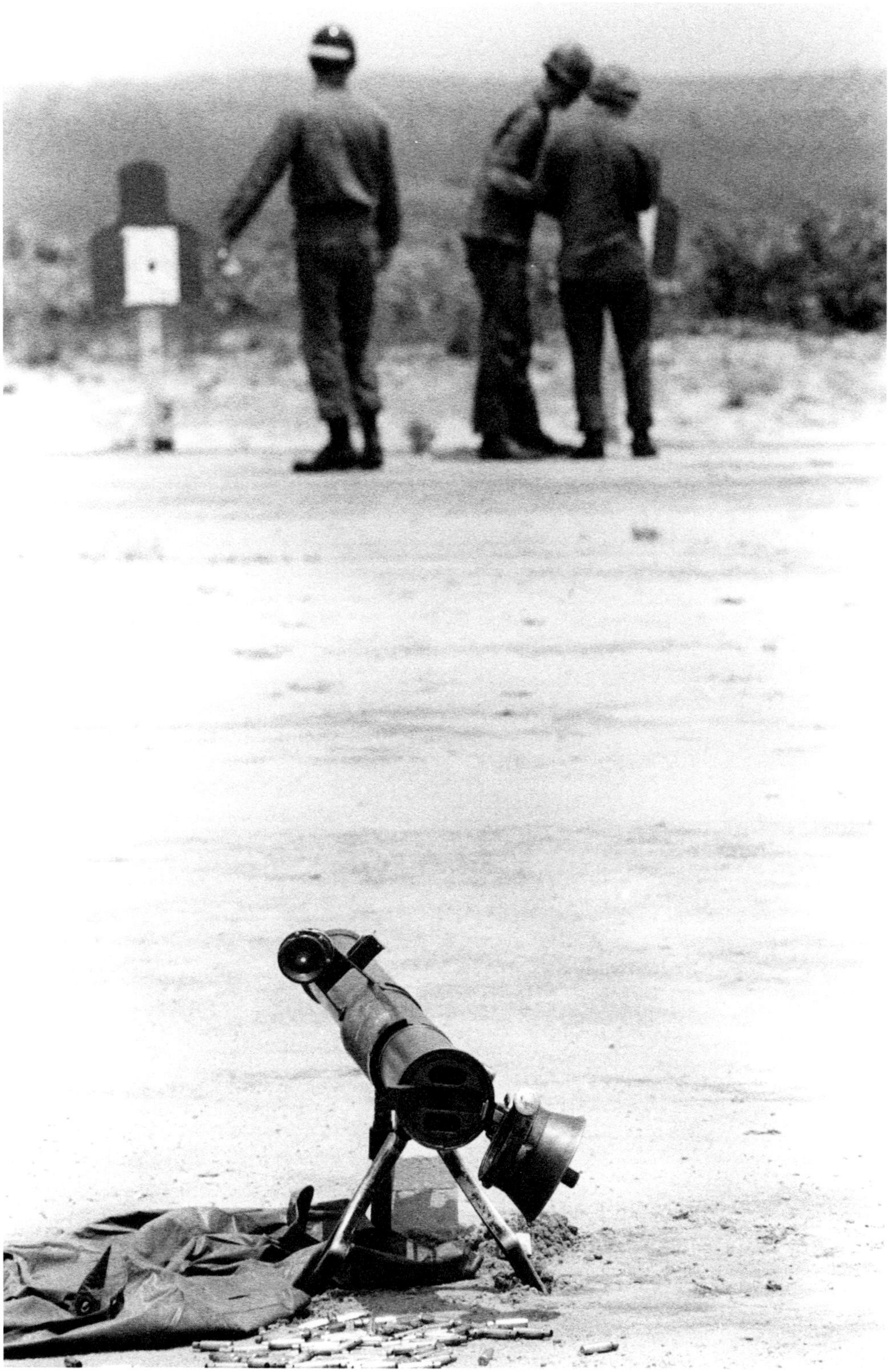

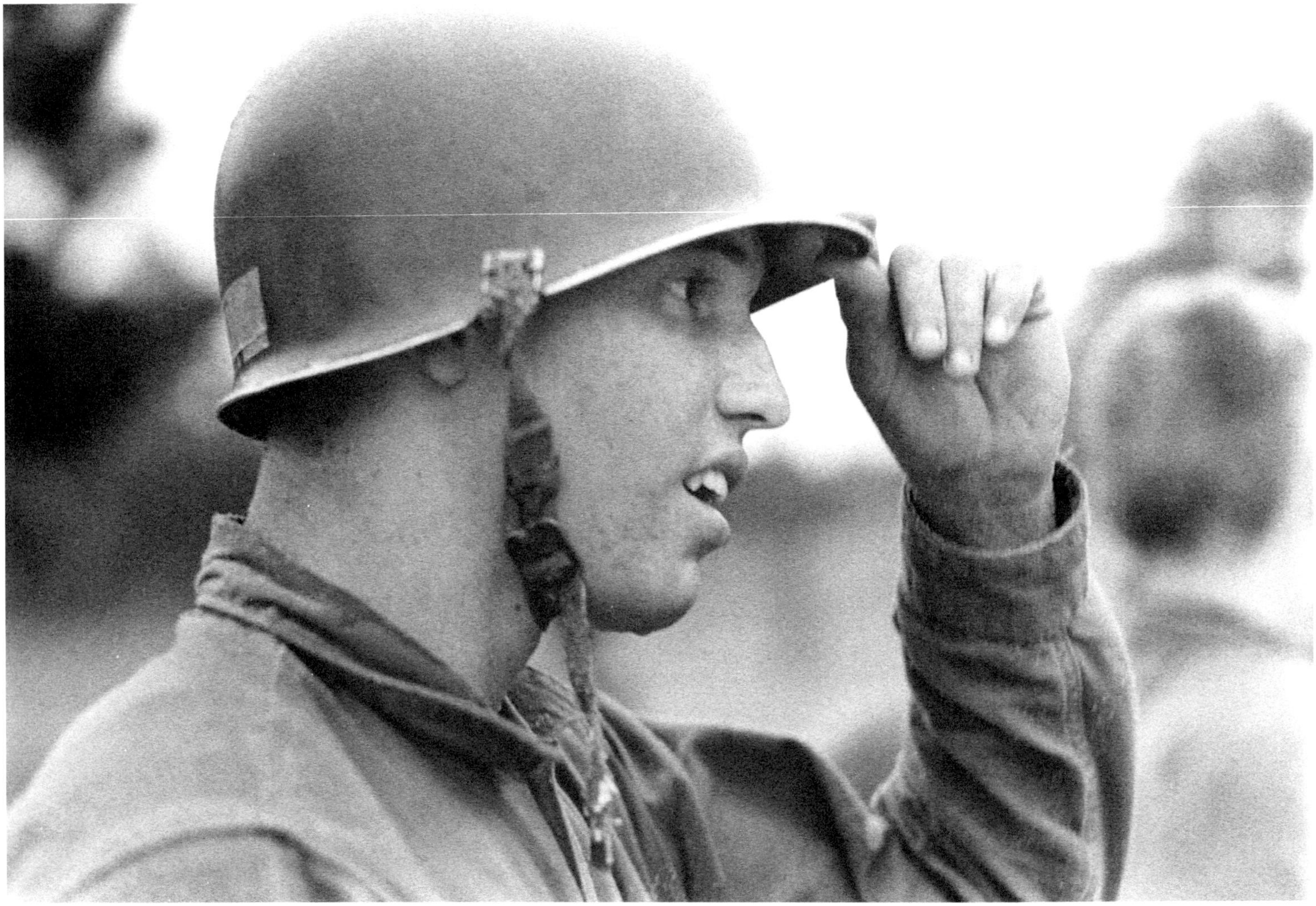

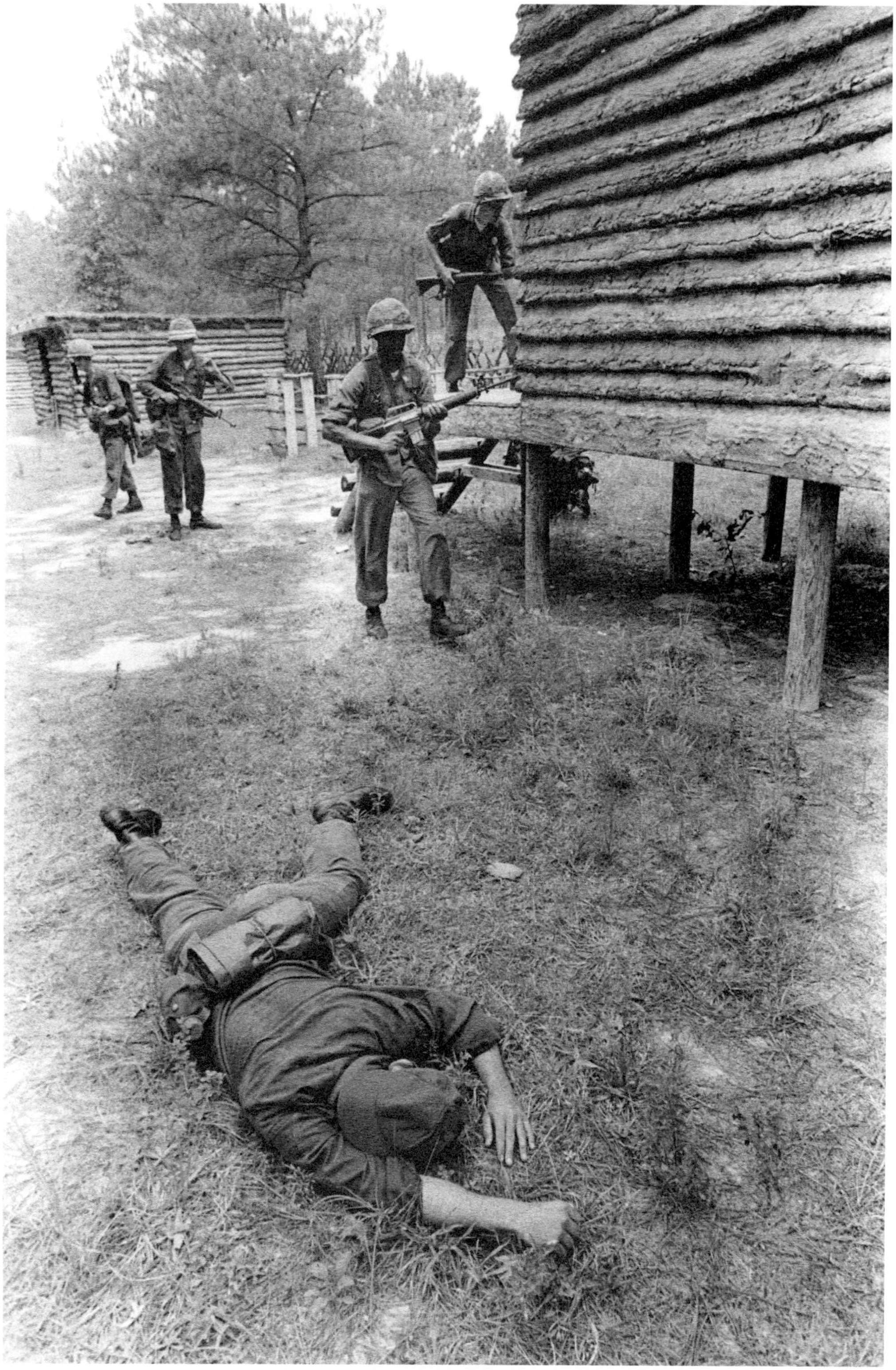

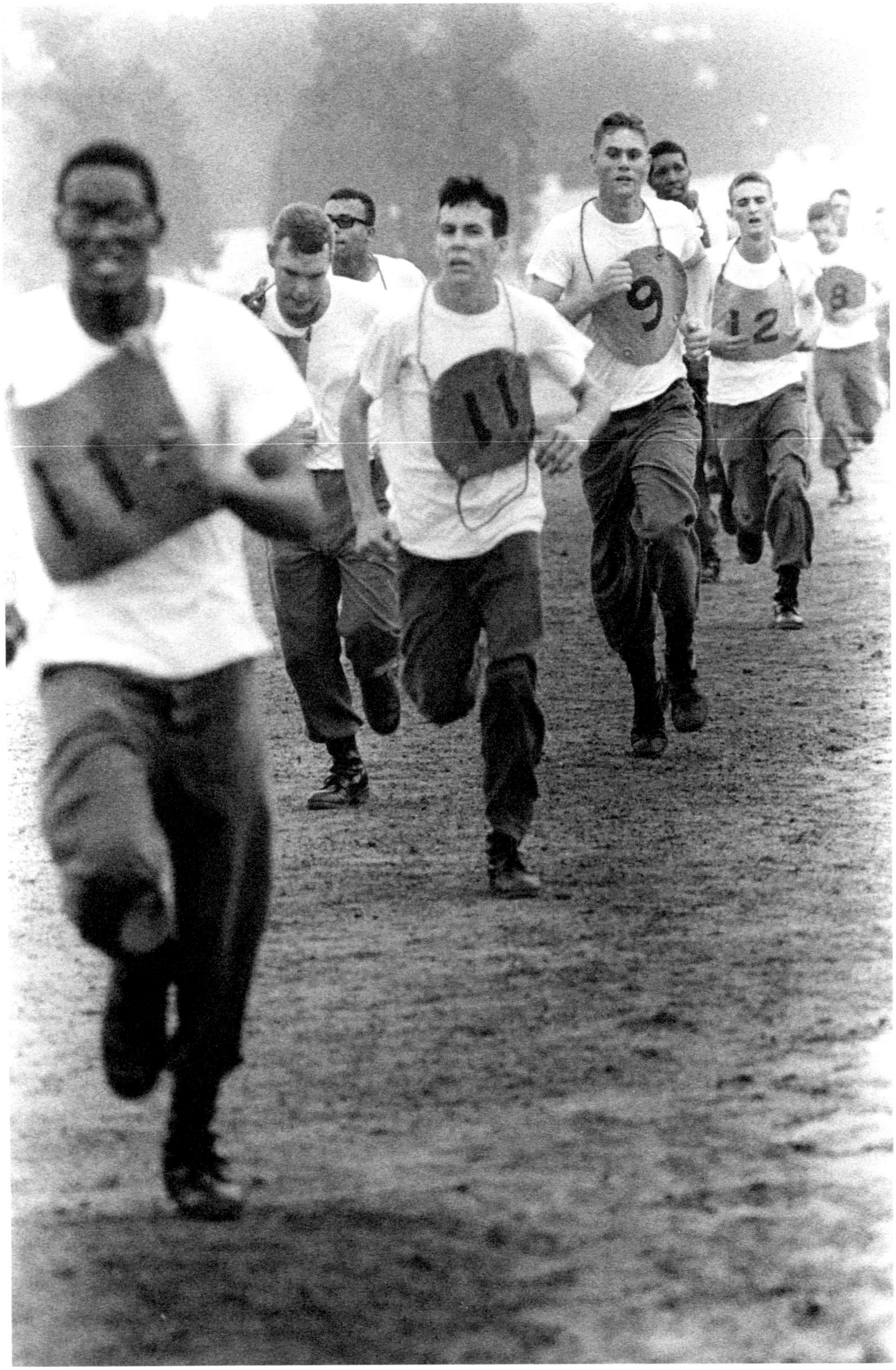

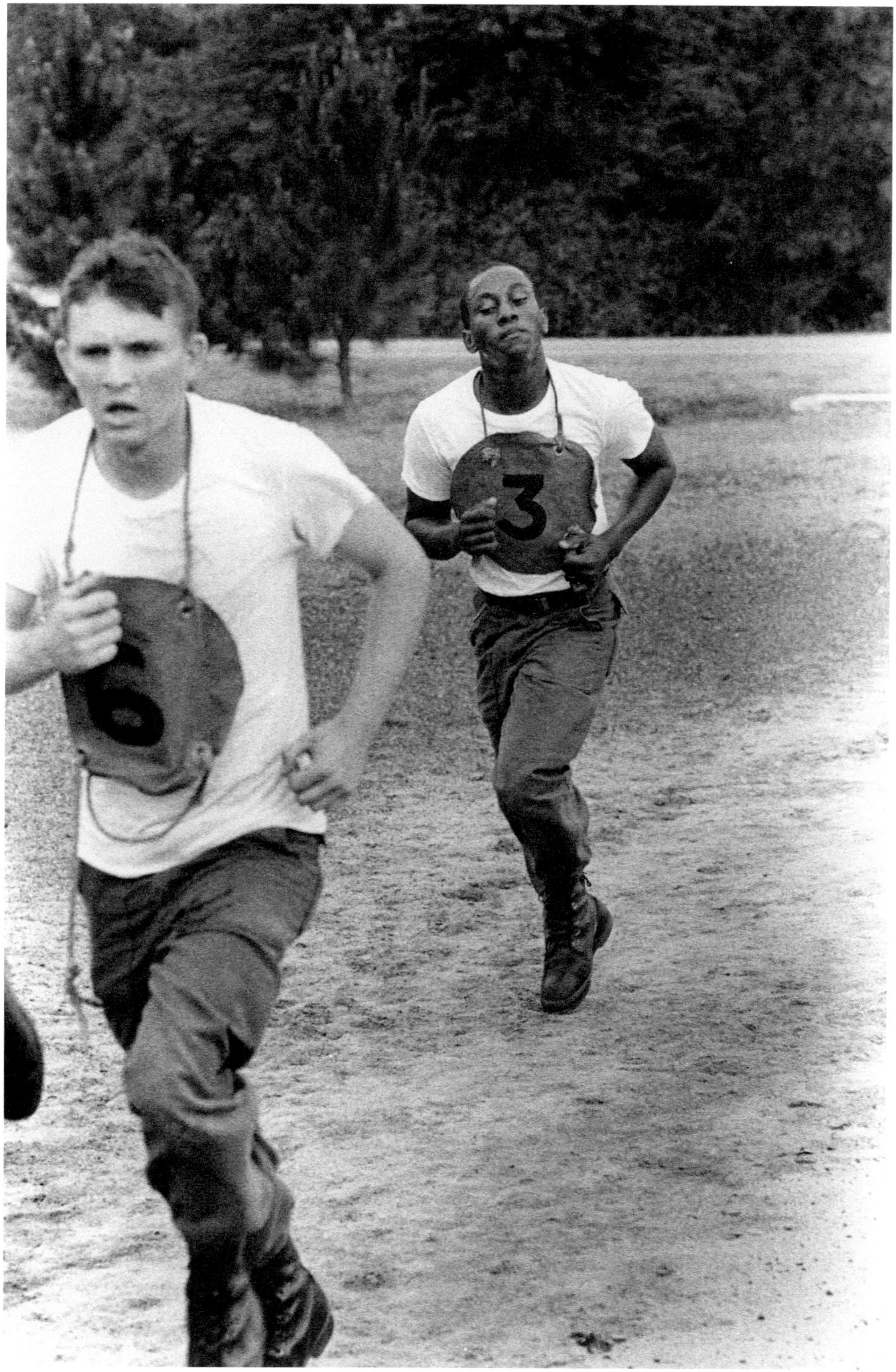
6
3

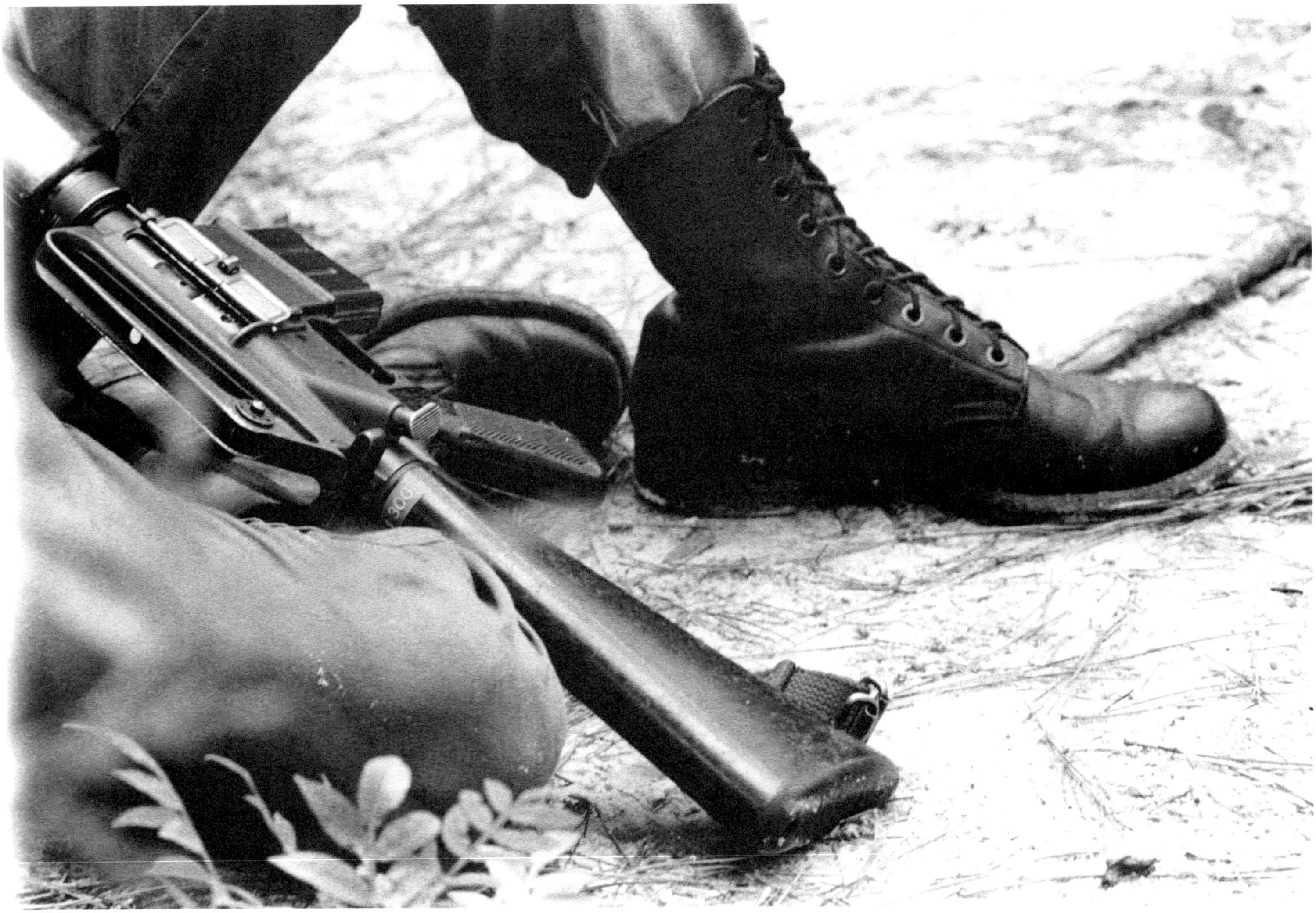

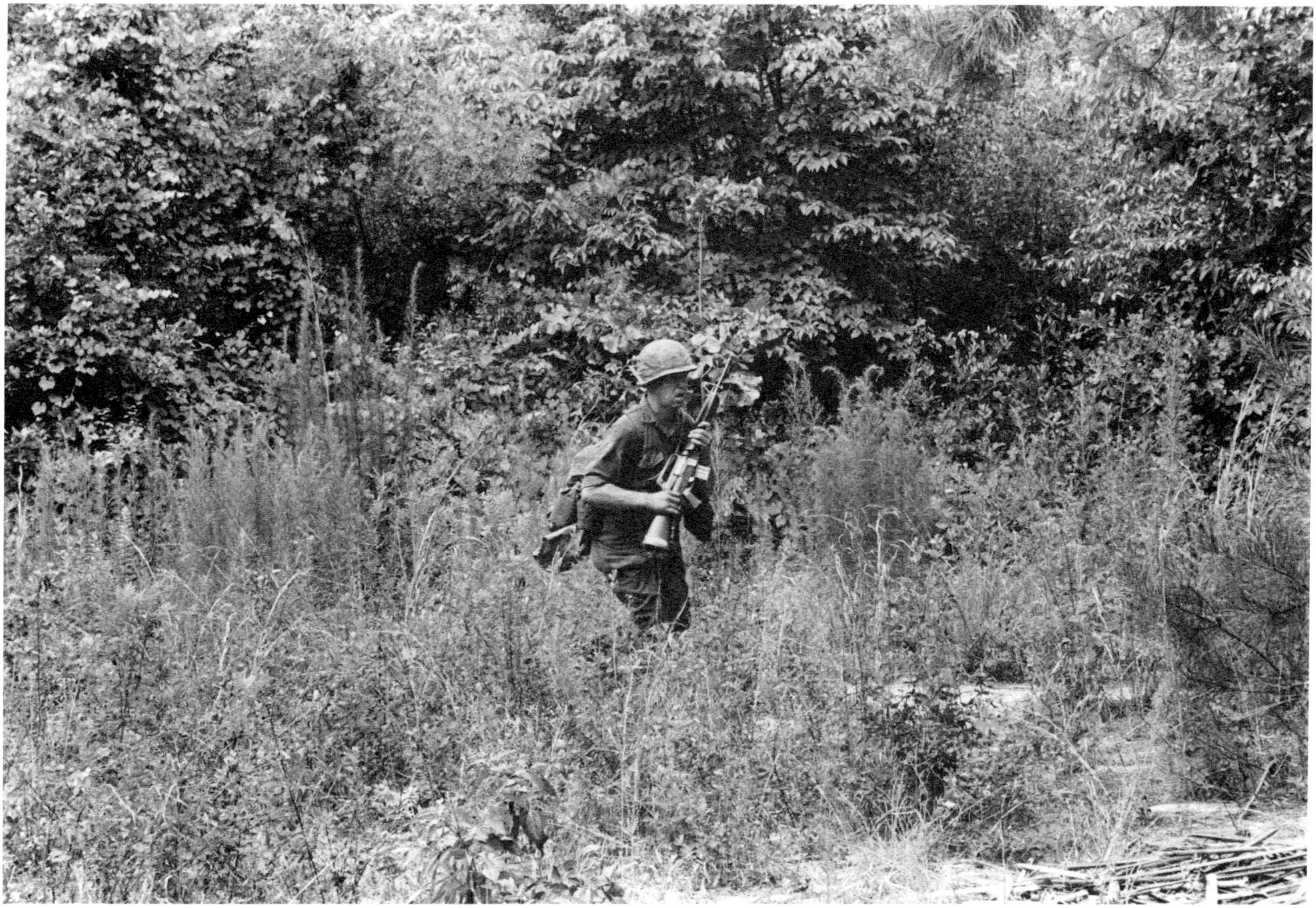

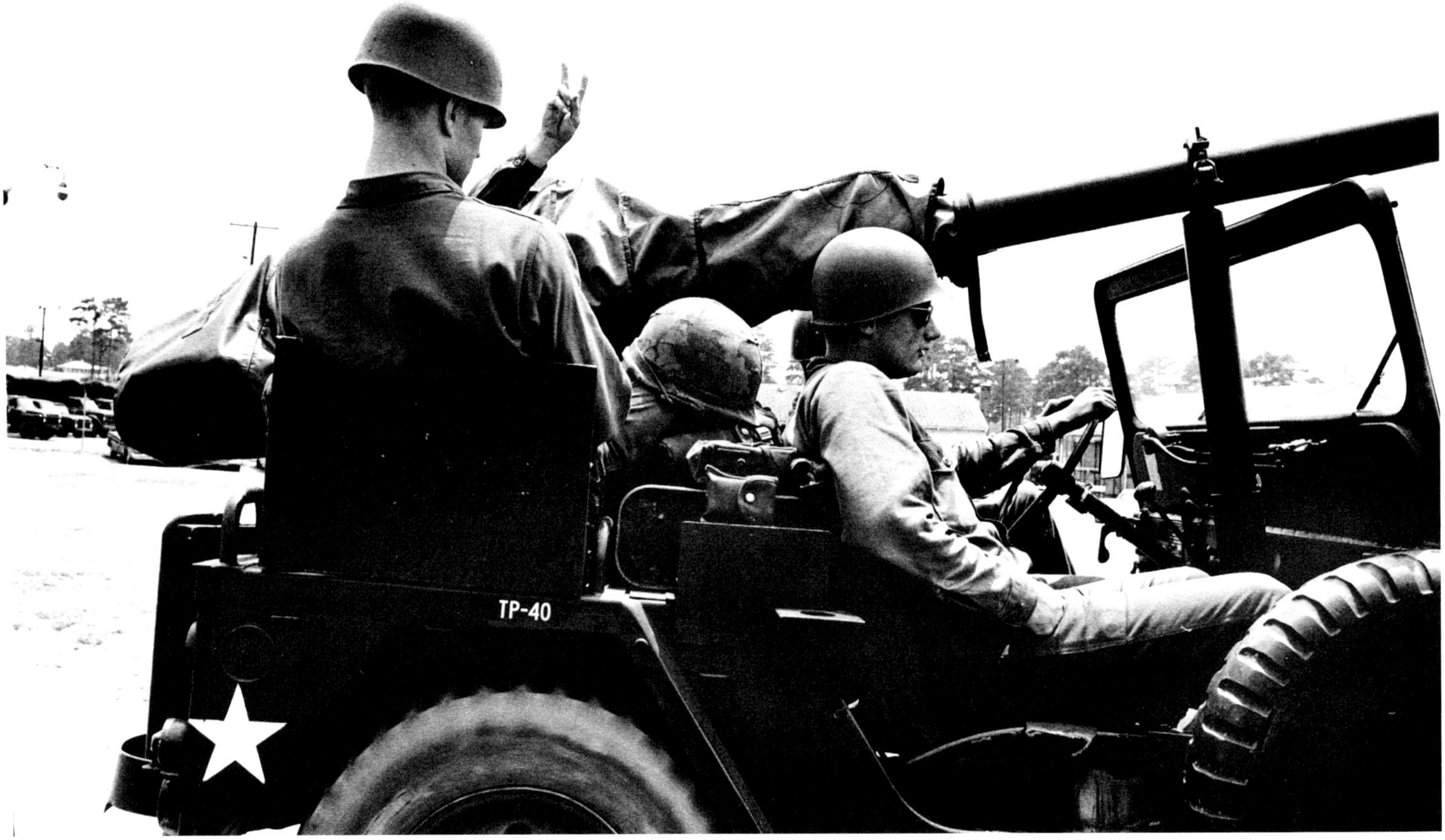
TP-40

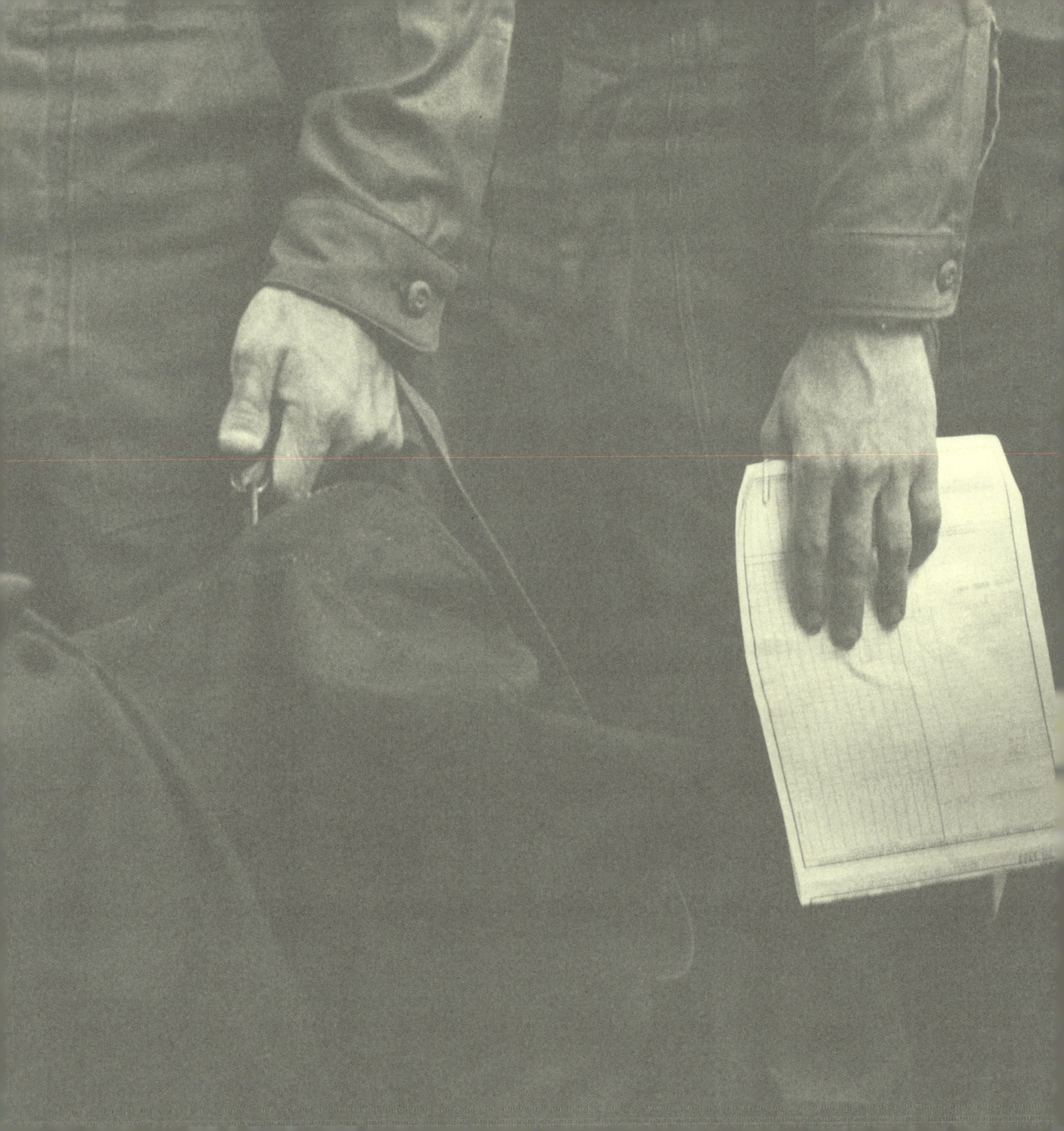